The Big Onion Guide to New York City

THE
Big Onion Guide
New York City ^TO
TEN HISTORIC TOURS

**SETH
KAMIL**

AND

**ERIC
WAKIN**

WITH A FOREWORD BY
KENNETH T. JACKSON

NEW YORK UNIVERSITY PRESS
New York and London

NEW YORK UNIVERSITY PRESS
New York and London

Library of Congress Cataloging-in-Publication Data
Kamil, Seth.
The Big Onion guide to New York City : ten historic tours /
Seth Kamil and Eric Wakin ; with a foreword by Kenneth T. Jackson.
p.   cm.
Includes bibilographical references (p.   ) and index.
ISBN 0-8147-4748-5 (pbk. : alk. paper)
1. New York (N.Y.)—Tours. 2. Historic sites—New York (State)—
New York—Guidebooks. 3. Walking—New York (State)—New York—
Guidebooks. 4. New York (N.Y.)—History.   I. Wakin, Eric.
II. Big Onion Walking Tours (New York, N.Y.) III. Title.
F128.18 .K34 2002
917.47'10444—dc21   2002000746

New York University Press books are printed on acid-free paper,
and their binding materials are chosen for strength and durability.

Manufactured in the United States of America
10 9 8 7 6 5 4 3 2 1

CONTENTS

FOREWORD

THIRTY-FOUR YEARS AGO, when I first began teaching courses about New York City at Columbia University, few walking tours of the city were available. The historic preservation movement was in its infancy, and Pennsylvania Station had only recently been yanked down. Although Gotham was the subject of dozens of new books each year, serious scholarship on the city was rare. The world has changed a lot in the past third of a century. I write this in the immediate aftermath of the World Trade Center disaster, at a time when New Yorkers are talking of both remembrance and rebuilding. I believe that New York will do both in ways that only New Yorkers can. Indeed, rebuilding is as much—perhaps more—a part of the city's history as building is. For what is New York but the world's greatest palimpsest, with each generation building on that which preceded it? Just as the city rebuilt after the fires of 1776 and 1835, just as it did after the Draft Riots of 1863, and just as it has done throughout the twentieth century, New York will rebuild, reform and remain. My confidence in New York's continued success derives in part from the history and accomplishments of Big Onion Walking Tours, which was founded by two graduate students of mine.

They, like myself and many New Yorkers, came from somewhere else and grew to love the city.

Big Onion's founders began giving tours on an ad hoc basis in 1990 for museums and small groups with the idea to help pay for graduate school (no easy task) by sharing what they were learning about the city with other interested people. It was slow going at first. Then, one day in 1991 the *New York Times* called to ask if there were any public tours being offered that winter, so a schedule was created, regularizing what had been an occasional venture. By being out there at a designated time every weekend year-round, rain or shine, Big Onion was following a managerial concept pioneered in New York almost two centuries earlier by the Black Ball Line shipping company. On January 5, 1818, a passenger and cargo ship, christened the *James Monroe*, left a South Street dock right when the company said it would, even though this meant setting sail in a blizzard and without a full cargo. No big deal? Turns out it was. Guaranteed departure schedules were an innovation that helped make New York the most successful entrepot the world has ever seen. Impatient New Yorkers, ever in a hurry, loved regularity then and still do. Scheduled packet ship departures were what I call one of the dozen decisions that changed New York. You'll see some of the others on the walking tours in this book—the great democratic Central Park; the gorgeous Brooklyn Bridge; the grid street system; the remarkable subway; Robert Moses' successes and failures; tenements reformed by legislation; and an urban architecture restructured by the 1916 zoning laws.

New York is fundamentally a walking city, so what better way is there to see it? The reason Big Onion Walking Tours has succeeded is that it makes the city's history accessible and understandable—not to mention entertaining. This is no small feat given New Yorkers' unforgiving nature and the difficulty of running any business here, let alone one founded by graduate students. Big Onion began with only three tours—Immigrant New York, the Jewish Lower East Side, and Ellis Island. Today there are almost thirty, all of which peel back the layers, like an onion, to reveal what's beneath.

Big Onion's first great success was on Christmas Day, 1991, when just over twenty people showed up for the First Annual Christmas Day tour of the Jewish Lower East Side. They thought that was a lot of people. So many have come to the last few Christmas Day tours that multiple guides at staggered times are required! For the first few years, Big Onion had only two guides—its founders. By 1993 they started hiring others. They've made and kept a commitment to hire graduate students—especially in history and related fields—as guides. At first, guides came from Columbia University, where Big Onion was founded. Since then they've hired students from CUNY Graduate Center, Fordham, New York University, and the University of Pennsylvania. Big Onion's "veteran" guides have gone on to teach at Dartmouth, Holy Cross, Princeton, UC Santa Cruz, Union College, and Yale. In 2001, there are twenty-five guides on their way to becoming veterans. Big Onion offers two kinds of tours. Public tours—"show ups"—that anyone can join without a reservation for two hours of walking. These walks attract tourists as well as those from the city. Over 40 percent of those going on tours live within fifty miles of the city. New Yorkers are not an easy group to please, yet 60 percent of the people who take a tour are repeat customers. The other kind of tours Big Onion offers are private. Any and all of its tours are available for groups 365 days a year. Groups come from schools, synagogues, churches, unions, law firms, colleges and universities, investment banks and so on. And most of these groups book a tour every year.

Finally, Big Onion works and has worked for the premier cultural and educational institutions of the city. I'm proud to have Big Onion as the programming partner of the New-York Historical Society. This book illustrates the commitment of serious historians to the city we all love.

KENNETH T. JACKSON

Jacques Barzun Professor of History and Social Sciences
Columbia University

President
New-York Historical Society

INTRODUCTION

NEW YORK IS the finest walking city in North America. Our terrain is primarily flat; virtually every street has a sidewalk; and each city block is different from the one before. Many think of New York as a massive city. We prefer to think of it as a series of neighborhoods, each with unique characteristics and features, not unlike a distinct collection of towns. New Yorkers speak not about which borough but about which neighborhood they call home. Living and playing in the Upper East Side are distinctly different from the same activities in the Upper West Side or in the East versus the West Village. For many of us, the ideal job would be no more than ten blocks from our home. And for most of us, the conveniences of daily life already exist between home and that mythological job.

New York neighborhoods are more than just a place to call home; they are also places to explore and adventure. While a subway, bus, or car may be the best way to reach these neighborhoods, the only way truly to see them is on foot. To experience the full fabric—the sights, sounds, smells, and tastes—of New York neighborhoods, a person must walk them. We are a city of some 8 million inhabitants. Listen to the vast array of languages we speak. See the homes, shops, and street life. Wander into a local market or restaurant and taste the flavors of the city.

Since 1991, Big Onion Walking Tours has led visitors and residents alike on ventures into New York's historic districts and ethnic neighborhoods. Big Onion specializes in social history—the weaving together of historical facts, important events and people, and the architecture of our city into a well-told story. All our guides have advanced degrees in American history or in a related field, and the chapters of *The Big Onion Guide to New York City* were written by veteran Big Onion guides.

With this book we share a series of our most special walking tours. Each walking tour in this guide is adapted from the tours we lead year-round in the city. Each explores a unique and special slice of New York City. While walking the city, please keep in mind that New York is a living, evolving place. The tours we present here are up to date as of winter 2002. It is inevitable that, over time, buildings will be replaced, community groups will move, and sites will close. We encourage readers not only to use the self-guided tours enclosed herein but to join our walking tours.

Each of our walking tours, if walked at a leisurely pace, should take between two and three hours. All tours begin and end at or near subway stations. These are outdoor walking tours. Many of our walks stop in front of historic sites and cultural institutions, so feel free to break from our tour and wander inside.

Seven of our chapters venture into Manhattan neighborhoods:

Our book begins in Lower Manhattan, the site of our colonial walled city. Written by Leonard Benardo, this tour explores the history and architecture of what is both the first area of settlement and the city's, and nation's, contemporary financial district.

Our second walk is "Immigrant New York," the multi-ethnic Lower East Side. This tour, written by Seth Kamil, is the tour that got Big Onion Walking Tours off the ground. It delves into the heart of what makes New York special—its multiplicity of cultures and people.

Our gay-and-lesbian history tour was crafted by Eliza Byard. This tour spans the East and West Villages and combines the historical and contemporary worlds of New York's thriving gay and lesbian communities.

Continuing uptown, Mark Elliott developed our Four Squares tour. Combining commercial and residential Manhattan, Four Squares demonstrates the variety of our city with a "short" walk from Fourteenth to Twenty-third Streets, east to west across the city.

Eric Wakin left the Manhattan street grid and created our Central Park tour. While technically not a neighborhood, Central Park is truly Manhattan's greatest work of art and what makes the island livable.

The Upper East Side tour shatters the myth that this neighborhood is a uniform district of apartment houses. Leading this walk is Leonard Benardo, who introduces the history and people of one of Manhattan's most overlooked residential neighborhoods.

Our final Manhattan walk explores Harlem. Cindy Lobel combines the historical development of the neighborhood with a detailed discussion of Harlem's people, arts, and cultural legacy.

These seven tours will lead walkers into what we feel are some of the most interesting and important of Manhattan's neighborhoods.

We also venture beyond Manhattan. Though it is the best-known and most explored borough, at the same time, with only 22.6 square miles, it is geographically the smallest of the five boroughs. With 1.5 million residents, Manhattan is the third largest borough in terms of population.

With these facts in mind, we have included two Brooklyn walking tours. Prior to the Consolidation of Greater New York in 1898, Brooklyn was the third largest city in America. Today it is the second largest and most populous borough, with more than 2.4 million people.

Our first Brooklyn walk takes you through Brooklyn Heights and across the Brooklyn Bridge. In writing this tour, Eric Wakin explores what was New York City's first suburb and a landmark district. The walk continues with a stroll across the great wonder of the nineteenth century—the Brooklyn Bridge.

Our second Brooklyn tour is Green-Wood Cemetery, the city's most pristine and elaborate garden cemetery. As told by Seth Kamil, Green-Wood is the perfect site to delve into the history of the people who have made this city great. With its unique architecture and sweeping vistas of Manhattan and New York harbor, Green-Wood is truly special.

Finally, Seth and Eric have created "The Other Boroughs: A Driving Tour." This is a daylong driving tour of New York beyond Manhattan and, to our knowledge, a truly unique experience. The driving tour is designed for individual cars. Unfortunately, due to restrictions on city bridges and highways, it cannot be walked or biked. It may seem a bit out of place for a walking tour company to write up a driving tour, but this tour has been carefully designed to lead the driver—and reader—through parts of the city that are less accessible by foot. We do encourage people to park the car and walk when possible. Although designed as one continuous route, it is possible to spread out the tour over the course of days, and you may want to think of it as four boroughs in four discrete pieces.

The creation and development of this project would not have been possible without the help and support of a great number of people. Thanks to Stephen Magro, our editor at New York University Press, who first contacted us and encouraged us to write this book. Thanks also to our colleagues and fellow Big Onion guides, mentioned above, who contributed chapters to this work. And thanks to Professor Kenneth T. Jackson of Columbia University, who got us both interested in the history of New York City so many years ago.

We would like to recognize the efforts of Nicole Wells of the New-York Historical Society, Stefan Saks of the New York Public Library, Anthony Toussaint at the Schomburg Center, and Maricela Herzog of NYC & Company for assisting in the gathering and production of the images. Thanks also to Kenneth Taylor of Green-Wood Cemetery for allowing us to write about Green-Wood. Thanks to Despina Papazoglou Gimbel of NYU Press for editing. Thanks to Bruce Cohen of the Bruce Cohen Group for his enthusiastic support and ideas over the years. Thanks to Matt Rosenberg for correcting (some) of our errors and Phil Mattera of the National Writers Union for his excellent advice.

Thanks to everyone who has ever come on a Big Onion Walking Tour for coming out rain or shine, 365 days a year, to join us as we walk the city we love.

Above all others, we would like to thank, and dedicate this book to, Traci Farber Kamil and Michele Barc and Dane Leach, for supporting us and putting up with many early weekend mornings we left them to explore the city.

SETH KAMIL AND ERIC WAKIN
New York, 2001

Big Onion Walking Tours
www.bigonion.com

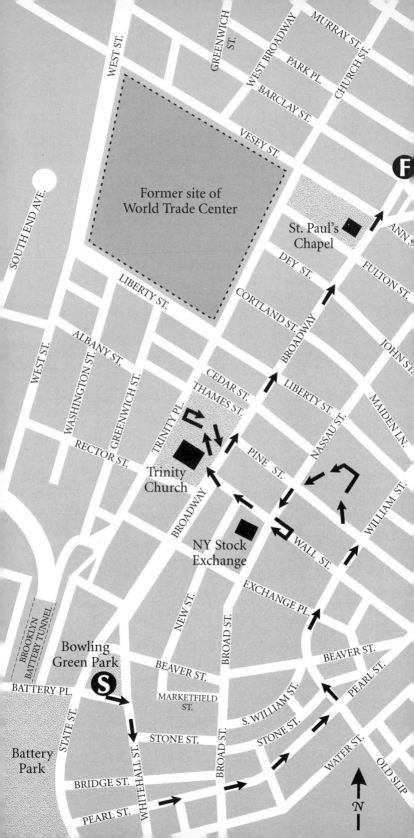

1 WALL STREET
The Architecture of Capitalism

➤ Start: Trains 4 and 5 to Bowling Green or the N/R to Whitehall Street. Begin facing north on Broadway (facing the bull) from the inside of Bowling Green Park.

NEW YORK CITY was founded on money. The Dutch, several years after Henry Hudson's initial tour of duty in 1609, laid claim to a "new" Amsterdam. Their goals were not to advance the cause of human liberty but to get rich. Unlike Pennsylvania Quakers, New England Puritans, or Maryland Catholics, who came to the New World to worship God as they saw fit, the Dutch had their hearts set on trade and exploitation. Beaver trading was the prime avenue to this end and, tragically, slavery a means to achieve it. The Dutch, whose winding streets are all that remain of their four-decade control of the island, were swept away bloodlessly by the British.

The period of British rule, mostly uninterrupted from 1664 until the conclusion of the Revolutionary War in 1783, saw the further development of New York as a center for commerce and early industry. Far more interested in money than politics, New Yorkers' adjustment to British leadership was none too difficult. Despite the devastation wrought by the war, independent New York regained its financial footing rather quickly, spurred on by commercial wizards such as Alexander Hamilton and geographic advantages such as the city's location on the mouth of two rivers. With the institutionalization of the stock exchange, the rise of business and manufacturing, and the riches guaranteed by the digging of the Erie Canal, New York City became the premier financial center in America.

The twentieth century only furthered the empowerment of New York's moneyed classes. New York had become the great symbol of wealth and power, with Wall Street representing the embodiment of that prestige. The first skyscrapers emerged around Wall Street's canyons during the initial years of the twentieth century and many could claim to be the world's tallest at different points in time. The postwar period secured America's economic hegemony, reflected in the transition to glass and steel edifices dotting the downtown skyline. Yet, from the 1990s to the present—with globalization the new rallying cry and markets turning ever more quickly toward virtual exchange—the future of New York's "downtown establishment" is being rethought. And, to be sure, the supreme tragedy of the World Trade Center disaster has changed our conception of the Wall Street environs forever. While both the world and global capitalism will recover, its near-term effects are anybody's guess.

This walk will shed light on New York City's downtown financial history as we take a winding jaunt through many streets originally laid down by the Dutch in the seventeenth century. In fact, it will traverse the basic borders of New York City—those that lasted until the second quarter of the nineteenth century. Throughout you will see how the Wall Street area has evolved—very much as politics and economics have—over the course of the past three centuries.

• • •

Standing here at the bottom of Broadway, it is remarkable to imagine that over the next twelve miles lies the longest avenue in America. But until the second quarter of the nineteenth century, New York City went no farther than City Hall, a fifteen-minute walk to the north. At Broadway's base you find Bowling Green Park, New York City's first official park (1733), which possesses a rich history due to the business and leisure activities of the Dutch and English. It has been pasture for cows, parade ground for soldiers, and, yes, a bowling field for colonists. "Taxation and recreation," one might say, illustrates the park's varied history.

By 1770, King George III was rewarded by the colonists with a gilded statue in the center of the park for his alleged efforts in repealing the Stamp Act; a year later the fence was added, one of Lower Manhattan's few colonial-era remnants. It was here that, in 1776, George's statue was beheaded by enraged colonists and members of the Sons of Liberty, hours after they read the Declaration of Independence in what is now City Hall Park. Supposedly, George's molten lead was then cast into musket balls later used to shoot Tory soldiers. The fence around Bowling Green is one of the oldest—if not the oldest—in the city. Iron crowns adorned the gateposts until American revolutionaries sheared them off. Touch history; you can actually feel where this happened.

➤ **Turn around 180 degrees and gaze at the wonders of the U.S. Custom House.**

While the Custom House is now the site of both the Museum of the American Indian and the U.S. Bankruptcy Court, at one time it was the primary point for revenue collection in the United States. Before the advent of the income tax in 1913, this was where the government made its money. And since New York was by far the leading port city in America, there was a huge amount of money to be made. As historian Henry Hope Reed once noted: If City Hall was run by the Democratic machine, the Custom House was certainly Republican. In fact, it was Republican Chester Arthur who, before becoming president on the death of James Garfield, as collector of customs of the Port of New York, set the wheels in motion for the construction of this building.

The 1907 Cass Gilbert masterpiece is a great example of New York City's beaux arts heritage. *Beaux arts* translates literally as "fine arts" and derives from the great French school, the École des Beaux Arts. But in the New York urban context, the term takes on a larger meaning. Here "beaux arts" refers to those buildings that evince civic pride, that express a grandeur and stateliness to match their civic function, whether that function be to house trains, books, or tax collectors.

In front of the Custom House are Lincoln Memorial sculptor Daniel Chester French's limestone statues representing Asia, America, Europe, and Africa, from left to right. Notice on the facade of the building how Gilbert skillfully illustrates various symbolic examples of commerce: atop the building's cornice are twelve marble statues of history's most successful commercial states. Although you can't see it, the name Germany was effaced during World War I and replaced with Belgium! And look who's gazing ahead from within every capital: none other than Mercury, Roman god of commerce (as Hermes, he is also the Greek god of transportation and can be seen in the heroic statue adorning Grand Central Station a few miles north). Stroll into the museum to view the oval rotunda which is decorated with a series of 1930s Works Progress Administration (WPA) murals by Reginald Marsh.

John D. Rockefeller. Rockefeller's Standard Oil Trust erected its first building at 26 Broadway in 1886. The current structure on the site, finished in 1924, was home to Standard Oil (which evolved into Exxon-Mobil) after the breakup of the trust in 1911. Photo courtesy of the New-York Historical Society.

From the steps of the old Custom House, have a look up Broadway at No. 26 on the east side of the street, on the corner of Broadway and Beaver, at the building with the cast-iron oil burner on the top. The lantern is expressive of the building's function: it housed Standard Oil, John D. Rockefeller's monopolistic firm. However, by the time this tower was built in 1924, the flame had long been extinguished—Standard Oil Trust was broken up a decade earlier. It was in 1911 that the U.S. Supreme Court required the Standard Oil Holding Company to be dissolved and its directors to relinquish their control over its numerous subsidiaries. Rockefeller himself had presided over the petroleum business until that year. Standard Oil's offices remained here until the 1930s, when Rockefeller Center was constructed. In 1796, the town residence of another financial giant, Alexander Hamilton, stood on this site.

Even if Bill Gates's net worth is a hundred times greater than Rockefeller's ever was, the latter's largesse in turn-of-the-century figures is the more significant. And the ravages and rewards of capitalism remain better depicted by old John D. in New York than by young Bill G. in Redmond.

For sheer architectural pleasure, take a moment and admire the graceful and humane way in which the base of the building follows the course of Broadway north. Where else but America would a veritable Greek temple end up on top of a building!

➤ Now look across the way, on the west side of the street.

Across from Rockefeller's building stands 25 Broadway, the former central ticket office of the Cunard Shipping Line. Cunard, one of many steamship companies in that once hugely profitable industry, was the leader of the pack. The Cunard Building was put up in 1921 to house the company that ran the fastest and most luxurious liners in the world. In the age of expensive cruises and mass immigration, this was big business. In fact, in the late nineteenth- and early twentieth-centuries, this bottom stretch of Broadway was known as Steamship Row. Step inside (but not on Sunday) to see some spectacular wall frescoes and maps outlining some of the old Cunard routes.

➤ Walk south on Broadway along the eastern side of the Custom House as it turns into Whitehall Street. Continue walking to Pearl Street.

On the corner of Pearl and Whitehall Streets, at 33 White-hall, is the National Association for Securities Dealers, bet-ter known by its acronynm—NASDAQ. For those of you who rode the turbulent markets of the past few years, this is the building for you to love or hate. Unlike the New York Stock Exchange (see below), NASDAQ's visitor center is not located in the neighborhood but in Times Square. In days past, this was the site of the Whitehall Induction Cen-ter, now immortalized in Arlo Guthrie's classic *Alice's Restaurant*, and the site where Guthrie was "injected, in-spected, detected, infected, neglected, and selected." It was here that Benjamin Spock, the famed baby specialist turned antiwar leader, and poet Allan Ginsberg were arrested in 1967 as part of Stop the Draft week.

> **Turn left onto Pearl Street and walk one block east to Broad Street. Stop in front of 85 Broad Street, located on the northeast corner of Broad and Pearl Streets.**

Goldman Sachs, the notoriously secretive investment-banking concern, is housed in this creatively built octag-onal structure that slices through Stone Street. The building was designed to conform to the irregular street pattern, and paving stones representing Stone Street ac-tually cut right through Goldman Sachs's lobby. The partnership between Marcus Goldman and Samuel Sachs dates from 1882, when they joined forces to further the commercial paper business that Goldman began thirteen years prior. Goldman Sachs has recently gone public, trading openly on the New York Stock Exchange. Is their incognito status endangered? Stay tuned.

During the construction of the site, from 1979 to 1982, a number of excavatory digs identified three-century-old fragments from Lovelace Tavern, once housed nearby. It was here that colonists gathered to deliberate municipal issues—a predecessor locale to the eventual first Stadt Huys, or City Hall, a block away on Coenties Alley and Pearl Street.

➤ **Look across Pearl Street at the southeast corner of Pearl and Broad, at Fraunces Tavern.**

Washington slept here? Well, in this case you might win the bet. What we know for certain is that at this site G.W. bade farewell to his loyal officers on December 4, 1783, nine days after the British evacuation and the end of the Revolutionary War. In one of his most memorable speeches, Washington said: "With a heart full of love and gratitude, I now take leave of you. I most devoutly wish that your latter days may be as prosperous and happy as your former ones have been glorious and honorable." The tavern, which was run at the time by an immigrant from the West Indies who would soon become Washington's steward, Samuel Fraunces, was a popular watering hole of the day. It was also the site where the Committee of Correspondence (later the Continental Congress) held its first meeting. Prior to its revolutionary history, the building was the mansion of Stephen Delancey (as in Delancey Street), a French immigrant who received it as a wedding present from his father-in-law Colonel Stephanus Van Cortlant, New York City's tenth mayor.

The building, a faithful reproduction—no original bits save a few bricks remain—was financed by the Sons of the Revolution in 1907. Its style is Georgian, named for those nefarious British kings and soon renamed "colonial" or "federal," in keeping with the antiroyalist mood of the newly independent states. Fraunces Tavern's modern history is more surreal: it was the site of a bombing in January 1975 by the Armed National Liberation Front (FALN), a group of Puerto Rican independence seekers, that killed four and injured fifty-three. Despite now-senator Hillary Clinton's resistance, President William Jefferson Clinton offered other members of the FALN a pardon in 1999.

Have a look at the block east of Fraunces Tavern on Pearl: this represents one of New York City's few remaining block-long groups of late eighteenth- and early nineteenth-century shipping offices and warehouses. Fortunately, these buildings were among the few that survived the Great Fire of 1835 unscathed. Thanks should go to the nonprofit New York Landmarks Conservancy for saving these buildings from the wrecking ball in the twentieth century. The area is now part of the Fraunces Tavern Block Historic District.

➤ **Walk north on Pearl Street two short blocks to Hanover Square.**

Here in Hanover Square sits lonely Abraham DePeyster, former mayor of New York City, colonial chief justice in the late seventeenth century, and prominent merchant, who once had a more princely view up Broadway, when he was planted in Bowling Green Park. Still, one could do worse than Hanover Square, a lovely former public common, today encircled by converted lofts and new condominiums. In fact, a return to the residential is a theme that is proliferating throughout Wall Street's canyons today, as space built for offices has become even more attractive as apartments for those who want to walk to work in the area.

The area around Hanover Square was once the center of New York City's publishing industry. William Bradford's *New York Gazette*, the city's first newspaper (1725), had its printing offices here. It was also the home base of Captain Kidd, the privateer turned pirate. Interestingly, Hanover Square retains the family name of the English kings. This is in sharp contrast to much of New York that changed its nomenclature after the Revolution.

On the west side of the square is India House at One Hanover Square. Built in the early 1850s, India House has had various incarnations. It was originally the Hanover Bank and later the New York Cotton Exchange, when cotton was king. Brownstone was once seen as unseemly for a proper home, but this building, as well as Trinity Church, helped change that. In the latter half of the nineteenth century, brownstone became a mark of dignity for New York's landed gentry. Today, India House is one of Lower Manhattan's most exclusive business clubs. It takes its name from nautical trips to (and Orientalist fantasies of) the East. Its original members were less concerned with the vagaries of banking and finance than with maritime issues.

Have a glance at the former headquarters of the infamous Kidder Peabody on 10 Hanover Square. They were housed here from 1969 through their Reagan-era junk-bond scandals, until their merger with Paine Webber in 1995.

Take a look eastward toward Old Slip by the river, which until 1973 housed the first Precinct Police (South Street at Old Slip). Finished in 1911 and considered to be New York City's first modern police station, it is designed in the form of a Renaissance palazzo. Now it is headquarters to the Landmarks Preservation Commission. Irony aside, without the latter institution, this and over a thousand other structures in New York City could have met the fate of Pennsylvania Station—destruction.

➢ **Leaving Hanover Square, turn left onto William Street and continue about four blocks to Wall Street.**

Along the way, at 56 Beaver, on the southwest corner of South William Street, is Delmonico's. This venerable New

York City restaurant was established in 1827 by the brothers Delmonico. The building, with a white marble portico reputedly from Pompeii, dates from 1891. Go inside to experience the *haute-bourgeois* flavor of nineteenth-century New York.

At 22 William, between Beaver and Exchange Place, is the City Bank Farmers' Trust Company Building, built in 1931. This building has always been a curiosity in the canyons of Wall Street; it departs from the rectilinear and pivots as if ready to blast off. The irregular site that it inhabits helped the architects push the envelope in their design. The bronze doors are the building's *pièces de résistance*; enjoy its sumptuous decoration filled with trains, boats, and airplanes. The interior uses over forty different kinds of marble and is laced with nickel and copper.

Look skyward for a few moments and bask in the glory of downtown New York's canyons. Could the Dutch ever have imagined that their twisted, circuitous roads would one day be dotted with towers of masonry and steel? Even present-day Amsterdam has nothing resembling a "small skyscraper"!

Wall Street—the locus of world capitalism, the *sine qua non* of corporate finance, the epicenter of the blue suit. This is perhaps the most famous street in all of America. And rightly so. Since the first market opened here under a buttonwood tree down on William and Wall after the Revolutionary War, Wall Street has been the lasting American symbol of wealth and power. Even if it seems a tad passé to envision one street as the embodiment of financial capital in an age when capital is virtual, the name Wall Street continues to resonate symbolically.

The "Wall" in the name indeed comes from an actual wall built by the Dutch that lasted from Governor Peter Stuyvesant, who had it erected in 1653, through the latter part of the seventeenth century, when colonists under British rule finally undermined it. The wall (known in Dutch as *De Wal*) was made of wooden planks stacked roughly nine feet high and was manned to keep both the British (until 1664) and the Indians away from New Amsterdam. Jews were at first banned from standing guard at the wall and were taxed instead. Asser Levy, a prominent Jewish resident, brought a suit against the Dutch West India Company, which eventually overturned Stuyvesant's ruling and allowed Jews to stand watch. Levy is now memorialized a little bit further uptown, on Twenty-third Street, by Asser Levy Place.

At the eastern end of Wall Street stood a number of slave markets; in fact, on the eve of the American Revolution, New York City was an ignominious second to Charleston, South Carolina, among urban slaveholding cities. It was not until July 4, 1827, with the approval of Governor Daniel D. Tompkins and the New York state legislature, that slavery was officially laid to rest (see more on slavery on page 26).

The building immediately to your right, at 55 Wall Street, was designed by Isaiah Rogers in 1842 to replace the Merchants Exchange, which, with four hundred other buildings, was lost in the Great Fire of 1835. It functioned as the U.S. Custom House during 1863–99. In its most recent incarnation, it was a branch office of Citibank, which was formed by the merger of First National Bank and the City Bank Farmers' Trust Company.

The building is notable for the amazingly seamless arrangement of its structure, where the bottom Ionic colonnade put up in 1842 (and each a single block of stone!) works hand in glove with the upper Corinthian colonnade built seventy years later. The mammoth lobby measures 198 feet long and is 132 feet in height, and it houses the largest display of Wedgewood china in the world around its central chandelier.

At press time, the Cipriani family, caterers extraordinaire and foes of New York City labor unions, notorious for hiring only nonunion labor, are converting this space into a banquet hotel on floor one and a hotel with 142 guest suites on floor two. For similar efforts by the same family, check out the conversion of the former Bowery Savings Bank building across the street from Grand Central Station on Forty-second Street, as well as the Rainbow Room at Rockefeller Center, which they also control. Across from 55 Wall Street we come to the J. P. Morgan Building. The Pulitzer Prize–winning architectural critic Ada Louise Huxtable, not known for her appreciation of the last several decades of New York City architecture, has sung the praises of Kevin Roche's rich postmodern monolith here at 60 Wall, and rightly so. The modern movement in architecture had become so moribund by the 1970s, producing a surfeit of third-rate flat-topped knockoffs, that it seemed the grace and grandeur of previous eras would be forever sundered from the future.

Roche, however, in one of the finer examples of postmodernism in contemporary architecture, has achieved a building that holds its own side by side with the pantheon of financial structures down and around Wall Street. And for a tall building, it does not impose upon or dominate its neighbors; it blends in quite nicely (enacting one of postmodernism's great critiques of modernism) as its own faux colonnade speaks convincingly to 55 Wall's colonnade across the street. In an interesting quirk, it was 55 Wall that sold its air rights to allow for the 55-story height of the J. P. Morgan Building. The vast interior atrium open to the public is lovely as well.

To your left, at 40 Wall Street, was originally the Bank

of Manhattan. It's hard to imagine that 40 Wall, polished, waxed, and stylized by New York's very own Donald Trump, once was of unique importance in the history of American skyscraper construction. But it was. New York City has had a number of terrific rivalries in its past: Dodgers/Yankees, Robert Moses/Jane Jacobs, Bronx Science/Stuyvesant. But in terms of the building trade, it's worth retelling the story of the Bank of Manhattan versus the Chrysler Building during the summer of 1929.

Longtime professional rivals, former partners William Van Alen and Craig Severance were hard at work trying to outdo each other in the battle for dominant skyscraper height. While the Great Depression lurked just around the corner, New Yorkers were enthralled by the so-called race to the top. The Woolworth Tower held sway as New York City's tallest building, but Severance was convinced until the very last moment that his Bank of Manhattan would outdo Van Alen's automotive giant and dethrone Frank Woolworth. But hidden from view, and unveiled only at the final moment of the competition, was Chrysler's razor-sharp spire, which because of its additional 125 feet outdid 40 Wall and brought the Chrysler Building the fame of being the tallest. Severance's consolation prize? 40 Wall broke all records for speed; it was finished in eleven months, with over a million square feet of floor space.

For Van Alen's Chrysler building, success was short-lived. The Empire State unseated the Chrysler after only eighteen months. As for the Bank of Manhattan, in only five years it would drop to being the fifth tallest building in the United States. Today it's at number 30 and counting.

Are the tallest buildings in the world in New York City? or perhaps Chicago? Better head east—Far East—as the giants are being built throughout China, Malaysia, and Singapore. Today, five of the world's tallest ten buildings are in Asia.

For many years, 40 Wall Street was the headquarters of the late Manufacturer's Hanover Trust (known by its avuncular nickname "Manny Hanny"). The site was home to the original Bank of Manhattan building in 1799.

➤ **Walk north along William Street, one block to Pine Street, and go up the steps on your left to Chase Manhattan Plaza.**

Finished in 1960, David Rockefeller's Chase Manhattan Bank Building is a shining example of sleek postwar modernism in action. The Chase building also helped usher in a new "democratic" era of bank building, where banks became transparent structures that could be "seen through" rather than maintaining the impenetrable fortress facades of tradition. As the best example of the contrast, take a look through the Chase building and have a peek at the Federal Reserve, an impenetrable fortress—as well it should be, to hold all the gold inside.

Standing on the plaza check out René Dubuffet's *Group of 4 Trees* sculpture; the AIA guide makes the clever remark that Dubuffet's white-painted concrete work has the effect of papier-mâché. David Rockefeller's commitment to modernist art and architecture is also seen in the sunken fountain below, courtesy of the fine Japanese American sculptor Isamu Noguchi. (One of New York City's lesser-known outer-borough treats is his sculpture museum in Queens.) For an additional taste of the fine arts, look north for a moment at Louise Nevelson Plaza. It is here that seven black sculpted objects by the noted American sit in a small plaza.

Chase remains one of the largest banking firms in the United States, with assets of almost $400 billion. Their historic merger in 1996 with Chemical Bank created what was, at the time, the nation's largest banking company.

Notice the modest, self-effacing marker announcing "The Trump Building" alongside the Pine Street facade of 40 Wall. Somehow, we don't think Craig Severance ever had this in mind.

Walk north to the other side of the plaza to the Federal Reserve Bank. Built like a fortress in 1924, this structure was made to resist the elements. It is not New York snobbery to recognize this as the most significant of the thirteen Federal Reserve sites. The limestone facade of the bank is noted for its capacity to weather in different tones. (Notice how they change from light to dark.) Take a closer look as well at the magnificent wrought-iron lanterns designed by the Philadelphian Samuel Yellin.

The Federal Reserve Bank was set up in 1914 in order to have a central bank, rather than one person, make decisions on policy. In 1907, for example, J. P. Morgan was responsible for mobilizing enough banking support to help stave off a collapse that could have rivaled the Great Depression. The Federal Reserve currently holds upward of $110 billion in gold bullion, mostly in foreign holdings (in other terms, one-quarter of the official monetary gold of eighty countries—more than Fort Knox!). Wheelbarrows are still in use transporting the gold bullion from one country's room to the next.

➤ **Double back, leaving Chase Plaza, and turn right and head west one block to Nassau Street. Walk south on Nassau Street one short block back to Wall Street.**

Westward, at 14 Wall, stands the Bankers Trust Building. Bankers Trust is no more (see Deutsche Bank for details), but Trowbridge and Livingston's pyramidal top, taken from antiquity's well-known mausoleum at Halicarnassus (fourth century B.C.), remains. It is one of the great pinnacles in a city bathed in sumptuous finishing touches. In fact,

The 1842 Federal Hall, formerly a subtreasury building and now a museum. George Washington took his first oath of office as president in the previous version of Federal Hall on this site, which also contained both houses of Congress and the departments of state, war and treasury. Photo courtesy of the New-York Historical Society.

J. P. Morgan shacked up in the pyramid to have a bird's-eye view of the construction of his own building across the street. The pyramid became for years the logo of Bankers Trust (although, in a testimony to the effect of downtown canyons, you cannot see the pyramid from Wall Street itself). Take a walk inside to have a peek at the bronze gates in the lobby. Exquisitely finished, they represent the various enterprises of capitalism, including metallurgy, shipping, mining, agriculture, and power.

On the northeast corner of Nassau and Wall stands Federal Hall National Memorial, the "Parthenon of Wall Street" as some have dubbed it. The site has a vigorous and significant past as New York City's second city hall, formerly the Custom House and subtreasury in the nineteenth century and currently a federal museum. When New York became the nation's capital in 1789, the building on this site was renamed Federal Hall. The current structure dates from 1842. In it the fledgling government of the United States operated for its first eighteen months. It contained both houses of Congress and the departments of state, war, and treasury. Before its federal function, here John Peter Zenger, editor of the critical *New York Weekly Journal*, was both tried and acquitted in 1735 of seditious libel in a case that was to be the lodestar for press and speech freedoms thereafter. The famed Stamp Act Congress met here in 1765 to draft the Declaration of Grievances against "taxation without representation." And the Declaration of Independence was read here on July 9. (It took some days to travel from Philly to New York; no e-mail access then.) The site even served as the British headquarters during the Revolutionary War!

Take a look at the dignified statue of George Washington sculpted by the master John Quincy Adams Ward (no relation to George Washington's successor). Just about where he now stands stood G.W. himself, in a plain brown suit on the second floor of the original building, taking the oath of office as the first president of the United States. In 1790, with the move of the federal capital to Philadelphia, the building on this site, designed by Washington, D.C.'s great master planner Pierre L'Enfant, was demolished.

Federal Hall's Greek-revival style was typical for the earlier nineteenth-century period, when Athenian democracy and the Greek independence movement led to a bumper crop of Doric-templed civic buildings throughout the nation. Only a short while later, when abolitionism gained steam in the North, Greece became associated with slavery rather than the *demos*, and those lovely classical buildings lost their place in the sun.

Set your gaze across Wall Street at the plain, unornamented, unsigned building on the southeast corner of Broad and Wall. Why the modesty? Why the restraint? Well, this is J. P. Morgan's bank building, and as Morgan wanted all to realize, if you didn't know what this building was, you had no business (literally and figuratively) being there. The only decoration on the facade of the building are the pockmarks that dot the Wall Street side, remnants of a bomb (blamed on anarchists) that killed thirty-one people and wounded hundreds in 1920. The scars remain because Morgan felt they were a testament to his invincibility.

Directly across Broad Street from Morgan's building is the *sine qua non* of capitalist institutions: the New York Stock Exchange (NYSE). Even if its address is, after all, on Broad Street, this is the best known of Wall Street's buildings. Its facade has contributed significantly to its status. In contrast to the severe Grecian temple of Federal Hall across the way, the NYSE's Roman trappings are all pomp and circumstance.

Take a look at the somewhat forlorn little tree out front on Broad Street. This isn't any old tree but a buttonwood (or sycamore). Its symbolism? Well, in 1792, twenty-four brokers met under a buttonwood (in actuality further east on Wall Street) and began trading the massive debt from the Revolutionary War. The so-called Buttonwood Agreement, *Gotham*'s Edwin Burrows and Michael Wallace tell us, "laid the foundations for a structured securities market without the now discredited auctions." Early the next year the traders moved into the Tontine Coffee House, which was located on the northwest corner of Water and Wall Streets. This site had been the locale for the infamous Royal African Trading Company, where the English bought and sold enslaved Africans.

Without question, the New York financial market has seen a multitude of changes since the crash of 1929. With the late-1990s boom cycle, the great crash has receded further into our cultural memory. But it was a full twenty-five years before the Dow Jones Industrial Average surpassed the summer highs of that fateful year. Even more telling, it wasn't until 1968 that the daily volume on the floor of the exchange surpassed the 16 million shares traded on Black Thursday. Today, 16 million shares are traded quite often on one company in the course of a day; the NYSE trades 16 million in each day's first few minutes.

Take a peek down Broad Street. It runs from Wall down to the tip of Manhattan. It was originally a canal dug by the Dutch in 1660 and filled in by their British successors in 1676.

SLAVERY

New York City was no stranger to slavery. It was, in fact, the largest slaveholding city in all the colonies until 1750, and the number-one place for slave importation and auctions.

Slaves arrived in the city as early as 1626, brought in small numbers from the Dutch West Indies. But on September 15, 1655, the **Witte Paert** docked with three hundred African slaves. This signaled New York City's beginning as a large-scale port of destination for the transatlantic slave trade. Many slaves were then shipped from New York to the Chesapeake, but by 1664, the city was 20 to 25 percent black.

Under the Dutch, slaves were provided with some medical care, food, and housing. The Dutch gave half freedom to some; this meant a degree of freedom in finding housing and employment, but even half-free blacks were required to work for the Dutch West India company when labor was needed, and children were company property. A few were allowed to settle outside the city on land grants, as a buffer between European settlers and Indians, and a few were free outright. Slaves could testify in court in cases involving whites and were allowed to serve in the militia during emergencies. In 1663, a group of half-free blacks petitioned for freedom in return for service to the Dutch under threat of English invasion. The Dutch agreed and gave some full freedom in 1664, but seven hundred remained in slavery.

The British recognized all residents' slave property after their conquest in 1664. They then made it more difficult each year for blacks to be free, restricted slaves freed by the Dutch, and eliminated half-free status. In 1677, British law dictated that all blacks brought to trial were presumed to be slaves, and in 1706, it decreed that conversion to Christianity did not affect slaves' status. The British needed labor. From 1730 to 1750 the black population grew faster than the white. By 1746, one in five New Yorkers was black, but that number declined to 16 percent at the time of the Revolution. In King's County at that time one-third of the residents were black, and more than half of whites owned slaves.

In the city, owners typically had two or three slaves who lived and worked in the master's home. Slaves also worked as coopers, tailors, bakers, tanners, carpenters, sailmakers, and masons and were able to hire out their own labor. New York City had 3,137 slaves by 1771. Under the British occupation, slaves fled to New York City in hopes of freedom. After 1781 the British evacuated many blacks, some of whom ended up as slaves in the West Indies. In 1784, the New York legislature granted freedom to slaves abandoned by departing Loyalists (property forfeiture). Others were freed for service to patriot causes.

In 1785, the New York Manumission Society began to work for the gradual abolition of slavery. The majority of both houses of the New York legislature wanted to abolish the institution, but could not decide on the future status of freed slaves; few wanted blacks to have equal civil rights. French fleeing Haiti near the end of the eighteenth century brought their slaves and increased New York City's slave population. The Gradual Manumission Act of 1799 freed males born after that year at age twenty-eight and females at age twenty-five. In 1820, only 518 slaves remained in New York City, and legislation emancipating all slaves finally took effect in 1827.

New York City saw several significant slave uprisings during the eighteenth century, most notably the 1712 uprising on Maiden Lane and Nassau Street (the present site of the Home Insurance

Company). It was here that more than fifty armed slaves gathered for an uprising that eventually killed nine white settlers before the slaves dispersed to the north. Ultimately nineteen participants were captured and executed in gruesome fashion—by hanging, burning, and goring—in order to intimidate the remaining slave population.

➤ **Walk west on Wall Street toward Trinity Church.**

The building at 1 Wall Street now houses the Bank of New York, which absorbed the original owners, the Irving Trust, in 1988; at the time the building had the highest real estate price tag of any site in New York City. Inside the three-story reception hall is one of the most glorious interiors in Manhattan, maybe even along the whole eastern seaboard. This is Art Deco at its most majestic: soaring, proud, and emboldened. Lewis Mumford called 1 Wall Street a building of "untrammeled imagination." It is one of the sad fates in architectural history that the golden age of Deco, reflected in a goodly number of powerfully massed tall buildings, came to a screeching halt with the onset of the Great Depression. At the very top of the fluted skyscraper is a gilded mosaic boardroom, testament to the extravagance of a different age.

Trinity Church (Wall Street and Broadway)—it is hard to imagine in an age when skyscrapers, giant corporate headquarters, and Starbucks dot the landscape, but there was a time when churches were all one could see on the skyline viewed from any part of the urban mise-en-scène. Trinity, at 280 feet, was the highest point in New York City until surpassed by the towers of the Brooklyn Bridge (which says a lot about commerce). That Trinity was in part a sanctuary for religious residents does not mean it didn't maintain close relations with the financial elements

The view west on Wall Street, from Broad Street to Trinity Church, with the steps of Federal Hall to the right. Kiernan's and the buildings to its left are on the future site of the New York Stock Exchange building. Photo courtesy of the New-York Historical Society.

of the city, nor that the two can be separated. Indeed, its location at the foot of Wall Street. is evidence enough of its relationship with the power structure's financial elite.

Trinity began as a land grant from Queen Anne to the colonists in the late seventeenth century. Many of the early belfrymen, pastors, and rectors now have New York City streets named after them (Chambers, Murray, and Reade Streets, for example). The church originally controlled all the land from Fulton up to Christopher Street.

Trinity Church has gone through three incarnations. The first church (1696–1776) was burned in the fire of 1776. The second saw its roof implode in 1839. The present building by Richard Upjohn has fortunately withstood the ravages of time.

Looking north up Broadway past the 280-foot Trinity Church spire, with the open space of the churchyard around it. This 1846 structure by Richard Upjohn is Trinity's third incarnation on the site; the church's original land grant included all the land from Broadway to the Hudson River, from Fulton to Christopher Streets. Photo courtesy of the New-York Historical Society.

Today the church is no stranger to wealth and influence; although many have been sold over time, parish holdings still bring in approximately $40 million per year. A curiosity from yesteryear: Trinity still maintains the rights to all unclaimed shipwrecks and beached whales along part of the Hudson River.

Take a walk around the churchyard and you will run into an illustrious gathering of New York City's prominent financial elite and early purveyors of freedom and liberty. Alexander Hamilton was buried here after his fateful duel with Vice President Aaron Burr in Weehawken, New Jersey; Robert Fulton, noted inventor of the steamship, is memorialized; and the churchyard provides the final resting places for William Bradford, publisher of New York's first newspaper; and Francis Lewis, the only signer of the Declaration of Independence buried in Manhattan. Opposite Pine Street, in the north part of the churchyard, stands the Soldiers/Martyrs monument. Erected in 1852, it stands as a memorial to soldiers who died during the American Revolution while imprisoned in Rhinelander Sugar House on Liberty (originally Crown) Street. There were only 6,824 combat deaths among the revolutionaries, 29 percent of the war's total fatalities. Another 18,500 died in captivity, more than half of them in New York.

➤ Take a quick detour through the graveyard on the north side of the church and down the set of stairs on the other side to Trinity Place, and have a peek at the American Stock Exchange.

The American Stock Exchange (AMEX) has its roots at the curbstone of Broad Street and Exchange Place, where curb brokers would literally stop at nothing to buy and sell. It was only in 1921 (after fifty-six years!) that the New York curb market found a home. In 1953 it was officially designated the American Stock Exchange. The AMEX is currently becoming a subsidiary of NASDAQ.

➤ **Return to Broadway and walk north to No. 120, the Equitable Building, filling the block between Pine and Cedar Streets.**

Standing on Thames Street opposite 120 Broadway offers the tourist an ideal crash course in New York City's first zoning ordinance. The extreme mass of the Equitable Building, where the floor area was thirty times the site's area and the shafts went straight up—all the way to the fortieth floor—was a bit discouraging. Forty-five acres of floor space all on a site that was just over an acre in size! Forget pork bellies; light and air are the most desired commodities on this block.

Among other things, the new ordinance called for a "zoning envelope" that restricted pure shafts darting straight into the sky and forced what became known as the "setback"—the stepped-back, stairlike recesses one sees as buildings grow taller. Spurred on by the exquisite drawings of Hugh Ferris, setbacks became a design challenge for architects, each trying to outdo the next in terms of geometry and flair.

The top three floors of the Equitable were for a long time taken up by the Banker's Club, one of the most affluent and well heeled clubs in the city. The Equitable has long since moved out.

➤ **Continue walking north on Broadway and take a breather in Liberty Plaza.**

You may be wondering how, in this dense and overoccupied downtown district, an open-air plaza (with benches!)

was able to emerge. If only we could credit the magnanimity of Wall Street bankers. In point of fact, it was the great Seagram Building on Park Avenue, with its pristine plaza and open space, that convinced the city to find incentives for developers to allow more public use. Thus was born the 1961 zoning ordinance, which encouraged and rewarded builders who provided public space integrated with private buildings.

Directly west of the plaza once stood the complex of seven buildings, the World Trade Center, spotlighted by the "twin towers"—Towers 1 and 2—the third tallest buildings in the world. In the greatest act of terror to occur on American soil, over three thousand persons lost their lives on September 11, 2001, when two hijacked planes were crashed into the twin towers, resulting in horrible fires and the buildings' implosion. As we write, it is too early to know what will become of this now tragic space. But in New York's unceasing effort to rebuild that which is torn down—part of the genetic make-up of America really—it is unlikely that the area will remain fallow far into the future. Yet the question remains how and in what way to memorialize, a question long debated at the site of the African burial ground, which still lies just north near City Hall.

Take a look across Liberty Street at the U.S. Steel Building at 1 Liberty Plaza. This building contrasts nicely with the Marine Midland Bank across Broadway to your right. Designed by the same firm seven years later (in fact Chase, also by Skidmore Owings and Merrill, was designed seven years before Marine Midland) it possesses none of the grace and attention to detail of Marine Midland. One could argue that, having been designed for U.S. Steel, it maintains an understandable girth and bulge, but this does not excuse the tiny and inhuman base. U.S. Steel itself exists today as USX.

THE LATE GREAT SINGER BUILDING

On the site of today's U.S. Steel/1 Liberty and the outdoor plaza stood one of the great downtown buildings in New York, the Singer Building. Perhaps the mourning wasn't as great as when Pennsylvania Station was slaughtered in 1963, but the Singer Building's demolition brought tears of rage consistent with its long-standing importance in New York City's skyline. Its tragic epitaph notes that it is the tallest building ever to be demolished.

As this book goes to press, a rare occurrence has happened in New York City: a bad building has lost the battle with developers. Say goodbye to the Columbus Circle Coliseum, a colossal disaster that New Yorkers had to live with for nearly fifty years and that is now being replaced by AOL-Time Warner's headquarters.

It was uncommon in the late 1960s and during the 1970s—impossible, is more like it—for a real estate developer to think about the quality of his building as a means of attracting lessors. Standard operating procedure called for structures that were materially inexpensive and expeditiously completed. The end result is best witnessed in much of the banal and uninspired last-gasp modernism that dots the canyons of Third and Sixth Avenues. But in the case of the Marine Midland Bank Building (140 Broadway), Harry Helmsley was ahead of his time.

Helmsley was moved to hire one of the great international style architects, Gordon Bunshaft of Skidmore Owings and Merrill (who also designed the Chase Manhattan building behind it in 1960), as well as the sculptor Isamu Noguchi (whose fountain you saw in Chase's plaza). The result is a sleek, refined, matte-glass exterior that adds dignity to this stretch of Broadway. Noguchi's moving contribution is an orange cube (well, to be exact, it's a rhombohedron—a six-sided figure) with a cut-out hole.

Marine Midland Bank is the principal U.S. subsidiary of

the London HSBC Holdings, P.L.C., one of the world's largest banking and financial services organizations.

➤ **Continue north on Broadway five blocks, to the corner of Barclay Place and the Woolworth Building at 233 Broadway.**

Where have you gone, Frank Woolworth? It was the revolutionary genius of Woolworth to open a set of stores where the buyer could touch, feel, and examine every item he or she thought of purchasing. Sounds sentimental in an age of virtual commerce, but it made Woolworth a mint.

The tallest building in the world from 1917 to 1929, the Woolworth is symbolized by its trademarked name the "Cathedral of Commerce." Sadly, the great cathedral closed its famous stores in the mid-1990s and sold its Gothic-style tower in June 1998 for $155 million to the Witkoff Group. But there is a happy ending: because of landmark rulings, once a building has been landmarked it forever retains the name of the original structure. Hence, forevermore, the Woolworth will be the Woolworth. (The same holds true for the Equitable, Lever House, and many others; the Pan Am Building, however, is only a memory.)

The exterior of the building is dressed up in late Gothic style, perhaps the best use of the period we have in New York. Everything is right in this building: its materials, specifically the terra cotta used throughout the facade; the clear and articulated form of the base, shaft, and tower. There is simply nothing extraneous. For most New York building enthusiasts, it is the archetype of a skyscraper.

Take a look where possible at the extraordinary interior as well. The central guards won't let you wander too far off, but you have time to appreciate several magnificent gargoyles, including Cass Gilbert (the architect) and Woolworth himself counting the nickels and dimes with

Cass Gilbert's "Cathedral of Commerce"—the Woolworth Building—just after it was completed in 1913. For many New Yorkers, the building's perfect form makes it the archetype of skyscrapers—and Frank Woolworth paid for its entire cost with $13 million in cash. Photo courtesy of the New-York Historical Society.

which he (literally) paid for the building. (Since Frank Woolworth paid in full with $13 million in cash, the building never had a mortgage.) It's a fitting coda to this downtown romp through New York's financial district.

When finished with Woolworth's sumptuous interior, go across the street and enjoy the newly redesigned City Hall Park. The park has been landscaped as a nineteenth-century meeting ground with actual gaslights and other accoutrements.

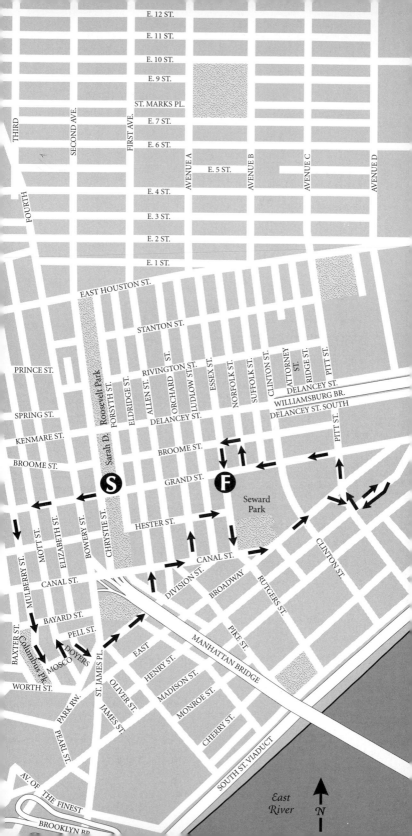

2 THE LOWER EAST SIDE

Immigrant New York

➤ Start: B/D/Q station at Grand Street at Sara Delano Roosevelt Park.

THE LOWER EAST SIDE is probably the single most significant multiethnic neighborhood in America. For the past two hundred years it has been the first area of settlement for numerous migrant and immigrant communities, and it continues to be so today. This walking tour is an introduction to the many layers of ethnicity in the Lower East Side.

What is the Lower East Side anyway? The geographic boundaries of the neighborhood have varied over the years, and New Yorkers continue to argue about where it begins and where it ends. The contemporary neighborhood is bordered to the north by Houston Street, to the west by Lafayette, and to the south and east by the East River. But the Lower East Side should also be thought of as a living multiethnic neighborhood—one not necessarily constrained by geographic boundaries.

Early eighteenth-century maps show the area as the location of the country estates of established Dutch and

English settlers of New York. Early property owners included the Stuyvesant, Delancey, Rutgers, Depeyster, and Roosevelt families. After the American Revolution, the estates and farms began to make way for smaller semirural and then almost suburban settlements.

By the mid–nineteenth century, the Lower East Side had accelerated process of urbanization and began to see its first significant influx of immigrants. By the 1840s the largest numbers of ethnic residents were Irish, Germans, and free blacks. A half century later these groups had largely moved northward and were replaced by southern and eastern Europeans from Italy, Russia, Poland, and elsewhere. Most of today's immigrant residents are Latino and Asian immigrants.

According to U.S. Census records, in 1930 the section of the Lower East Side bordered by Delancey, East Broadway, Bowery, and the East River was home to almost eighty-thousand residents. Over half of them were foreign born, mostly immigrants from Poland, Russia, Austria-Hungary, and Italy. In 1990, despite increased immigration to New York in recent decades, the population of the Lower East Side was only forty-seven thousand, of which about a third were foreign born, mostly from China, Hong Kong, and the Dominican Republic. It is important to note that there is a substantial Puerto Rican population on the Lower East Side, but they are not counted as immigrants by the Census Bureau because Puerto Rico is an American commonwealth and its residents are American citizens.

The pattern of arrival, settlement, and migration to the second area of settlement is a complicated process. Some families live in the neighborhood for only a brief time while others call the Lower East Side home for generations. Countless individual decisions drive families and groups to move into or out of a neighborhood: wanting a bigger apartment; marriage; work; not wanting to live with newer immigrants. And some folks remain in a neighborhood regardless of changes around them.

Further complicating our understanding of the place called the Lower East Side are the labels immigrants are assigned on arrival in America. As we will see on this walking tour, the various neighborhoods may bear such names as Little Italy and the Jewish East Side, but in reality there were (and are) multiple Italian communities within Little Italy, and a vast array of Jewish immigrants settled in the Jewish East Side. In the end, there is no single Lower East Side. This is a deeply textured neighborhood with a tremendous and complex array of immigrant groups.

Beginning our tour at Sara Delano Roosevelt Park illustrates the tremendous changes in the Lower East Side over the past century. Seven blocks of tenement houses were destroyed from 1932 to 1936 to create this "green" space. Construction was part of a Depression-era plan to employ thousands of laborers using federal relief funds. The city proclaimed "eminent domain" over the existing tenements, removed the tenants, and tore the buildings down. Like most public spaces in New York, the park is named for a significant New Yorker—Franklin Delano Roosevelt's mother. Sara was raised in a manor house, now long gone, on Chrystie Street.

In 1900 the Lower East Side was the most densely populated spot on earth. It had 850 residents per block and nearly 1,000 per acre. In fact, a single square block adjacent to the park—bordered by Canal, Hester, Eldridge, and Forsythe Streets—housed 2,628 people in 1890. This block currently houses no residents. The contemporary buildings on the block are a school and a few manufacturers. Other blocks in the neighborhood were destroyed to build the approaches to the Manhattan and Williamsburg Bridges in 1903 and 1909, forcing tens of thousands of people out of their homes. Many people stayed in the neighborhood, but more began to move uptown and to outer boroughs in the years leading up to World War II.

➤ **Walk west on Grand Street past Chrystie Street toward the Bowery.**

We begin our walk in the area some call the New China-town. Thousands of immigrants from mainland China have moved to these blocks in the past ten or fifteen years. Walking along Grand Street between Chrystie Street and the Bowery, note the incredible array of fish and produce stores that line the street. This block in particular has become one of the best food shopping blocks in Chinatown. But note, it is shopping for residents—not for tourists. Pay close attention to how the Lower East Side functions as a commercial district on some blocks while it simultaneously attempts to cater to tourists with cafés, restaurants, and souvenir shops on others.

THE BOWERY

In 1637 the Bowery was created by New Amsterdam governor Willem Keift to connect the distant Dutch farms of what we now call the East Village with the city, which was south of Wall Street. Some historians claim that Bowery derives its name from **bowerij,** the Dutch word for farm, but others state it is from **de bowerie,** the road to the farms. Either way, it connected the city to the countryside. By 1776, the Bowery connected New York City with Boston, Massachusetts.

During the mid-nineteenth century, this bucolic roadway became increasingly commercial and simultaneously gained a reputation for being New York's Skid Row, a place of saloons, sailors, homeless men, and a wide array of activities condemned as unsavory by the middle class. In 1884, more than a quarter of all the police arrests in Manhattan took place here. In that same year there were eighty-two saloons on the Bowery, an average of more than six per block.

In the early twentieth century, the Bowery was a geographical divider between Little Italy (to the west) and the Jewish Lower East Side (to the east). Not only was this a major commercial street, but between 1878 and 1955 an elevated train ran the length of the Bowery. Prior to electrification, the soot and burning embers falling from the engines made crossing under the tracks dangerous and unpleasant. Furthermore, the El tracks shrouded the Bowery in darkness, adding to the seedy and dingy atmosphere.

Beginning in the early 1970s, commercial development by Chinese immigrants began moving up the Bowery from Chatham Square, and by the late 1980s, gentrification began to spread south from Cooper Square. Despite these changes, in 1999 there were still eight flophouses and three charitable missions on the Bowery.

The Hotel Providence stands on the southeast corner of Bowery and Grand Street, at 125 Bowery. This is one of the eight surviving Bowery "flophouses." These private hotels emerged on the Bowery in the early 1870s. The largest was the Mills Hotel on Bowery and Rivington Street, which had five hundred rooms and slept over one thousand men.

Today, for $8 to $15 per night, a male resident can get a four-by-eight-foot cubicle with a cot and a hanging light. There are shared toilets and baths on each floor. By looking through the windows, you can see how the second floor of the Hotel Providence is a common space with tables and chairs; the rooms are on the upper floors. The rooms are nicknamed "cages" because the walls do not go to the ceiling. Just above the door jamb, the wall and ceiling are replaced with a wire screen. Theoretically

Steve Brodie's Saloon at 114 Bowery around 1890. Brodie won a $200 bet for jumping from the Brooklyn Bridge in 1886 and used the money to open his saloon, which included a mural of his leap painted behind the bar. Photo courtesy of the New-York Historical Society.

this is for ventilation, but it also creates a cagelike space, open at the top, with limited privacy.

Across the Bowery from the Hotel Providence stood Steve Brodie's Saloon, at 114 Bowery. Steve Brodie, a national champion racewalker, jumped from the Brooklyn Bridge in July 1886. He collected a $200 bet for surviving his leap and used the money to open his saloon here. On the wall behind the bar he painted a large image of himself falling between the bridge and the water. While a regular saloon, Brodie's also quickly became a prime tourist spot. For a "small consideration" Brodie would retell his story to visitors. Should anyone not believe his tale, he would point to the signed affidavit from the nearly dozen witnesses who saw his leap. A cloud of suspicion does remain—those who signed were members of Brodie's gang. For years after Brodie's death, an old man would pretend to be Brodie and recount the tale, much to the delight of the tourists.

On the northwest corner of Bowery and Grand Street, at 230 Grand, is the old Bowery Bank building. Built in

1890, this was one of the many smaller banks that filled the city before banking consolidation and the financial crashes of the late nineteenth and early twentieth centuries. Wrapped around the Bowery Bank is the Bowery Savings Bank (1894–95, designed by Stanford White). The street address of the L-shaped Savings Bank is 130 Bowery and is one of the few landmarked buildings on the Lower East Side. As we go to press, this magnificent building is no longer open to the public, as the bank's offices have moved to 116 Bowery.

The Bowery Savings Bank was created in 1834 by three prominent New York businessmen: Hamilton Fish, Peter C. Stuyvesant, and Anson Phelps. The original 1834 safe box is displayed as part of a small historical exhibit in the restored main banking room. While the Bowery is popularly known as "Skid Row," it has been a significant commercial district for more than a century.

➤ **Continue walking west on Grand Street, three blocks toward Mulberry Street.**

Di Palo's Fine Foods on the northeast corner of Mott and Grand is one of the few remaining Italian stores (except for those along the two-block stretch of Mulberry Street north of Canal) in the midst of New Chinatown. DiPalo's was opened by Savino Di Palo, the great-grandfather of the current owner, in 1910. In 1925 it moved to its present corner, where it has remained ever since. The Di Palo family comes from the Puglia province in Italy.

Puglia is a rural area known for its dairy farmers and cheese-makers. Savino brought his trade to America and the family shop still makes its own mozzarella and other cheeses. The small shop has a selection of goods that rivals any of its more famous uptown competitors, such as Balducci's in Greenwich Village and Zabar's on the Upper

West Side, and at far better prices. The current owner, Louis Di Palo, has kept the shop as it was when it opened. The low marble counters are reminiscent of the Italian kitchen table and are designed for conversation as well as commerce, and the entire front of the store is maintained at cheese-curing temperature.

Diagonally across Mott Street, at 203 Grand Street, on June 22, 1905, Dr. Vincent Sellaro founded the Order of the Sons of Italy in America. Sellaro sought to create an organization that fulfilled a dual mission: first, to encourage Italian immigrants to work together despite their provincial or local origins; second, to maintain the Italian languages and customs in America. The Sons of Italy has grown into a national umbrella organization, bringing together more than 750 different Italian social clubs, family societies, and fraternal orders. It is similar to other ethnic umbrella groups such as the Chinese Consolidated Benevolent Association and the Irish Ancient Order of Hibernians.

ITALIANS IN NEW YORK

Between 1880 and 1920, nearly 4.1 million Italian immigrants came to the United States. No other ethnic group in American history has sent so many in such a short period of time. While Manhattan had fewer than twenty thousand Italian residents in 1880, by 1930 more than 1 million New Yorkers were of Italian descent. Today, more than 80 percent of the residents of what used to be Little Italy are Asian. The Italians, like the Irish, German, and other immigrants before them, have migrated from the neighborhood.

Italians left their homes in Italy for at least five reasons, all of which are linked to great poverty—especially among southern Italians, who formed the bulk of immigrants to New York. Although Italians chose to leave Italy, "push" factors influenced millions of landless farmers—contadini—to leave. First, extreme poverty in southern Italy made it a place to escape from. Second, heavy local and national taxation further impoverished Italians. Third, a sudden population surge in the latter half of the nineteenth century made jobs and land even scarcer than they had been. Fourth, the growing industrial disparity between northern and southern Italy and the subsequent rise in the Italian cash economy replaced the traditional barter system. Finally, recurring agricultural and economic crises increased the misery.

Although Italians came to America for economic opportunities not available at home, they also had the highest rate of return to their homeland of any immigrant group. Over a third of Italians who emigrated to America returned to the old country at one point in their lives, some to visit and but many to stay. Italian immigrants in the New World—whether they stayed or not—annually sent millions of dollars back to their families.

Immigration was such a prominent part of Italian life that once, when the Italian prime minister visited southern Italy, the mayor of Moliterno greeted him "on behalf of the eight thousand people of this community, three thousand of whom are in America, and the other five thousand preparing to follow them."

Banca Stabile (189 Grand Street at the southwest corner of Grand and Mulberry Streets) is an 1865 Neapolitan family bank that served the varied needs of the Italian immigrants. The tin ceilings, terrazzo floors, large vault, and brass tellers' cages have all been preserved. Beyond its role as a bank, Stabile also provided currency exchange, translation services, and steamship-ticket sales. Look inside at the cashiers' cages, which are still labeled "tickets," "money exchange," and "foreign transfers."

➤ Walk south on Mulberry Street four blocks toward Mosco Street.

Looking north on Mulberry Street toward Mulberry Bend from just north of Mosco Street, around 1890. All the buildings on the left side of the street were torn down a few years later to build Mulberry Bend Park (now Columbus Park). Photo courtesy of the New-York Historical Society.

As you walk along the first two blocks of Mulberry Street between Canal and Grand, you are walking on most of what remains of Little Italy. And today's version is a conscious effort by the local businesses to preserve an "Italian" flavor to the space. Why? Money. The neighborhood supposedly attracts as many tourists as Greenwich Village or Rockefeller Center.

All that remains of commercial Little Italy can be found here. The Italians who once made this stretch little Naples have moved out. Most of the residents are Asian, although the shops and restaurants are often still owned by Italians.

Despite the "touristification" of Little Italy, there is still tremendous history on these blocks. The oldest building in this area now houses Paolucci's Restaurant at 149 Mulberry, between Grand and Hester Streets. Originally built as the Van Rensselaer residence in 1816, it is a perfect example of an early nineteenth-century merchant house. The first floor was for the family's carpet and dry-goods shop and the basement was for storage. The family lived on the upper floors, with servants or slaves residing in the attic with the dormer windows. In the 1880s it became the Italian Free Library, with a collection of Italian-language books for neighborhood residents.

The Franciscan Fathers who care for the Shrine of San Gennaro (Saint Januarius) have a rectory at 109 Mulberry Street, just north of Canal Street. Look at the plaque on the gate into the rectory courtyard: it commemorates the death of Private First Class Frank Vallone, United States Marine Corps, who died fighting in Vietnam in 1968. Today the Church of the Most Precious Blood is home to the Co Bac Si Thuong Truc, or the Refugee Social Services, and the Vaco Youth Center, serving the community of Vietnamese Catholic immigrants. In Private Vallone and the Co Bac Si Thuong Truc are writ the rapid changes that take place in the Lower East Side.

Directly behind the rectory, at 113 Baxter Street, is the entrance to the Church of the Most Precious Blood. The church was built in 1901, one of the peak years of immigration to the Lower East Side. From the late nineteenth century to the mid–twentieth, Mulberry Street was the home of Italian immigrants from Naples. The religious center for many in this community was here at the Shrine of San Gennaro.

San Gennaro, the patron saint of Naples, was martyred by the Romans at Pozzuoli in A.D. 305. After his beheading, the legend goes, his blood was gathered by an old couple and preserved in a vial. This blood liquifies twice a year—the miracle of San Gennaro—on the first Sunday in May and on September 19.

Two thousand years later, in 1917, four Neapolitan businessmen on Mulberry Street decided to celebrate Gennaro's martyrdom, and a great New York tradition was born. Every year for ten days in mid-September, Mulberry Street from its southern end at Canal Street all the way up to Houston Street is closed for the Feast of

San Gennaro. Although most of the "feast" today consists of endless sausage and *zeppole* stands, a bust of San Gennaro is paraded through the streets by the faithful during the feast. In between parades, the saint's bust sits in the window of the Mulberry Street Cigar Company at 140 Mulberry.

➤ **Continue walking south on Mulberry Street across Canal Street.**

Canal Street was the great divide between Little Italy and Chinatown for many New Yorkers for much of the twentieth century. This ethnic border no longer exists, as you've seen walking along Grand and Mulberry.

Canal Street was dug as a canal, beginning in 1805, to drain the Collect Pond to the south (an upcoming site). It was filled in and paved over to make way for the progression of urban development. Because Canal Street is a direct connection between Brooklyn (via the Manhattan Bridge) and New Jersey (via the Holland Tunnel), it is incessantly clogged with traffic.

As you cross Canal Street, notice the immediate change. Mulberry Street above Canal is an Italian tourist district with restaurants, outdoor cafés, and gift shops. Mulberry below Canal is a residential and commercial Chinese neighborhood. The tables outside the Italian restaurants have been replaced by streetside vendors, fish markets, and houseware shops.

One block south of Canal, on the northeast corner of Bayard and Mulberry, is a red-brick building that used to be New York City Public School 23. Tens of thousands of immigrant children went to this elementary school from 1893 to 1976. The school was closed when a new one opened on Division Street (a later stop). Rather than tear down the building, it was converted into a community center for the contemporary Chinese neighborhood. Inside, the Museum of the Chinese in the Americas holds exhibits tracing the history of Chinese immigration to America and the process of Americanization.

Diagonally across the street and stretching southward is Columbus Park. Built between 1892 and 1894, this park was the first open space designed and built for the neighborhood. The person most responsible for its creation was Jacob Riis, the Danish American photographer and writer who chronicled the lives of poor New Yorkers in the late nineteenth and early twentieth centuries.

To create this park, the city destroyed an entire block of tenement houses, displacing their residents by right of eminent domain; that is, the city took the property from its owners for the public good—or so the city would argue. The residents would argue differently, of course. The park was first called Mulberry Bend Park, but Italian residents rechristened it Columbus Park in 1911. The structure at the north end dates back to the late 1890s, a time when public concerts and patriotic celebrations were presented to the neighborhood.

As you continue walking along the park, note how Mulberry Street curves. This sharp crook is the infamous Mulberry Bend, an area with individual tenements that both residents and contemporary newspapers named Ragpickers' Row, Bandits' Roost, and Thieves' Alley. Jacob Riis wrote about it in his patronizing *How the Other Half Lives* (1890):

> Where Mulberry Street crooks like an elbow within hail of the depravity of the Five Points, is the Bend, foul core of New York's slums. . . . Around the Bend cluster the bulk of tenements that are stamped as altogether bad, even by the optimists in the Health Department. . . . In the scores of back alleys, of stable lanes, and hidden byways, of which the rent collector alone can keep track, [the

poor] share such shelter as the ramshackle structures afford with every kind of abomination rifled from the dumps and ash barrels of the city. . . . There is scarce a lot that has not two, three, or four tenements upon it, swarming with unwholesome crowds.

Columbus Park sits atop the former Five Points District and the old Collect Pond. Prior to 1790, the site immediately to the west was a beautiful freshwater pond, surrounded by low hills and the country cottages of wealthy New Yorkers who lived farther downtown. In 1790 the primary landowner, Sarah Delancey, daughter of British colonial governor James Delancey, leased much of her property to a consortium of forty-six butchers. These butchers established a slaughter yard along the shore of the Collect. Bone-boiling and leather-tanning shops soon followed, all contributing to the rapid pollution of the pond. This early nineteenth-century environmental hazard was drained by the City of New York along the aforementioned Canal in 1805. In an early public-works project, city government hired workers to level the surrounding hills and fill the pond, extended streets, and renamed the area Paradise Square. The area was then subdivided into lots and sold to real estate speculators.

Unfortunately for the new residents, the Collect had been formed by a series of underground springs and natural water sources. With the constant dampness of the ground, Paradise Square quickly began to decay. The upper-middle-class residents of the area began moving to the newer neighborhoods of Greenwich Village and St. John's Park in today's TriBeCa. This outflow of people coincided with an influx of poor Irish Catholic immigrants. Paradise Square had become Five Points, so called because three streets—Park (now Mosco), Worth, and Orange (now Baxter)—came together forming a five-pointed intersection. The exact location of the intersection that gave the neighborhood its name is at the southwestern tip of Columbus Park.

IRISH IN NEW YORK

The Irish are one of the oldest immigrant groups in New York City. In fact, Colonial Governor Thomas Dongan, who served in 1683, was Irish, and the first post-Revolution mayor, James Duane, was an Irish American. The first St. Patrick's Day parade was held in 1766. In 1784 the Society of the Friendly Sons of St. Patrick was formed, the first specifically ethnic self-help organization in the city. Most of the early Irish immigrants were Protestant and middle class.

Mass Irish immigration began in the 1820s and peaked during the Irish famine years of 1845–1855. By 1860, roughly one in six city residents claimed some Irish heritage. Most of these later Irish were poor Catholics. They arrived in New York at a time of tremendous urban and industrial growth, and many were able to find work as unskilled laborers. By 1855, 86 percent of the city's laborers and nearly 75 percent of its household servants were Irish born.

As the Irish population increased, so too did their cultural and political significance. The Irish were instrumental in the founding of the New York City police and fire departments and other branches of city government and civil service. They were invited into the Democratic Party through Tammany Hall and by the 1870s came to dominate the organization. Tammany Hall became known as a rampantly corrupt political machine, but to the thousands of immigrant Irish it was a crucial institution that offered tremendous social welfare. All Tammany asked in return was a vote. It was Tammany that was behind the 1880 election of William Grace, New York's first Irish Catholic mayor.

While large-scale Irish immigration continued well into the twentieth century, the center of Irish settlement changed. The Irish Lower East Side gave way to the Italian Lower East Side as the next great wave of immigrants reached this neighborhood.

Almost at the corner of Mosco Street, 32 Mulberry Street is a wonderful example of the layers of history in this area. Take careful note of the old (and barely visible) hand-painted sign above the modern electric one for New Jeannie's Restaurant. Somewhat obscured under untold layers of paint, the name of the previous restaurant—Moneta's—is still legible.

On the south corner of Mosco and Mulberry Streets, at 28 Mulberry, is a building with marble pillars and a terra-cotta eagle as entrance ornamentation. Currently the Wah Wing Sang Funeral Corporation, this was Antonio Cuneo's 1881 bank. Cuneo, a Piedmontese immigrant, arrived in America in 1855. He began selling nuts and fruit from a pushcart and slowly built a real estate and banking empire. Cuneo sold this bank to Felice Tocca a few years later.

In 1887 a United States congressional investigation found that the bank operated under the *padrone* system, a labor arrangement where the bank, for a fee, operated an agency in Naples that coordinated prepaid steamer tickets and requests for underpaid labor. This system, outlawed in 1885 by the Contract Labor Law, brought immigrants into the country to undercut America's industrial and unskilled wages. The Contract Labor Law was supported by both the Daughters of the American Revolution and the American Federation of Labor. It simultaneously protected American workers from having wages undercut by immigrants and mandated that immigrants be paid a living wage.

Next door to Cuneo's bank was the Bacigalupo Funeral Parlor. Its ornate terra-cotta and marble entranceway shows traditional funeral details of shrouded urns and angels. Much of this detail is obscured by a modern awning.

At the southern end of the block, where Mulberry intersects Worth, was the Cow Bay section of Five Points. Cow

Bay was the largest free-black neighborhood in Manhattan in the early nineteenth century. In 1805, nearly 1,200 out of the 1,960 free blacks in Manhattan lived in this general area. By 1825 the community had built seven churches. African Americans remained in the neighborhood throughout the century.

Historians debate whether or not the free blacks coexisted peacefully with the Irish immigrants. Older historians claim these were two separate, competing, and often warring communities. Newer research, however, indicates that they not only coexisted on the street but even shared houses. Historian Graham Hodges reports that a dozen intermarried couples were living here in the late 1860s.

> **Walk east on Mosco up the short hill to Mott Street.**

When you reach the top of the hill, walk a few feet to your left to see the Church of the Transfiguration at 29 Mott Street. Originally built in 1801 as the English Lutheran First Church of Zion, this Georgian-style church served the farmers of the surrounding area. In 1827, as the neighborhood became increasingly Irish, the Lutheran congregation leased their building to the Catholic Church, which ultimately bought it in 1853. If you look carefully at the facade, you will notice that different stone was used for the church and the steeple. The steeple was added after 1853.

The parish was founded in 1827 on Ann Street in Lower Manhattan by Padre Félix Francisco José Maria de la Concepcion Morales y Valera, New York's first Spanish-speaking priest. Born in 1788 in Havana, Cuba, to a prominent family, Valera was an outspoken voice for Cuban independence from Spain. After his expulsion from Cuba, he moved to New York and became a leader of this church and its Irish parishioners. The plaque on the church calls Valera

"Father to needy Irish immigrants" for his role in establishing this parish. At a time of great tension, he was an early advocate for Catholic and Protestant dialogue and presided over Transfiguration's growth into the largest immigrant parish in Manhattan.

By the early 1880s, the Irish began to migrate out of the parish and Italians began using the basement for services. Although the two congregations worshiped the same God, their styles of worship were different enough and the communities separate enough that they didn't worship together. In 1902 an Italian priest, Father Cappo, moved the Italian community upstairs into the main chapel to sit with the Irish. With Italian immigration, this became the church of Enrico Caruso, Jimmy Durante, and Mother Cabrini, the first naturalized American saint.

By the 1960s the congregation had become increasingly Chinese; today the congregation is almost exclusively Chinese. Note the Mass schedule outside the church: Mass is given in Cantonese, Mandarin, and English. Recent members of the congregation are Father Ignatius Kung, the bishop in exile from Shanghai, and Father Dominic Tang, the archbishop in exile of Canton. Both were imprisoned in the 1960s during the Chinese Cultural Revolution. They remained jailed for nearly twenty years before being released on the condition that they leave China.

If you go into the church, note the stained-glass window on the left-hand side of the foyer. The image in the window is of St. Patrick. Directly below the window is a memorial photograph of Mother Cabrini. The sanctuary, which was restored in 1999, has maintained the form it held in its Protestant past with its high-vaulted ceiling and sweeping balcony.

➤ **Walk north on Mott Street one block to Pell.**

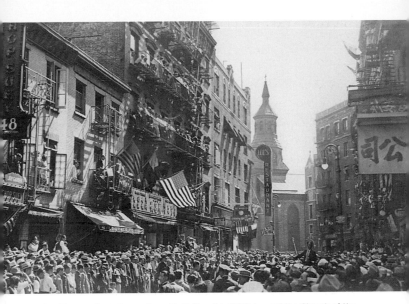

Looking south past crowds on Mott Street in 1937, toward the Church of the Transfiguration in Chinatown. Photo courtesy of the New-York Historical Society.

CHINESE IN NEW YORK

Of all the immigrant groups that have passed through the Lower East Side, the Chinese have had the longest continuous presence. A small group of Chinese, predominantly sailors, lived here as early as 1850. In 1859, the **New York Times** estimated that some 150 Chinese lived in the district, working as sailors, cooks, and vendors.

Following the completion of the transcontinental railroad in 1869, the conclusion of the California Gold Rush, and increased anti-Chinese nativism throughout the nation, Chinese immigrants moved from rural America to cities, including New York. Mott, Pell, and Doyers Streets became home to two thousand Chinese within a decade.

America's anti-Chinese bigotry culminated in the passing of the Chinese Exclusion Act in 1882. With this law, the Chinese became the first and the only ethnic group to be excluded from admission into, and denied citizenship of, this country.

When the law was passed, the majority of Chinese living in America were men, and these Chinese laborers were not allowed to bring their wives to the United States. The result was a Chinese community that became known as a "bachelor society." In New York, the ratio of Chinese young men between the ages of fifteen and twenty-one to Chinese young women of the same age range was 3,961 to 100 in 1910. By 1940 the ratio had somewhat improved—896 to 100.

The United States revoked the Chinese Exclusion Act in 1943, allowing a very small number (105 per year) of Chinese Americans once again to come to America and, for the first time, to become naturalized citizens. However, Chinese immigration did not significantly increase until the Immigration Act of 1965, which replaced the existing national quota laws with numbers based on broad hemispheric definitions. The new law also included a "uniting the families" provision, allowing migration based on familial connections rather than job skills. The Chinese quota changed overnight, from 105 immigrants allowed per year to nearly 20,000. The result in this neighborhood was phenomenal—the Chinese population increased from 11,000 in 1960 to nearly 150,000 by 1995.

There are multiple Chinatowns within this one small area. The heart of Old Chinatown can be found on Doyers, Pell, and lower Mott Streets. The majority of the communal societies and long-established businesses are by and for the Guangdong (Cantonese-speaking) Chinese residents. This area is surrounded by a number of newer neighborhoods populated by immigrants from Fujian Province in China, Hong Kong, Taiwan, and other Asian countries.

On the third floor of the building at 12 Mott Street, south of the Church of the Transfiguration, was the former New York headquarters of the Kaoshen (High Mountain) Club, a secret political organization founded by Dr. Sun Yat Sen in 1895. This was the local chapter of Sun's secret revolutionary party, the Hsing Chung Hui, which helped overthrow the Chinese emperor in 1911. After spending most of his life as a revolutionary, Sun went on to become the first president of the Republic of China, but only for a month. A junior high school on Hester Street is named for him.

Across the street from the Church of the Transfiguration, at 32 Mott, is Quong Yuen Shing & Co., (also known as the Mott Street General Store). This store was founded by the Lee family in 1891. Originally a grocery, it is the oldest continuously operating shop in Chinatown. In the early days of Chinatown it served as a post office, meeting place, message center, bank, and, of course, store. The store has maintained its original interior and exterior and offers a unique glimpse into the commercial life of Old Chinatown.

Take a brief detour north to the tallish white-faced building on the west side of the street. This is home to the Lee Family Association. This social organization was established to assist the extended Lee family with monetary, legal, and medical aid. It assists all Chinese with the surname Lee. All immigrant groups who have come to New York in substantial numbers have set up these mutual-aid societies. Apart from family organizations, immigrant groups often establish aid societies based on occupation or on the town or region they came from.

For Chinatown, the umbrella organization that oversees many of the various social organizations is the Zhonghua Gong Suo—the New York Chinese Consolidated Benevolent Association (CCBA)—at 62 Mott Street, with the Taiwanese flag flying from the roof. Just like the Sons of Italy, this is a self-help and protective organization for Chinese immigrants. It was founded in 1883 in response to the Chinese Exclusion Act. The CCBA served as the spokesperson and advocate for the community, settled disputes among the Chinese organizations, collected funds to hire lawyers to defend the interests of Chinese in court, and sponsored various social welfare programs.

For a long time the CCBA was seen as the "informal government" of the Chinese community, bringing together more than sixty different family and fraternal associations. Since the 1960s this organization's influence in the community has declined, as Chinese and Asian residents of Chinatown have become more diverse and no longer come primarily from Guangdong Province.

➤ **Walk east on Pell Street one short block toward Bowery.**

The intersection of Pell and Mott Streets is the center of historic Chinatown. Prior to the founding of the *Ming Ch'i Daily* in 1915, the community had no regularly published daily newspaper. Instead, on this intersection stood a bulletin board that provided residents with news of the old country as well as neighborhood announcements and job postings.

As you walk these narrow and curved streets of Chinatown, you will notice that they predate urban development and the automobile. Pell Street, which appeared on maps beginning in 1776, is named for John Pell, a prosperous butcher. Mott Street is named for Joseph Mott, also a butcher. The street names are our last link to those very early residents of this neighborhood.

Further along Pell Street, at No. 24, is the former Sun Wui Association, the last wooden pagoda building in Chinatown. It remains as a great example of symbolism in Chinatown architecture. The roof is a pagoda with two fish, symbols of good luck and abundance. (The word for fish in many Chinese languages is the same as the one for profit or surplus.) The colors are red, gold, and green. Red is a symbol of good luck; gold represents money or wealth; and green stands for growth and flowering. Many signs in Chinatown are a combination of these three traditional colors.

Until recently, this building was home to the Chinese Theatrical and Musicians Union.

The Hip Sing Tong, the most powerful individual fraternal organization in Chinatown, is at 16 Pell Street in the building labeled Pell Street Social Club. The tongs illustrate the two sides of immigrant communal organizations. "*Tong*" has the same meaning as *wui*; both mean "association." But *tong* is a charged word carrying insinuations of criminal activity and danger. The tongs are secret societies that originated in China several hundred years ago. They began arriving in New York in the early 1880s to protect their members' business interests. Over the years, numerous tongs have been investigated and indicted for criminal activities—extortion, prostitution, gambling. But at the same time they also serve important community functions for those outside the established political order. For example, the Hip Sing Tong contains a federally insured credit union for members and offers business loans and student scholarships.

➤ **Return on Pell and walk south-southeast on Doyers Street to the Bowery/Chatham Square.**

In the nineteenth century, scores of seedy saloons lined Doyers Street. Novelist Rupert Hughes wrote in 1904 that these saloons were filled with

> soldiers, sailors, workingmen, cooks, ladies of the pavement and their impresarios who live upon their earnings. At a rickety piano sat a hardworking mechanic in shirt sleeves, whose most artistic effect was a so-called mandolin attachment, which gave the decrepit instrument a still tinnier sound. A youth in a striped sweater stood alongside and roared out dismal melodies in a saturated voice.

Where the Chinatown Post Office now stands at 4–6 Doyers Street was one of the most famous of these saloons: Callahan's. Neighborhood saloons hired singing men and scantily clad women as waiters and waitresses to attract customers. Callahan's hired two of the most popular young Jewish men to sing: Asa Yoelson and Israel Baline. When these two were able to move out of the neighborhood they changed their names, to the more familiar (and American) Al Jolson and Irving Berlin.

Doyers Street ends at an intersection that is an urban planner's nightmare—Chatham Square. Ten different streets collide at this one site. The square is named for William Pitt, the earl of Chatham, an eighteenth-century English prime minister who became a local hero when he argued against the impending war with the British colonies in America. Directly across from Doyers Street, on the southeast corner of Catherine Street and Chatham Square, stands a feeble attempt by the Manhattan Savings Bank (now HSBC Holdings) to cloak a financial institution in a Hollywood version of a Chinese temple.

➤ **Cross Bowery to the 1962 Benjamin Ralph Kimlau Memorial Arch, standing on an island slightly south of Doyers.**

The arch is dedicated to all Chinatown residents who died serving in the American armed forces during World War II. The war was a crucial turning point in Chinatown. Prior to the 1940s, numerous books, plays, movies, and reporters described the Chinese as opium addicts, gangsters, and the "Yellow Peril." The war began to change that perception. For most Americans, World War II began in December 1941 with the Japanese attack on Pearl Harbor, but for Chinese Americans it began in 1932 after the Japanese invasion of Manchuria. When America entered the war, numerous

American propaganda films presented the Chinese as patriotic and loyal. Then, other Americans slowly began to see
Chinese in an entirely different light.

> **Continue across and south about a block onto St. James
> Place.**

At 55–57 St. James (between St. James Place and Oliver
Street) is the First Cemetery of the Spanish and Portuguese
Synagogue, Shearith Israel. Built in 1654, this site is both a
National Historic and a New York City Landmark. It is the
oldest Jewish cemetery in the United States and one of the
oldest cemeteries in New York City. Buried here, among
others, are Jewish American soldiers who fought in the
American Revolution and Benjamin Mendes-Seixes, one of
the founders of the New York Stock Exchange. When the
cemetery was established, it was over a mile north of the
city limits. Dutch governor Peter Stuyvesant, New York's
first prominent anti-Semite, ordered it built outside New
Amsterdam proper. This congregation still exists and
meets at Seventieth Street and Central Park West.

Adjacent to the cemetery and just out of view is St.
James Church. This beautifully maintained 1837 Greek
revival church is one of the centers of New York's Irish
history. Also part of Father Valera's 1827 parish, this is
the "sister" church to Transfiguration. It is credited as
the founding site of the first American chapter of the
Ancient Order of Hibernians. The Hibernians were
formed in Ireland in 1565 as a Roman Catholic social and
benevolent society. Established here in 1836 in the midst
of a strong anti-Catholic and anti-immigrant moment in
New York history, the Hibernians brought together Irish
Americans in the name of charity, brotherhood, and self-
defense. It is an ethnically specific umbrella organization

very similar to those we have already seen for Italians and Chinese immigrants.

➤ **Walk north past Chatham Square and then head east onto Division Street.**

New York City has a wonderful tradition that allows neighborhood residents to name public places and schools. The 1976 elementary school P.S. 214, located just opposite Market Street, is named for Yung Wing. Both the school and the man serve as role models for the predominantly Chinese immigrant children who learn here. Yung Wing (1828–1912), was born near Macao, China. He came to the United States as a student visitor in 1847, entered Yale University, and, in 1854, became the first Chinese person to graduate from an American college. After graduating, Yung Wing resolved to devote most of his life to the modernization of China and returned there. While primarily an educational reformer, he also served as a Chinese diplomat in the United States. Despite his lack of American citizenship, he remained in America until his death in 1902. He is buried in Hartford, Connecticut.

Along your way to Eldridge Street, you will walk beneath the Manhattan Bridge, the third bridge connecting Lower Manhattan with Brooklyn. Designed by engineer Gustav Lindenthal in 1905, the bridge was the divider between Chinatown and the old Jewish East Side. This rather unattractive structure is greatly enhanced by the newly restored 1916 colonnade that stands at the Canal Street entrance to the bridge. Built by the architects Carrere & Hastings, this triumphal arch is a wonderful example of the City Beautiful movement, which, from 1890 to World War I, saw New York City invest in the beautification of urban neighborhoods. Trees were planted on sidewalks; "slums" were cleared to create parks, and architectural enhancements were built.

> Cross under the bridge and take your second left to walk north on Eldridge Street. Continue one block toward Canal Street.

JEWS IN NEW YORK

The East European Jews began arriving in large numbers in the early 1880s and almost exclusively settled in the Lower East Side. These immigrants attempted to reestablish their Old World institutions and traditions in America. In this attempt they came together not as Jews but by country and area of origin, creating ethnic enclaves of Russians, Poles, and Hungarians within the larger Jewish immigrant community.

Describing these immigrants as "Jews" is problematic. First, it is against American law to ask the religion of an immigrant or a citizen. It is therefore difficult to determine from immigration data how many Jews came to America, although estimates range widely, from 3 to 5 million. We know how many Russians or Poles immigrated but not how many Jews or Catholics. Second, Jewish immigrants came from a variety of countries, thus creating a number of Jewish communities within the neighborhood. Unlike most Italian immigrants, most Jews were fleeing political or religious oppression and were viewing America as a permanent home. For every one thousand Jews to come to America through Ellis Island, only three chose to return to Europe.

The eastern part of the Lower East Side was the most densely populated. By 1894, the population had reached a density of almost one thousand people per square acre. The population of the Lower East Side climaxed with some 542,000 residents in 1910. Yet the population quickly declined with the building of the subways and the development of new neighborhoods uptown and in the outer boroughs. By 1915, the heart of Jewish Manhattan was no longer this area but East Harlem.

At 12–16 Eldridge Street stands the Congregation Khal Adath Jeshurun and Anshe Lubz Synagogue, popularly known as the Eldridge Street Synagogue. Built in 1886–87 by the Herter brothers, German architects, in a Moorish revival and Romanesque style, this synagogue was named a National Historic Landmark in 1996.

While the exterior rose window is similar to those erected by various Christian groups, it is distinctly Jewish. It contains twelve rondels, or smaller windows, representing the twelve tribes of Israel. Also note the recurring patterns of two tablets (the Ten Commandments), five windows (the five books of the Torah), and three sets of stairs leading to four sets of doors (Jewish biblical matriarchs and patriarchs). The interior is a beautiful Orthodox synagogue complete with women's balconies and designed overall in Moorish/Sephardic style. The Eldridge Street Synagogue Project is currently reconstructing the building.

➤ **Walk east along Canal Street two blocks toward Orchard Street.**

The wide Allen Street thoroughfare on your way east is very different today than it was in the heyday of the Jewish Lower East Side. Prior to 1932, the street was only thirty-two feet wide and was completely covered by an elevated train. In that year the buildings on the east side were torn down and the street was widened to 138 feet to accommodate the automobile.

The city removed the elevated train in 1942. At that time the city planned to build the Second Avenue subway to connect the northern Bronx with Wall Street. Construction finally began in 1972 but was soon discontinued for lack of money and fears about construction disrupting commerce. New York, like so many other American cities, became beholden to the automobile at the expense of public transportation. Only in the late 1990s, after years of economic prosperity and federal regulations to limit auto exhaust, did the city begin to reconsider the project. In 2000 a voter referendum on a municipal bond to build the subway failed to pass.

On the southwest corner of Canal and Orchard, notice the tall building taking up most of the block. It's the former Jarmulovsky Bank. Founder Sender Jarmulovsky is a fine example of how one could "make it" and then "lose it" all on the Lower East Side.

Jarmulovsky began his banking career with his savings from his peddler days. He built this building in homage to himself in 1912, although Jarmulovsky's bank predated this building. The bank essentially catered to poor immigrants, especially those sending money back to family in the Old World as financial support and to help emigration. Jarmulovsky died of old age a few months after his building was completed. His sons continued the family business. By 1914 the bank had established quite a clientele—at least until the outbreak of World War I. The war led many Jewish depositors to withdraw their money and send immediate help to family caught in Europe. Furthermore, the immigrant depositors held no confidence in paper money and demanded silver and gold coins. The "runs" on the banks caused the state superintendent to close the Jarmulovsky bank on August 4, 1914, but not before the family was ruined. The *New York Times* reported:

On August 5, two thousand people demonstrated in front of Yarmulowsky's bank; three days later riots broke out in front . . .

and one hundred policemen were called to restrain a mob of fifteen hundred enraged depositors. . . . On September 5, five hundred people gathered in front of M. Yarmulowsky's apartment, forcing him and his family to flee.

Throughout this part of the neighborhood there are street signs that proclaim you are in the "Historic Orchard Street Bargain District." These signs were hung by the local business improvement association in an attempt to bolster commercial activity. This is a controversial group, comprised mostly of the older Jewish businesses from the surrounding blocks. By using the term *historic* they are, in some ways, excluding the two important new arrivals—the new Chinese businesses and the even newer (and hipper) shops, bars, and restaurants that are flocking to the area.

➤ **Walk north on Orchard Street one block to Hester Street.**

Four buildings, 27–33 Orchard Street, are excellent examples of "pre-law" tenements. These are some of the oldest multifamily buildings on the Lower East Side. A pre-law tenement is a multifamily dwelling built before 1879. These older buildings were built before modern housing laws and are some of the least desirable housing in New York City.

Each building contains sixteen apartments, four on each floor. Each apartment is, on average, three rooms totaling 270 square feet—that's a kitchen, bedroom, and living room, each only nine feet by ten feet. The only windows in each apartment are two in the living room facing the street or the backyard, depending on whether it is a front apartment or a back one. There is no elevator, and before 1901 there was no indoor plumbing. The residents shared outhouses and hand pumps in the backyard. The outhouses were cleaned out twice a year. Today the apartments have indoor plumbing and heat, but they are still only three small rooms.

Note the smoke damage on the upper floors of No. 31. This building had an accidental fire in December 1997. When it burned, a total of ninety-six people lost their homes. That is an average of six people per apartment.

Compare these older tenements with the more ornate ones in the neighborhood. As the neighborhood aged and elevated trains and subways offered newer neighborhoods to residents, builders and landlords began to decorate the facades of later tenements as enticements for tenants. Despite the ornate exterior, most are identical inside—small, dark, and cramped rooms. An excellent example of the 1890s ornate tenements are a few doors back on Orchard Street. Walk back and view the terra-cotta details on 14–16 Orchard Street. The two rows of Jewish stars surrounded by twelve pomegranates are exceptional in detail. Contrary to popular lore, these were never "Jewish" buildings. Rather, the decoration was meant to entice Jews to live here.

Hester Street, between Orchard and Essex, was the site of the Khazzer Mark—"Pig Market" in Yiddish. Here Jewish and Italian peddlers set up pushcarts to sell an incredible array of goods. Why Pig Market? Jacob Riis gives this description of turn-of-the-century Hester Street:

> There is scarcely anything else [other than pork] that can be hawked from a wagon that is not to be found, and at ridiculously low prices. Bandannas and tin cups at two cents, peaches at a cent a quart, "damaged" eggs for a song. . . . The crowds that jostle each other at the wagons and about the sidewalk shops, where a gutter plank of two ash-barrels does the duty for a counter! Pushing, struggling, babbling, and shouting in foreign tongues, a veritable Babel of confusion.

Looking west on Hester Street from the corner of Norfolk Street in 1898. Today, the pushcarts are gone and the corner in the photo would be in the middle of Seward Park. Photo courtesy of the New-York Historical Society.

Pushcart peddling was abolished by Mayor Fiorello La Guardia in 1935, after it was determined that the average peddler was not only making a decent living but was paying minimal taxes. La Guardia had enclosed markets built throughout the city and offered peddlers a bargain—heated and ventilated buildings complete with police for safety and theft deterrence—all in exchange for getting a license and paying taxes. Unfortunately, the space in the new markets was nowhere near enough to house all the peddlers chased off the streets.

➤ Take a right and walk east on Hester Street two blocks to Essex Street.

While walking toward Essex Street, it is impossible not to note the small, three-acre Seward Park in front of you. Built in 1901 and named for Abraham Lincoln's secretary of state William Seward (1801–1872), this was the first park built in this part of the neighborhood. The City of New York tore down three blocks of tenement houses and displaced nearly three thousand people to create this open space. Why choose these particular blocks? Seward Park sits atop three of the most densely crowded blocks of 1900 New York. Just as we saw at Columbus Park, this was not simply a philanthropic act for the immigrants of the Lower East Side but an early attempt at "slum" clearance and neighborhood population control.

This park is best known as a gathering point for striking garment workers during their numerous work stoppages. In 1909, 1912, and 1916, thousands of workers gathered here and gazed south toward the Jewish Daily Forward Building, waiting to hear reports on their demands for a living wage and an eight-hour day.

➤ **Walk south on Essex Street one block past Canal to East Broadway/Straus Square.**

Straus Square is the small traffic triangle with the marble pillar directly in front of you. The square's namesake is Nathan Straus, the great financier, philanthropist, and a leader of the New York Jewish community. Straus is best remembered for sponsoring the 1919 program to bring free sterilized-milk stations to children throughout the country. The marble column is a tribute to the Jewish men and women of the neighborhood who gave their lives in both world wars and the Korean War. It was presented by the Morris Dickstein Post No. 462 of the Veterans of Foreign Wars in May 1953.

Look directly across the square to the southeast at the old Forverts (Forward) Building at 173 East Broadway. Built in 1912 and designed by George A. Boehm, the twelve-story Jewish Daily Forward Building was a towering presence over the neighborhood. This building used to have the name Forverts inscribed across the top, along with a huge clock.

From 1901 until 1951 the *Forward* (*Forverts*) was edited by Abraham Cahan, a Russian Jewish immigrant, who made the *Forward* the most widely read Yiddish paper in the world. Cahan used the paper as an Americanizing tool—a way to introduce the East European Jewish immigrants to American life. He also wrote extensively about American politics and culture. The most widely read section of the paper was the "Bintel Brief" (the "Bundle of Letters"), a section in which readers could present their concerns and problems and receive an answer from the editors.

The *Forward* moved from this space in 1975. The Forward Building was then purchased by the New York Ling Liang Church, an evangelical Protestant missionary church and Bible publisher. The church building, located within the former socialist Yiddish newspaper building, was sold in 1999 to a developer who is transforming the space into luxury condominiums. This will be the first luxury doorman condo in the Lower East Side, a clear sign of things to come—increasing gentrification.

➤ **Walk east on East Broadway three long blocks toward Montgomery Street.**

At the southeast corner of East Broadway and Jefferson is the Educational Alliance, known as "the Edgies." Built in 1889, the alliance was established by "uptown" German Jews as an attempt to Americanize the East European immigrants by providing day and evening classes in English, citizenship, and hygiene. The alliance also coordinated the immigration process for all Jews arriving at Ellis Island and was the center for all American relief to Jews in Nazi-occupied Europe. Furthermore, the Educational Alliance helped create a Legal Aid Bureau and the

American Desertion Board, which aided in the search for fathers and husbands who had abandoned their families. The alliance still provides for the community through a series of events and classes in the arts, sciences, and vocational skills.

The main building was renamed for David Sarnoff after its 1960s renovation. Sarnoff's life is a veritable Horatio Alger story. Born in Russia in 1891, the eldest of five children, Sarnoff arrived in America at age nine. The family's first American home was a fourth-floor walk-up on Monroe Street, for which they paid $10 a month. Within days of his arrival, the young David Sarnoff began earning money by picking up copies of the Yiddish newspaper *Tageblatt* at 4 A.M. and selling them on the streets around his home. For every fifty papers he sold, he earned twenty-five cents. Sarnoff eventually graduated from newsboy to working at a newsstand. At night he enrolled in English-language classes at the Educational Alliance. Next he became a messenger at the Commercial Cable Company. From there his career took off: he eventually became president and CEO of RCA. Sarnoff was instrumental in the RCA creation of NBC television in 1926.

Further east, the converted double tenement at 229 East Broadway was the first home of the Hebrew Sheltering and Immigrant Aid Society, now known as HIAS. Founded in 1892 to provide burial services for Jews who had died on Ellis Island, by 1897 the organization had grown to provide job training, legal aid, temporary housing, and interpreter services for Jewish immigrants. HIAS quickly became a national organization, offering aid in Boston, Philadelphia, and Baltimore as well as New York. While primarily concerned with Jewish arrivals, HIAS was a strong advocate for unrestricted immigration and by 1914 was one of the most outspoken voices that stood in opposition to immigration restrictions.

In 1921, HIAS moved from this site to the former Astor Library in the East Village. In the same year, the Young Israel Synagogue of Manhattan purchased the HIAS site. Young Israel, an international Orthodox movement, was founded in 1912 in the Lower East Side at a time when many young Orthodox were greatly concerned with what they saw as the "damage" being done to Jewish practices by the growing popularity of the Reform movement, socialism, and Jewish crime.

The spark that led to the founding of Young Israel came during a Friday-evening lecture on American Judaism by the Reform rabbi and Zionist Stephen S. Wise at the nearby but now-razed Clinton Hall. During the course of the evening lecture, collection baskets were passed around the hall. This action, which violated the Jewish law against the use of money on the sabbath, outraged many of the young Orthodox in the audience, who stalked out. With the assistance of local civic leader, Benjamin Koeningsberg, they called on Dr. Judah Magnes to discuss possible responses. To counter the growing Reform sentiment, Magnes agreed to give a series of lectures on Orthodox religious themes at the Kalvarier Synagogue on Pike Street (now a Buddhist temple), and Young Israel was born.

The rest of this block of East Broadway is known as "Shteebel Row." A *shteeblach* (room) is a Jewish synagogue based in a house. Most of these tenement buildings contain synagogues. Each has a sign in Hebrew and English. Note how the communities are created based on place of origin rather than on Jewish religious denomination. Jewish immigration was divided by one's *landslayt*, or homeland, and synagogues in this neighborhood reflect that distinction.

➤ **Continue east on East Broadway, turn right (south) at Montgomery Street, and then left (east) onto Henry Street.**

At 263, 265, and 267 Henry Street are three 1827 Federalist buildings that are National Historical and New York City Landmarks. It was here in 1893 that Lillian Wald began the Henry Street Settlement. With the assistance of philanthropist Jacob Shiff, she began the Visiting Nurse Service to care for the ill and infirm. Rather than require a visit to a medical office, these nurses would bring care to the people in their homes. The Henry Street Settlement House is still a strong anchor of nonsectarian assistance for the neighborhood; they run an arts-and-theater center around the corner on Grand Street. Prior to being added to the settlement house, no. 267 had been the Hebrew Technical School for Girls, a trade school for immigrants.

➤ **Turn around and walk back west the half-block to Pitt Street (or Samuel Dickstein Plaza). Turn right on Pitt Street and walk two short blocks to Grand Street. Turn left onto Grand and begin walking toward the west.**

St. Mary's Church on the corner of Grand and Ridge Streets is the oldest Catholic church building in all of New York City and its third parish, founded in 1827. Originally built in 1833, the structure's brick facade and double spires were added in 1871 by architect Patrick C. Keely. St. Mary's is dramatically different from the other houses of worship in the Lower East Side. This building has served the Cath-olic community since it was first erected. No other house of worship has served one religion for so long in this neighborhood.

When the Catholic Church abolished mandatory Latin Mass in 1965, it enabled buildings such as this to become diverse gathering places for believers. St. Mary's currently offers Mass in English and Spanish, thus opening its doors to a wider community. Certainly there are older churches, but they have gone from Lutheran to Catholic, as we saw at the Church of the Transfiguration, or from Baptist to Jewish, as we will see later.

Continue west on Grand. There are only two buildings standing on the north side of Grand Street between Clinton and Suffolk Streets. No. 402 is a wonderful example of an 1830s merchant house. The shop would have been on the street level and the family would have resided in the floors above. Next to the merchant house is a fine example of a dumbbell tenement (as opposed to the pre-law tenements we saw on Orchard Street). The change in tenement law came in 1887. The crucial addition was the airshaft, along with the requirement for a window in every room. The airshafts failed, however, in their mission to provide fresh air to the apartments. In the end they resulted mostly in residents losing square footage of usable space. We are given this description of a dumbbell tenement from an 1888 journal:

> They are great prison-like structures of brick, with narrow doors and windows, cramped passages and steep rickety stairs. . . . The narrow court-yard . . . in the middle is a damp foul-smelling place, supposed to do duty as an airshaft. . . . In case of fire they would be perfect death-traps, for it would be impossible for the occupants of the crowded rooms to escape by the narrow stairways, and the flimsy fire-escapes which the owners of the tenements were compelled to put up . . . are so laden with broken furniture, bales and boxes that they would be worse than useless.

➤ **Continue walking along Grand Street until you reach Norfolk Street. Turn right and walk north on Norfolk one block to Broome Street.**

At 60 Norfolk is the Beth Hamedrash Hagadol (Great House of Study). Built in 1850 as the Norfolk Baptist Church and purchased by a Jewish congregation in 1885, it

View north on Bowery from Grand Street to Cooper Union, with the Bowery Savings Bank to the far left and the two tracks of the elevated railroad that used to darken the street clearly evident. Photo courtesy of the New-York Historical Society.

is the oldest Russian (Ashkenazic) Orthodox congregation in the United States. The congregation was formed in 1852.

In 1899, this was the pulpit of Rabbi Jacob Joseph, the first and only chief rabbi of New York's Orthodox community. Joseph, a native of Vilna, Lithuania, came to America in 1888 with high hopes for leading the growing Orthodox Jewish population. However, because of the diverse Jewish communities, the multifaceted neighborhood was unable to sustain a single chief rabbi.

Once the largest Russian synagogue in the country, the congregation is now rather small. The synagogue is open for daily prayer and should be visited to see the beautiful Gothic interior. In January 1967, Beth Hamedrash Hagadol was made a New York Historical Landmark.

➢ **Walk Broome Street west one block to Essex.**

Broome Street is worth pondering for a moment. In 1946, Robert Moses, urban planner, head of the Triboro Bridge and Tunnel Authority, and great builder and destroyer of New York, wanted to build the Lower Manhattan Expressway across Broome Street. This expressway was to connect the Holland Tunnel with the Williamsburg and Manhattan Bridges. It would have run at a height of about one hundred feet above the ground and would have caused the devastation of this neighborhood. Luckily, Moses was foiled.

➤ **Walk Essex Street south one block to Essex and Grand.**

Before you reach Grand, be certain to note the very small plaque on the wall to your east at what would be 60 Essex Street. This was the site of Sinsheimer's Cafe. It was here that the B'nai Brith (Sons of the Covenant) was organized by immigrant German Jews on October 13, 1843. Just as we have seen for other immigrant groups on the Lower East Side, it was founded as a self-help and defensive organization to protect American Jews in the face of anti-immigrant sentiment. It is the oldest Jewish fraternal organization in America.

➤ **From this point you can walk east on Grand Street five short blocks back to where we began.**

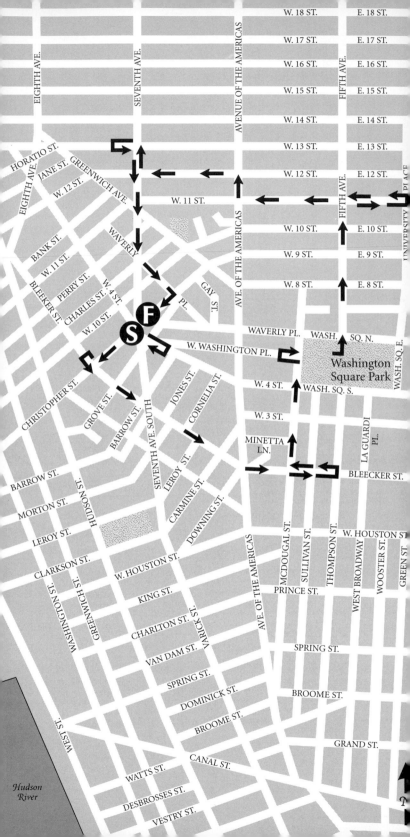

3 GREENWICH VILLAGE

A Gay and Lesbian Mecca

➤ Start: We begin at the Christopher Street station for the 1/9 subway, located at the intersection of Christopher Street, Sheridan Square, and Seventh Avenue South.

SOME CONTEMPORARY TRAVEL guides refer to New York City as having the largest lesbian and gay population of any city on earth, and for many years, Greenwich Village was the center of this community. While the geographic center of gay and lesbian life in the city has been shifting in recent years (for men, up to Chelsea, and for women, out to Brooklyn), Greenwich Village remains the focus of legend and history, and a walk through the streets of the Village will take you past landmarks from more than one hundred years of the lesbian and gay past.

Greenwich Village is also home to the gay-and-lesbian rights movement's most sacred site: the building that once housed the Stonewall Inn, site of the legendary Stonewall riots. The three days of unrest that took place there in June 1969 are widely considered the spark that launched the modern lesbian-and-gay liberation movement. (See page 106 for more on the Stonewall Inn.)

With its mix of immigrant, elite, and artistic populations, the Village was a refuge for lesbians and gay men
from all walks of life for nearly a century before the riots.
They prized the anonymity and freedom of its streets, tenements, and boarding houses and the relative openness of
its bohemian society. Once the subway was extended down
Seventh Avenue South, the Village was accessible from all
parts of the city and became known as "the place where the
Bronx meets Brooklyn" for a taste of wild nightlife. As an
enclave within the bustling metropolis of New York City,
Greenwich Village became an oasis for men and women
from around the world.

There is evidence of homosexual activity in New York
from the time of the earliest Dutch settlement in Manhattan. Early court records and legal codes in New Amsterdam and New York set down prohibitions against the "sin"
or "vice" of sodomy, and several prosecutions were re-
corded in the seventeenth century. By the late 1800s, New
Yorkers and other American city dwellers were well aware
of gay men and lesbians in their midst. In 1889, the *American Observer* wrote: "There is in every community of any
size a colony of male sexual perverts who are usually
known to each other and are likely to congregate together."
In Greenwich Village at the time, clubs featuring waiters in
drag had become a top tourist attraction.

Lesbian lives were far less visible on the streets of U.S.
cities, but awareness of women's relationships with each
other grew in certain circles. In the late nineteenth century,
relationships between women were common within communities of educated women of some financial means.
Temperance leader Frances Willard, who herself had several romances with other women, observed, "The loves of
women for each other grow more numerous each day.
That so little is said about them surprises me, for they are
everywhere."

As you walk through the streets of the Village, this chapter will point out some of the traces of years of lesbian and gay history that are, indeed, everywhere.

SODOMY LAWS IN NEW AMSTERDAM AND NEW YORK

Historians investigating lesbian and gay history in New York before self-identified subcultures began to emerge in the late nineteenth century turn to legal and court records for evidence of gay life. The earliest and most macabre evidences related to homosexuality in New York City are the criminal statutes prohibiting "sodomy," which date back to the first European presence. Sodomy laws were established in all the European colonies in North America, although each colony defined the crime slightly differently. The term was sometimes used to encompass a variety of homosexual and heterosexual activities deemed unnatural. Only a few sodomy laws covered sexual acts between women, which tended to be covered by prohibitions against "lewd and lascivious" behavior. In New York and New Amsterdam, sodomy was narrowly defined to cover only sex between men.

In 1613, when the Dutch established their rule over New Amsterdam, sexual activity between men was punishable by death. In 1665, when the English duke of York established his laws for the colony, sodomy remained among New York's eleven capital crimes. Executions for sodomy in New York City were gruesome: on June 25, 1646, a black man named Jan Creoli was sentenced to be "choked to death and then burnt to ashes" for having sex with another man, and on June 17, 1660, Jan Quisthout pleaded guilty to the same charge and was condemned to be "tied in a sack and cast into the river and drowned until dead."

The New York state legislature repealed the death penalty for sodomy in 1796, though sexual activity between men in New York City remained a crime (subject to much lesser penalties) until 1980. Sodomy laws were ubiquitous in the United States until

1962, when Illinois became the first state to repeal its statute. Today, while many other states have followed suit, sodomy laws remain on the books in nearly twenty states.

➤ Walk east along Sheridan Square (the street, not the square itself) to the southeast corner of Barrow Street and Washington Place. We know this intersection is confusing. With your back to the newsstand that sits on top of the uptown 1/9 stop, look for the very tall brick building with the bas-relief of a seahorse just above the ground-floor door that is facing you. That's Sheridan Square, and if you keep the seahorse building on your left, you're heading in the right direction.

Café Society, an integrated club known as "the wrong place for the right people," was in the basement of the two buildings (one is 1 Sheridan Square) that meet at the corner of Barrow Street and Washington Place across from the end of Sheridan Square. From 1938 to 1950 the owner ran a club where, he said, "black and white worked together behind the footlights and sat together out front." In the late 1940s, *New York Confidential* referred to Café Society as "one of the most famed cabarets" in the Village, New York's neighborhood for "long-haired men, short-haired women, and those not sure exactly what they are." The gossip-laden guide also noted with alarm that the president of the corporation operating the club was the wife of "America's No. 2 Communist," and that the club's patrons "hopped across the race fence." Just the bohemian locale to scandalize visitors to Greenwich Village.

Over the years, Café Society hosted performances by such jazz greats as Billie Holiday, Lena Horne, Sarah Vaughan, and Art Tatum. Its patrons included a number of prominent figures in lesbian and gay history and the history of the American left, including Eleanor Roosevelt (see page 103); Lillian Hellman, sometime Village resident and the author of the lesbian-themed drama *The Children's Hour*; and Paul Robeson.

In the late 1930s, a young man named Bayard Rustin frequented Café Society both as patron and performer. (He also liked the Village Vanguard, across and up Seventh Avenue.) An aspiring singer who was attending City College at the time, Rustin would go on to become a key figure in the Civil Rights movement. However, despite playing a crucial role in the triumphant 1963 March on Washington—the civil rights march that produced Dr. Martin Luther King Jr.'s "I have a dream" speech—Rustin was continually limited and hindered by homophobia from within and outside the movement.

Rustin was a committed disciple of nonviolence who went to prison as a conscientious objector during World War II. He was an important lieutenant of A. Philip Randolph during the 1940s, before an arrest in California for soliciting another man for sex forced him to take a lower profile in organizing efforts. During the Montgomery bus boycott, Rustin went south and worked with King behind the scenes, helping him make nonviolence his strategic focus. Rustin was one of King's closest advisers until the early 1960s, when a rival civil rights leader threatened to spread the false rumor that King and Rustin were having an affair. To avert a scandal, King distanced himself from Rustin.

In 1963, A. Philip Randolph brought Rustin back into the fold, making him his deputy for the planning of the March on Washington. Despite attacks by Strom Thurmond, who denounced Rustin from the floor of the Senate as a pervert and a Communist, the march was a success. Those in the know called Rustin "Mr. March," but he never received the public credit he deserved before his death in 1987.

> ➤ Return to Seventh Avenue South and, crossing the avenue, walk west on Christopher Street one block and then turn right on Bleecker, going a few buildings to No. 337, the former home of Lorraine Hansberry.

Lorraine Hansberry was an African American playwright whose *A Raisin in the Sun* brought a groundbreaking portrayal of black family life to Broadway when it opened in 1959. The play ran for two years, and Hansberry became the first black playwright to win the New York Drama Critics Circle Award for Best Play of the Year.

Hansberry was married to Robert Nemiroff, but during the 1950s, she wrote a number of anonymous letters to *One* magazine and *The Ladder*, publications of "homophile organizations" that were just beginning to campaign for gay rights. Nemiroff was aware of her lesbianism. The couple divorced in 1964 but remained close.

Her letters reveal an understanding of the links between sexism and homophobia and describe her own discomfort with more obvious and "out" butch-femme couples. In a letter to *The Ladder* in 1957, she wrote: "Someday I expect the 'discreet' lesbian will not turn her head on the streets at the sight of the 'butch' strolling hand-in-hand with her friend in their trousers and definitive haircuts. But for the moment it still disturbs. It creates an impossible arena for discussion with one's most enlightened (to use a hopeful term) heterosexual friends."

THE EARLY ACTIVISTS: THE DAUGHTERS OF BILITIS AND THE "HOMOPHILE" MOVEMENT

The Daughters of Bilitis (DOB), founded in San Francisco in 1955, was part of the first wave of the organized gay rights movement. From 1956 to 1970, the DOB published a magazine called **The Ladder,** to which Lorraine Hansberry wrote in the late 1950s.

The first New York chapter of the Daughters of Bilitis was organized in 1958 by activist Barbara Gittings and, from 1963 on, had its headquarters nearby in a basement office at 26–32 Charleton Street, nine blocks south of Hansberry's apartment. The New York chapter of the DOB was at the forefront of public actions in support of gay rights, including the "Annual Reminder" marches in front of Independence Hall in Philadelphia from 1963–1969 and the 1965 picket in front of the White House to protest regulations prohibiting federal government employment of gay men and lesbians.

The DOB was one of the "homophile" organizations founded in the 1950s that began the fight for "full citizenship for homosexuals." The other homophile organizations were the Mattachine Society (founded in 1950) and ONE (founded in 1954). Created in the midst of the repression of the McCarthy era, homophile organizations took a conservative approach to activism, asking, for example, that members "dress appropriately" for public demonstrations—men in suits and ties and women in skirts and dresses. The emphasis of early homophile activism was on enlisting the support of medical experts and members of the clergy, appealing to the idea that homosexuals were deserving of sympathy rather than scorn.

➤ Turn around and walk back (east) on Bleecker two blocks to the intersection with Seventh Avenue South. Cross Seventh Avenue and pick up Barrow Street on the other side, and immediately on your right you'll see Greenwich House.

By the late 1800s, the streets of the Village south of West Fourth Street and Washington Square Park had become the city's second most important Little Italy. Greenwich House (27 Barrow Street), a settlement house founded by Mary Simkovitch in 1904, is a reminder of that aspect of the neighborhood's past. The settlement house provided classes in English for members of the community, cooking lessons for immigrant women dealing with unfamiliar American ingredients, and activities for the neighborhood's children when they weren't in school. Further evidence of the former Italian presence is visible along Bleecker and Cornelia Streets, where Italian businesses and restaurants survive.

This immigrant neighborhood was one in which gay men might seek companionship relatively openly. In *Gay New York*, historian George Chauncey describes evidence of the "relative acceptance" of homosexual relations in New York City Italian and Jewish immigrant communities in the early years of the twentieth century. This does not mean that gay men were accepted for who they were but that having sexual relations with another man was not seen as absolutely out of the question for men who might otherwise think of themselves as "normal." You could have certain kinds of homosexual sex and not have to think of yourself as "a homosexual."

Evidence from the past shows that gay men might actually approach other men in the streets of New York. In 1915, the second edition of Havelock Ellis's groundbreaking work on *Sexual Inversion* included the observation: "The great prevalence of sexual inversion in American cities is shown by the wide knowledge of its existence. Ninety-nine normal men out of a hundred have been accosted on the streets by inverts, or have among their acquaintances men whom they know to be sexually inverted. Public attitude toward them is generally a negative one—indifference, amusement, contempt. The world of sexual inverts is, indeed, a large one in any American city, and it is a community distinctly organized with words, customs, traditions of its own."

As you walk through the streets to the east of Seventh Avenue South, you will notice the tenement buildings that line most streets. These, like the tenements of the Lower East Side, were built to house a growing immigrant population in the late nineteenth century. Later these buildings provided a base of cheap housing stock that made the neighborhood accessible to the starving artists and writers of "New Bohemia."

➤ **Return to Bleecker Street and turn left, walking east six short blocks (crossing Sixth Avenue) to Kenny's Castaways at 157 Bleecker Street (just before Thompson Street).**

Bleecker Street was notorious in the mid– to late nineteenth century, second only to the Bowery in its reputation as a rough and racy part of town. Greene and Mercer Streets were among the busiest red-light districts in the city. In the early 1890s, in the building that now houses Kenny's Castaways, an entrepreneur started a drag club called the Slide.

Drag clubs came into fashion in the late nineteenth century. The most famous was Columbia Hall (a.k.a. "Paresis Hall," after a kind of madness that comes from syphilis) at 392 Bowery. These were places where straight patrons might come to gape, but they were also centers of gay male social activity and relatively safe gathering places to meet other men.

The Slide quickly became infamous. In 1892, the *New York Herald* reported that the Slide was becoming a tourist attraction for out-of-towners seeking a glimpse of the low life in the city: "It is a fact that the Slide and the unspeakable nature of the orgies practiced there are a matter of common talk among men who are bent on taking in the town. Let a detective be opportuned by people from a distance to show them something outre in the way of fast life, the first place he thinks of is the Slide, if he believes the out-of-towner can stand it."

The Slide was a drag club on Bleecker Street that was both a center of gay male social activity and popular with straight visitors who wanted to observe. These histrionic **New York Herald** headlines helped inflame public sentiment against the Slide, which police closed in 1892. Illustration from the **New York Herald**, January 5, 1892.

A vice cop described his visits to the Slide and the men he encountered there: "Men of degenerate type were the waiters, some of them going to the extent of rouging their necks. In falsetto voices they sang filthy ditties, and when not otherwise busy would drop into a chair at the table of any visitor who would brook their awful presence." The Slide was closed by the police in 1892. (Down the block at 183 Bleecker Street, a sex club called the Black Rabbit, featuring gay-themed acts, managed to stay open until 1900, when it, too, was raided by the police.)

Across the street from the Slide is an apartment building now called the Atrium. Above the modern lettering one can still see the shadow of its old name, "Mills House No. 1."

The Mills Houses were male residence halls created by the philanthropist Darius O. Mills. (The other Mills House was on Rivington Street on the Lower East Side.) This one was built in 1896. Mills intended to provide sanitary and moral accommodation for unmarried working men. As historian George Chauncey notes, these inexpensive rooms were home to a number of working-class gay men, including a few who ended up in court for homosexual activity.

FROM "URANIAN" TO "QUEER": EVOLVING NAMES FOR HOMOSEXUALITY

The "love that dare not speak its name" has, in fact, had many—in medical journals, in the records of vice cops and the courts, and in the codes and slang used by gay men and lesbians themselves.

In the 1860s, a gay German writer and activist named Karl Heinrich Ulrichs wrote a series of articles about his theory of "Uranians"—people who were physically male or female but had spirits of the opposite sex. Ulrichs derived his new term from Plato's **Symposium** and wanted to create a respectable label for a nature that he insisted was not sick or sinful. Ulrich rejected the terms **pervert** and **sodomite,** which were commonly used by the public and the police to refer to gay men. The first known use of the word **homosexual** was in a letter to Ulrichs written by a friend in 1868.

In the late nineteenth century, as doctors and psychologists began to study human sexuality, they discussed a condition similar to what Ulrichs described that they termed "sexual inversion"—the condition of being a man trapped in a woman's body or vice versa. Those who suffered from the condition were known as "inverts." **Degenerate** was a term eugenicists used for gay men and lesbians. Like the mentally unfit or the physically disabled, gay men and lesbians were considered less than human, and their degenerate state justified measures to segregate them from "normal" people.

The slang of the New York streets had a range of words for

gay men and lesbians. **Fairy** was the most common word for a homosexual man in the early years of the twentieth century, though gay men themselves would use it only to refer to more effeminate men, using **queer** as the more universal term. Black gay men and lesbians would refer to being "in the life" to identify themselves to one another. The word **gay** itself was originally used in the nineteenth century to refer to prostitutes ("gay women"). The gay men who frequented the city's rougher neighborhoods and often kept company with prostitutes adopted the term as a code word among themselves. Police records make it clear that the cops didn't crack the code until the late 1940s, when the great mobility of World War II had led to the nationwide use of the word by gay men and lesbians.

➤ Turn around and walk west two blocks on Bleecker to MacDougal Street, then turn right on MacDougal and up one block to Minetta Lane.

Until the time of the Civil War, the southeastern section of Greenwich Village was home to one of New York City's largest African American communities, in an area known as "Little Africa." Many of the buildings along Minetta Lane and Minetta Street survive from that period. Among Little Africa's many residents in the 1860s was a young black woman from Connecticut named Addie Brown, who worked as a domestic servant. One of her employers, a prosperous African American man named John H. Jackson, had a house on Sullivan Street and ran a hotel on Broadway. From her room in Jackson's house, Brown wrote letters to her dearest love, Rebecca Primus, a black woman from Hartford with whom she had an intimate and passionate "romantic friendship."

Their correspondence is one of the most remarkable

documents of romantic friendship between women that survives from the nineteenth century. It is also one of the few examples of black women's writing that survives from the mid-1800s. The record we have of their relationship is, unfortunately, uneven: 120 of Brown's letters to Primus have survived, but none of Primus's replies.

Brown's letters reveal a close and passionate connection between the two women. In 1859, Brown wrote to Primus: "How did I miss you last night. I did not have anyone to hug me up and to kiss. No kisses is like yours." On another occasion Brown wrote: "O Rebecca, it seem I can see you now, casting those loving eyes at me. If you was a man, what would things come to? They would after come to something very quick."

Primus's family in Hartford were aware of the intensity of the women's bond. In 1866, Brown visited Primus's family and reported a remarkable statement that Primus's mother made to a gentleman caller to their home. After the visitor made a disparaging remark about Brown and Primus's affection for each other, Mrs. Primus defended them, saying, Brown reported, "that I thought as much of you as if I was a gentleman. She also said if either one of us was a gent we would marry. I was quite surprised at the remark." Both Primus and Brown eventually married men, though the letters reveal ambivalence and tension about their decisions.

WORDS INTO ACTION? THE EVIDENCE OF "ROMANTIC FRIENDSHIP"

What would you make of this excerpt from a letter written by a man to another man in 1777: "I wish, my dear Laurens, it might be in my power, by action rather than words, to convince you that I love you." What would you make of the fact that this letter was written by Alexander Hamilton to a fellow soldier in the Continental Army?

Historians have long debated what to make of the numerous examples of effusive, loving, and sometimes passionate correspondence between men and between women that survive from the eighteenth and nineteenth centuries. We know that many men and women had what historians have termed "romantic friendships" with people of the same sex. The eighteenth and nineteenth centuries were tremendously homosocial—that is, people tended to have their most important emotional relationships with others of the same sex. What historians debate is the extent to which these relationships might ever have been sexual.

The evidence of romantic friendship in the 1800s—with the notable exception of the Brown-Primus correspondence—tends to be from the letters and diaries of wealthy white men and women. Among those whose letters reveal such attachments are Ralph Waldo Emerson, Margaret Fuller, and Susan B. Anthony.

After the Civil War, romantic friendship among men became increasingly suspect and faded from view. Paradoxically, however, at about the same time, a new institution for women emerged from the tradition of romantic friendships. Some women began to form long-term partnerships with other women—arrangements that came to be known as "Boston marriages"—and some even set up households together. (The term **Boston marriage** derives from the prevalence of such relationships among propertied white women in Boston and from the novel **The Bostonians,** by Henry James, which depicts such a relationship.)

Boston marriages were relatively acceptable in the late 1800s and seem not to have provoked great scrutiny from the public, who seem to have accepted that two older single women might choose to live together without considering the sexual possibilities of such a relationship. With the advent of new medical and psychological attention to "inversion" among women at the turn of the century, however, these pairings fell under suspicion; people began to look askance at these "unnatural" relationships.

➤ **Continue walking north on MacDougal Street, keeping the Empire State Building in view, eventually stopping at Washington Place but taking note of the sites described below along the way.**

MacDougal Street was the main drag of New Bohemia and the Village's first Christopher Street. This was the center of lesbian and gay life and the place where the city's first gay and lesbian businesses outside of the seediest neighborhoods, were established in the 1910s and 1920s. By the 1930s, the west side of Washington Square Park was a major cruising area known as the "meat rack" or the "auction block."

Eve Addams's Tea Room, located at 129 MacDougal Street, was New York City's first lesbian bar. "Eve Addams" was Eva Kochever, a Polish Jewish immigrant who started her business here in 1925. Outside the door hung a sign that read "Men admitted but not welcome." In 1926 police raided the bar. Kochever was charged with writing an obscene book and with disorderly conduct. After serving a one-year sentence in a New York prison, she was deported to Paris in December 1927.

Beginning at the turn of the century, the Village's immigrant neighborhood to the south of Washington Square Park saw an influx of artists and writers who formed the core of New Bohemia. This community was tolerant of homosexuality in its ranks and even witnessed periods of what might be termed "lesbian chic," when women's explorations of lesbianism and bisexuality were in vogue. In a famous tale from the 1920s, poet Edna St. Vincent Millay conveys the spirit of the times in her exchange with an analyst. Seeking relief from persistent headaches, Millay asked an analyst's advice at a party. The analyst, not wanting to shock this lovely woman, said: "I wonder if it has ever occurred to you that you might perhaps, though you

The Greek revival townhouses along Washington Square North between University Place and Fifth Avenue, completed in 1833, are known as "The Row." Most now house New York University offices. Photo courtesy of the New-York Historical Society.

are hardly conscious of it, have an occasional impulse towards a person of your own sex?" Millay responded: "Oh, you mean I'm a homosexual! Of course I am, and heterosexual too, but what's that got to do with my headache?"

At 146 MacDougal was the Calypso Restaurant, where James Baldwin worked as a waiter in the early 1940s. The gay African American writer became friends with many locals who would come to see him at the restaurant, including Henry Miller, Paul Robeson, Marlon Brando, and Eartha Kitt. Baldwin met Brando when the two were students at the New School. Brando, who lived on nearby Patchin Place at the time, never tried to hide his own homosexual impulses. In 1956, Baldwin would publish *Giovanni's Room*, his second novel and one of the first to deal openly and centrally with homosexuality.

➤ **Turn left on Washington Place (not Washington Square South), which intersects Washington Square Park from the west, and walk about a half-block to No. 82.**

From about 1908 to 1913, 82 Washington Place was home to novelist Willa Cather and her partner Edith Lewis. Cather, author of such works as *My Antonia* and *Death Comes for the Archbishop*, had two central relationships with other women and referred to herself as "William" in letters that she wrote to a woman whom she admired while an undergraduate at the University of Nebraska. Cather and Lewis lived together at various addresses in Greenwich Village for nearly forty years, until Cather's death in 1947.

Cather lived at a time when women's relationships with each other were increasingly suspect, and she herself was clearly ambivalent about her life and loves. She took great care to destroy most of her personal correspondence before her death. In one surviving letter that she wrote in college, Cather laments her "unnatural" attraction to another woman.

Cather's correspondence with her mentor, author Sarah Orne Jewett, provides an illustration of the shifting situation for women who lived with other women at the turn of the century. Jewett was in a Boston marriage with Annie Fields from the 1880s through the early twentieth century. Jewett was not as ambivalent as Cather about the life she and Fields made together. The difference in the women's lives is also visible in their writing.

While Jewett's stories often center on two women, Cather's do not. In fact, some literary critics identify male leads in Cather's stories as stand-ins for Cather herself. In critiquing Cather's work, Jewett often remarked on Cather's choice to write about heterosexual pairs instead

Writer Willa Cather (1873–1947) lived in Greenwich Village for most of the last forty years of her life with her partner Edith Lewis. Although a lesbian, Cather didn't write openly about women's relationships with each other in her brilliant fiction, instead choosing to use heterosexual couples as stand-ins. Photo courtesy of the New-York Historical Society.

of focusing on relationships between women. In 1908, for example, Jewett wrote the following to Cather about Cather's story "The Gull's Road:"

The lover is as well done as he could be when a woman writes in the man's character—it must always, I believe, be something of a masquerade, and you could almost have done it as yourself, a woman would love her in the same protecting way, a woman would even care enough to wish to take her away from such a life by some means or another.

Uncomfortable with her own attraction to other women, Cather did not feel free to write so openly about women's relationships with each other.

➤ **Return to MacDougal Street (Washington Square West) and walk northeast through Washington Square Park, exiting at the Arch at Fifth Avenue.**

As you walk through the park, you're passing over the remains of probably thousands of bodies interred here in its years as a potter's field in the eighteenth century. The park and the neighborhood have gone through many changes since then. A yellow fever epidemic in 1822 forced many to flee downtown New York City for the "village." Many stayed and the area developed, growing further as population expanded northward. In the 1830s, luxury townhouses appeared on the northern edge of the park and some still remain. Tenements to the south came in the latter part of the nineteenth century. The Arch itself was designed by Stanford White (see our Four Squares Tour in chapter 4) in 1892 to replace a papier-mâché antecedent erected in 1889 to celebrate the centennial of George Washington's return to the city after the Revolutionary War.

➤ **Continue north on Fifth Avenue to No. 23.**

In her apartment at 23 Fifth Avenue, Mabel Dodge ran a weekly salon that became a center for Village artists and intellectuals. Openly bisexual herself, Dodge opened her doors to many unconventional women, including Emma Goldman, Margaret Sanger, and Gertrude Stein. (Stein's work *A Portrait of Mabel Dodge* was named in the hostess's honor.) Dodge was also one of the people who made possible the Armory Art Show, which opened in February 1913, bringing Marcel Duchamp's *Nude Descending a Staircase* and works by Picasso, Cézanne, and others to the protesting masses.

➤ **Continue north on Fifth Avenue to Eleventh Street. Walk east to University Place and then north to 86 University Place, the former site of the Bagatelle.**

The Bagatelle was one of the few lesbian bars in the city in the 1950s. The other popular ones were the Sea Colony (a more working-class bar on Eighth Avenue) and the Swing Rendezvous (on MacDougal Street). Audre Lorde, black poet and essayist, wrote about spending time at the Bagatelle in her autobiography *Zami: A New Spelling of My Name*. There was a tiny dance floor in the back, and the front room "smelled like plastic and blue glass and beer and lots of good-looking young women." Lorde describes that she and the other "out" black lesbians in the bars rarely acknowledged one another, and most of the women with whom she spent time, and with whom she slept, in her early years were white. While there were other places for women to go at the time, she said that "the Bag was always The Club."

➤ **If you would like to take an interesting detour that will add fifteen to twenty minutes to your tour, walk east several blocks on Eleventh Street to No. 125, the site of Webster Hall. (If not, backtrack on Eleventh Street to Sixth Avenue; cross over and go left a few doors to 457 Sixth Avenue.)**

Detour: From 1913 through the 1930s, Webster Hall was the site of the annual Greenwich Village Ball. (Today Webster Hall is a popular and mostly straight nightclub.) The masquerade balls were sponsored by various organizations and patronized by the Village's bohemian society, including many gay men in drag. By the early 1920s, gay men and lesbians were holding events of their own at Webster Hall.

In 1934, the *New York Herald Tribune* described the mixing, role-playing, and inversion that characterized the Greenwich Village Ball:

Blonds equipped themselves with dark hair. Caucasians came disguised as orientals. Mongoloid individuals blackened their faces and appeared as Ethiopians, Negroes powdered their skins and dressed as Scandinavian villagers. College boys masqueraded as hoboes. Waitresses and soda clerks wore full evening dress. Men danced with women in men's clothes. Women danced with men in women's clothes. And strange androgynous couples careened about the floor, oblivious to the workings of society and nature.

By the 1920s, drag balls were an established part of gay male culture in New York, particularly that of the black gay community of Harlem. The most famous and well attended of such events was the Hamilton Lodge Ball in Harlem, which began as the Masquerade and Civic Ball organized by the Grand United Order of Odd Fellows. By the early 1920s the ball was increasingly noted for the presence of "fairies." By the late 1920s it was known as the "Faggots Ball." Attendance at the ball ranged from four thousand to eight thousand (both spectators and participants) between 1927 and 1937.

The drag balls gave rise to the use of one of contemporary gay life's most familiar terms: *coming out*. Today, coming out is generally thought of as "coming out of the closet," emerging from terrified secrecy. Earlier origins of the phrase in the ball scene, however, were much less dark and sad. Participants in the balls used the term *coming out* with a wink and a nod to straight debutantes. As the *Baltimore Afro-American* put it in 1931: "1931 Debutantes Bow at Local 'Pansy' Ball: The coming out of new debutantes into

homosexual society was the outstanding feature of Baltimore's eighth annual frolic of the pansies when the Art
Club was host to the neuter gender at the Elks' Hall Friday
night." (*This is the end of the detour.*)

The house at 457 Sixth Avenue was the former home of
Murray Hall, a "ward heeler" for Tammany Hall, the machine behind Democratic politics in New York City from
the early 1800s through the 1950s. Hall was responsible for
"organizing the vote" in this district. Hall was married
twice and was known for being a heavy drinker and a
brawler and for being "sweet on women." In 1901, Hall
died, leaving a wife and an adopted daughter, and it was revealed that Hall had died of breast cancer. Hall was a
woman who had passed as a man for all of her adult life.

The *New York Times* gave the revelation extensive coverage over a number of days, as Hall's friends and associates reacted to the news. A lawyer friend quoted in the
Times recalled: "I've known him for a number of years. He
could drink his weight in beer and stand up under it. I saw
him play poker with a party of the Jefferson Market clique
one night, and he played the game like a veteran. And for
nerve, well, I just can't believe he was a woman, that's all."
(So much so that he still referred to Hall as "he.") Senator
Bernard F. Martin (D–NY) also averred: "I wouldn't believe it if Dr. Gallagher, whom I know to be a man of un-
doubted veracity, hadn't said so."

Passing women were not uncommon in the nineteenth
century. Local papers across the country carried items
about men revealed to be women, usually after an arrest or
at their death. Historians debate why women made the
choice to pass as men. Some might have understood themselves to be men born in female bodies (or "transgen-
dered," in contemporary terms). Some might have been
women who wanted the greater freedom and autonomy

that men enjoyed, some the work opportunities and higher wages available to men. Some might also have been women who wanted to make lives with other women. Many passing women were, indeed, married. While a wealthier woman had the possibility in the late nineteenth century of forming an independent household with another woman in a Boston marriage, working women did not have the financial independence that made such an arrangement possible.

> **Go north on Sixth Avenue one block to Twelfth Street, then west on Twelfth Street toward Seventh Avenue South.**

From the 1920s through the 1950s, the building at 171 West Twelfth Street was home to a number of lesbian couples, an extended network of friends and comrades-in-arms that included artist Nancy Cook and educator Marion Dickerman; activist Polly Porter and Democratic Party official Molly Dewson; and Grace Hutchins and her partner Anna Rochester, both leaders in the Communist Party. Many of these women, particularly Dickerman and Cook, were good friends with Eleanor Roosevelt, who had apartments of her own at 20 East Eleventh Street from 1933 to 1942 and at 29 Washington Square West from 1942 to 1949. Since her young adulthood, Roosevelt had been part of a circle of women reformers, many of them in long-term relationships with other women.

When Franklin D. Roosevelt became president, Eleanor became a fierce champion for women in government, and many of her friends got government positions during the New Deal. Molly Dewson served as director of the Women's Division of the Democratic National Committee and as a member of the Social Security Board. Among President Roosevelt's other appointees were Frances Perkins, the secretary of labor from 1933 to 1945 and the first woman cabinet member, and Grace Abbot, who was chief of the Children's Bureau. From within the government, these women could press for action on the issues they had pursued for years, such as wages and hours' legislation, workers' compensation requirements, and child labor laws.

Roosevelt herself had an intimate relationship with another woman. In 1932, an Associated Press reporter named Lorena Hickok was assigned to file stories on the new first lady. They quickly became fast friends. Hickok would eventually come to live in the White House. The nature of the Hickok-Roosevelt relationship has been hotly contested by biographers and historians, but their letters reveal a passionate intimacy—in 1933, for example, Hickok wrote to Roosevelt:

> I've been trying today to bring back your face, to remember just how you look, most clearly I remember your eyes, with a kind of teasing smile in them, and the feeling of that soft spot just North-east of the corner of your mouth against my lips. Good night, dear one, I want to put my arms around you and kiss you at the corner of your mouth. And in a little more than a week now, I shall.

Despite such effusive letters, many biographers strenuously insist that Roosevelt herself was not a lesbian.

➤ **Upon reaching Seventh Avenue South, cross the avenue and walk north to Thirteenth Street. Turn left (west) on West Thirteenth Street to No. 208.**

Since 1984, 208 West Thirteenth Street has been the home base for New York's gay and lesbian community. On any given day, the Lesbian and Gay Community Services Center, which is open to the public, will host dozens of meetings and events. With offices and meeting rooms for nu-

merous lesbian/gay/bisexual/transgendered (LGBT) organizations, its halls have witnessed many key moments in
lesbian and gay history.

On March 14, 1987, for example, novelist and activist
Larry Kramer rose at a center event—he had been scheduled to read from one of his novels—and delivered an im-
passioned plea for action on AIDS. Within a week the
AIDS Coalition to Unleash Power, or ACT UP, was
founded and rejuvenated lesbian and gay activism in the
Reagan era. ACT UP's defiant brand of in-your-face activism led to action on AIDS by pharmaceutical companies
and local, state, and national governments. While the organization has declined somewhat from its heyday in the
late 1980s and early 1990s, ACT UP meetings continue at
the center to this day.

> **Return to Seventh Avenue South, cross the avenue, and
walk down four blocks to Waverly Place. Turn left on Waverly Place and walk two blocks to Julius' in the nonde-
script stucco building at the corner of West Tenth Street.**

Julius', at 159 West Tenth Street, dates back to before Prohibition and is one of the oldest bars still open in the Village. A lively if somewhat down-at-the-heels neighborhood gathering place to this day, it was the site of an important early gay rights victory in New York State.

In 1966, the Mattachine Society of New York staged
what it called a "sip-in" in the bars of the Village, con-
sciously linking their action to the tactics of the civil rights
movement. At the time, if a bartender knowingly sold al-
cohol to a homosexual, the New York State Liquor Licens-
ing Authority (SLA) could rescind the establishment's
liquor license. Bars around the Village had signs in the windows that read "If you're gay, go away." However, many
bars that catered to lesbians and gay men were run by the

Mafia, which could afford to pay off the police and stay open despite serving homosexual patrons.

For the "sip-in," members of the Mattachine Society went from bar to bar, sat down, announced that they were homosexual, and ordered drinks. In most places, they were served. However, when they got to Julius', they were refused. Working with the City Human Rights Commission, the Mattachine Society brought suit, and in 1967 the New York State Supreme Court ruled that the liquor authority needed substantial evidence of indecent behavior (not just same-sex kissing or touching) to close a bar. Wearing clothes inappropriate to one's sex counted as such substantial evidence, a fact that would be important just two years down the road and just two blocks away.

➤ Continue along Waverly Place (Stonewall Place) one block to Christopher, then turn right on Christopher and walk to 51-53 Christopher Street, the Stonewall Inn.

This stretch of Christopher Street is widely considered the birthplace of the modern lesbian and gay rights movement. In 1999 the blocks around the site of the former Stonewall Inn were designated a National Historic Landmark: the Stonewall National Historic District, the first recognition of lesbian and gay history by the federal government.

The bar that once stood here at No. 53, the Stonewall Inn, was an unprepossessing place, crowded and popular on weekends but nothing fancy. (The bar that now stands here, called Stonewall, is not the original.) Like most other bars in the city that served a gay clientele, the Stonewall Inn was owned by the Mob, which paid off the local police in order to stay in business. Police raids and shakedowns for such establishments were the norm, and many bars had a light over the front door that would go on when the police were coming in order to alert patrons to approaching danger.

In the early morning hours of June 28, 1969, the patrons of the Stonewall Inn fought back against such routine police harassment, refusing to disperse quietly when the cops singled out several drag queens for arrest and sent the rest of the crowd into the streets. When one butch lesbian struck the cop who had hit her, the crowd unleashed a hail of coins and a flood of invective. The police were forced back into the bar, and the crowd attacked the building, trying to set fire to the bar and leading the cops to draw their guns. When riot police arrived they averted a possible shooting, but the invigorated crowd still refused to back down. The actions of that night sparked several nights of unrest and launched a new phase of gay and lesbian activism, "gay liberation."

On the first anniversary of the Stonewall riots, New York City witnessed its first Gay Pride march, up Sixth Avenue from Christopher Street to Central Park. Every year since, lesbians and gay men in New York City and around the world have remembered the Stonewall riots with parades and marches in the month of June. The riots quickly became the stuff of legend. One activist once remarked, "I am probably one of six people who lived in the Village at the time who does not claim to have been at the Stonewall riots."

The riots at the Stonewall Inn in 1969 sparked the Gay Liberation movement, a vibrant and in-your-face effort to eliminate antigay prejudice in American law and society. This effort was spearheaded by two organizations: the Gay Liberation Front (GLF), launched immediately after the riots, and the Gay Activists Alliance (GAA), which split off from the GLF after infighting over the scope of the work gay and lesbian activists should take on. Both the GAA and the GLF had their headquarters in Greenwich Village: the first GLF meetings were held in the space of an organization called Alternate U, at 534 Sixth Avenue at Fourteenth Street; and from 1971 to 1974, the GAA had its headquarters in a renovated firehouse at 99 Wooster Street.

The GLF and GAA were building on work done by the homophiles, but they had a new style and a new politics. The Gay Liberation Front saw itself as part of the larger New Left movement of the late 1960s and sought to incorporate gay liberation into the agenda of the radical politics of other organizations. The GLF's commitment to coalition politics led to friction within the group, as some members argued for an effort more centered on gay rights than on revolution.

In December 1969, a group of GLF members broke off to form the Gay Activists Alliance. The group sought to avoid the pitfalls of movement politics and the sometimes chaotic style of GLF organizing. The GAA had clear membership requirements and a constitution that prohibited endorsement of or alliance with "any organization not directly related to the homosexual cause."

Together, the GLF and the GAA transformed gay activism, responding to homophobia with "zap" actions directed at the offenders (a tactic that would reemerge in the 1980s with ACT UP) and creating a new level of visibility for the gay cause. The GAA Firehouse became a center of gay life and activism until it was firebombed in October 1974. That fall saw a rash of arson attacks on gay bars, homes, and offices, a reaction to the growing visibility and militance of gay liberation activism.

From a nation in which, as we have seen, gays were choked to death or drowned, we have become one in which being publicly gay is celebrated—in some places. Greenwich Village remains a center of established gay and lesbian life, which overlaps—as does gay and lesbian history—with the other lives and other events of these streets.

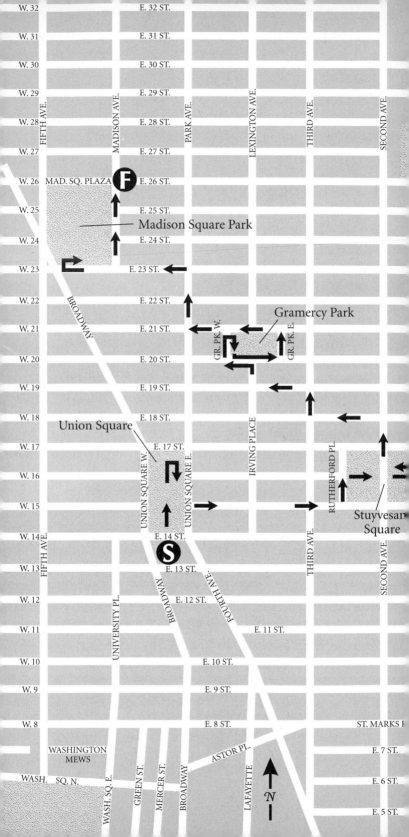

4 FOUR SQUARES
Union Square, Stuyvesant Square,
Gramercy Park, and Madison Square

➤ Start: The George Washington Statue, located on the
Fourteenth Street side of Union Square.

THE CITY SQUARE represents a civic ideal that op-
poses the environmental chaos that can result from un-
planned urban development. Especially on Manhattan Island, where real estate is limited by geography, unguided
urban growth tends to create overcrowded, densely packed
residential and commercial housing. The city square, by
preserving some of this jealously coveted real estate for
communal use, offers a slice of uncluttered, open space for
the public to enjoy. In city squares, one can retreat from the
bustle of the crowded streets to enjoy a relaxing hour on a
park bench beneath the cover of trees or to absorb the
warmth of sunlight on an expansive picnic lawn. By com-
memorating important events, honoring the memory of
leading citizens, or celebrating historical figures held in
high esteem, the public monuments that grace these
squares pronounce civic values. This carefully constructed
environment is intended to elicit a sense of community in
its inhabitants.

This walking tour visits four New York squares:
Union Square, Stuyvesant Square, Gramercy Park, and
Madison Square. None of these squares has been imper-
vious to historical change. Situated amid an astonishingly

fast-changing urban environment, these public spaces have been shaped and reshaped as the communities around them have changed. Originally designed to attract a "better class" of New Yorkers to form a quiet, residential neighborhood, only one, Gramercy Park, has maintained a fairly stable identity through its existence. Each square, however, has seen periods of decline and resurgence, of conflict and community.

The man most responsible for the founding of these squares in the 1830s was the lawyer and visionary real estate investor, Samuel Ruggles. At that time, the area between Fourteenth and Twenty-eighth Streets had begun to take shape as a genteel suburb on the northern outskirts of the city. Correctly anticipating New York's impending growth uptown, Ruggles purchased numerous undeveloped plots of land in the area that would become Union Square and Gramercy Park. Ruggles saw an opportunity to beautify these suburban communities and turn them into neighborhoods for the city's elite. By designing an exclusive, fenced park in the center of each square, Ruggles hoped to entice the wealthy to settle around them. The value of Ruggles's property grew after the Great Fire of 1835 prompted Manhattanites to migrate uptown in large numbers. In 1839, Union Square opened with an oval-shaped iron fence surrounding the park at its center. Ruggles built a four-story home for himself at Union Square, but his masterpiece, although he never lived there himself, was Gramercy Park, which opened in 1844.

At Samuel Ruggles's urging, the residents of what would become Madison Square also organized their neighborhood around a residential park that was constructed in the 1840s. The Stuyvesant family also began to develop public squares on their land, beginning with Tompkins Square (which we won't be visiting) in 1834. In 1836, Peter

Gerard Stuyvesant deeded the land that would become Stuyvesant Square to the city for $5.

The period during which Union Square and Madison Square remained residential enclaves for the wealthy was relatively short-lived. Geographically placed at the strategic center of the city, right along the highly trafficked path of Broadway, Union and Madison Squares rapidly became commercial and cultural centers as the city expanded northward. None of the original residential houses still stands at either Union or Madison Square. Elegant brownstones and townhouses from as early as the 1840s, however, can be found at both Gramercy Park and Stuyvesant Square, as well as on the side streets throughout the neighborhood. They are the remnants of the area's first epoch.

UNION SQUARE

Our tour begins on the southern side of Union Square, between Fourteenth Street and the monument of George Washington on horseback.

Looking around Union Square today, one sees the results of a revitalization effort that has been transforming this neighborhood over the past fifteen years. Although it was New York's most fashionable shopping and theater district in the late nineteenth century, Union Square experienced a long period of decline beginning in the 1920s. The department stores and boutiques that made up "Ladies Mile" moved further uptown, closer to the upscale residential districts of the Upper East and West Sides. Caught between the midtown and downtown business districts, Union Square and its environs were left to deteriorate. Union Square became known in the 1960s and 1970s as a site for drug dealers and a place for the homeless. A $3.6 million reconstruction project, launched in 1985, dramatically refurbished the park's neglected landscape and successfully addressed its safety problems. Crowning its restoration, Union Square Park was designated a National Historic Landmark in 1997 by the National Parks Service.

LADIES' MILE AND THE RIALTO

The proliferation of department stores along Broadway from Ninth to Twenty-third Street, terminating at Madison Square, earned this stretch the nickname "Ladies' Mile" in the 1870s. This development began in the 1860s when A. T. Stewart, owner of a dry-goods store near City Hall, decided to build a massive emporium on the corner of Broadway and East Ninth Street. In a cast-iron building that filled the entire block, A. T. Stewart's sold expensive furnishings, antiques, fabrics, and women's wear. The triumphant success of A. T. Stewart's brought a succession of upscale department stores to this stretch of Broadway, which transformed the character of the neighborhood. Tiffany and Company demolished James Renwick Jr.'s Church of the Puritans at Union Square to build its store in 1869. Orbach's established itself on Fourteenth Street at Union Square; W. & J. Sloane's and Arnold Constable's together took up the entire block between Eighteenth and Nineteenth Streets on Broadway; and Lord & Taylor's inhabited the elaborately designed building on the southwest corner of East Twentieth. The shopping district also included a stretch of Sixth Avenue two blocks west, where Macy's and B. Altman's opened.

Interestingly, the nickname "Ladies' Mile" took on a far different meaning at night. Above the department stores one could find lavishly furnished brothels that catered to the men of the upper class. These high-priced "Temples of Love" advertised themselves in publications such as the **Gentleman's Directory,** promising women who were not only beautiful but also charming and refined conversationalists. Outside the elite brothels, throngs of street-walkers worked Ladies' Mile after dark. By the 1890s, reformers complained that both Union and Stuyvesant Square Parks had become a place where "tramps [both] male and female haggle and dispute over their price."

While Broadway brought department stores, Union Square's other tributary, the Bowery, brought theaters. Dubbed "the Rialto" by **New York Sun** reporter Ted McAlpin, by the 1870s, Union Square had replaced the Bowery as the hub of theater activity in the city. In 1854 the Academy of Music, one of the largest theaters in the world, opened on Fourteenth Street near Union Square. The city's primary opera house, the Academy of Music hosted the American premieres of **Aida** (1873), **Lohengrin** (1874), **Die Walküre** (1877), and **Carmen** (1878). All of New York society pined for the prestige of owning an opera box at the academy. Despite a cost of as much as $30,000, the waiting list for boxes was long and included such names as Vanderbilt, Astor, and Gould.

Some referred to Union Square Park as the "slave market" because aspiring actors bargained for contracts with theater managers in impromptu negotiations within it. The Rialto's major theaters included Irving Hall, at Fifteenth and Irving Place; Wallack's Theatre, at Thirteenth and Broadway; the Hippotheatron, across from the Academy of Music on Fourteenth; and the Union Square Theatre. Nearby restaurants, such as Luchow's (opened in 1882), became legendary hot spots where celebrities and performers mingled and danced while critics wrote their reviews at the dinner tables. The popular tune "Yes Sir, That's My Baby" is said to have been written one drunken night by Gus Kahn on a Luchow's tablecloth.

At the south side of the park is Henry Kirke Brown's *George Washington*, dedicated on July 4, 1856. Considered by some to be the finest equestrian statue in the country, it depicts Washington's triumphant return to New York City on November 25, 1783. As British troops ended their seven-year occupation of the city at the close of the Revolutionary

War, Washington came personally to repossess the city he had lost to the British in 1776. At this spot, Washington and his officers were greeted by a crowd of jubilant citizens. Known then as Union Place, this grassy clearing north of the city was named for the juncture of Boston Post Road (later to become the Bowery) and Albany Post Road (later Broadway). As the statue depicts, Washington then headed southward, accompanied by the cheering crowd, down the path of Albany Post Road toward the city, where New Yorkers thronged the streets to catch a glimpse of him. For years afterward, the anniversary of this day would be celebrated in New York as "Evacuation Day."

➤ **Walk west toward the intersection of University Place and Fourteenth Street.**

K. B. Patel's statue *Mohandas K. Gandhi* (1986) stands in a floral bed known as the Gandhi Garden to the southwest of Union Square Park, where Fourteenth Street and Broadway meet. Donated by the citizens of India, this statue was originally intended to be placed at the newly established Washington Market Park in TriBeCa, but its neighborhood residents rejected it. It is fitting, however, that the great philosopher and practitioner of nonviolent protest should be honored at Union Square instead, which has a long tradition of (mostly) peaceful protest.

On September 5, 1882, the nation's first Labor Day parade ended at Union Square after marching up Broadway from City Hall. After that event, Union Square became the preferred site of labor rallies and mass political protests. Soapbox orators regularly drew crowds, while thousands would turn out to celebrate every May Day and Labor Day. Anarchist Isadore Wisotsky later recalled the atmosphere of Union Square in the 1910s: "We gathered to make revolution and stayed to talk. And how we talked—anarchism,

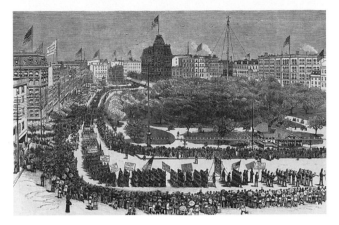

America's first Labor Day, as it was held in Union Square, September 5, 1882. The parade was organized by P. J. McGuire. McGuire's mottos—"Organize, Agitate, Educate." Illustration from **Frank Leslie's,** September 16, 1882, in John Grafton, **New York in the Nineteenth Century** (New York: Dover), 1977.

atheism, against the military, for birth control, against injustice, for socialism and for the rights of workers to organize. . . . The right to speak at Union Square was more precious than the bread we sweated to earn.

One of the most tension-filled protests at Union Square occurred on August 22, 1927. On that night, five thousand people gathered to hold a candlelight vigil for the anarchists Sacco and Vanzetti, who were about to be executed in Boston. The New York Police Department was so apprehensive of violence that it stationed machine guns on the nearby roof of Klein's department store. No incidents occurred. However, a few years later, police and protestors battled furiously in a bloody riot here on March 6, 1930. The demonstrators had come to Union Square that day, six months after the 1929 Stock Market crash, to celebrate International Unemployment Day, an event sponsored by the American Communist Party. When thousands of demonstrators attempted to march down Broadway without a permit, the police opposed them with force, igniting a violent conflict that resulted in hundreds of injuries.

➤ Enter Union Square Park and walk toward its northern
end. Stop at the statue of Abraham Lincoln, which stands
on a pedestal facing Seventeenth Street.

On the west side of the park is an elaborate fountain designed by the German sculptor Karl Adolf Donndorf
(1881), that was originally placed at the center of the park.
When the park was redesigned in the 1920s, *Independence
Flagstaff* (1926) by Anthony de Francisci became the center of the park. Erected to commemorate the 150th anniversary of the signing of the Declaration of Independence, this flagpole's massive base is adorned with a relief
sculpture depicting the forces of good and evil in a struggle
during the American Revolution.

On the north side of the park is a structure dating from
the 1920s that operates as an outdoor restaurant during the
summer months. Looking beyond it, one can see a richly
ornamented red-brick building facing the park on Seventeenth Street. Designed by William Schickel in 1881, it was
built as the headquarters of Century Publishing, whose
Century magazine was one of the most respected literary
journals of the 1880s. Currently it houses an expansive
Barnes and Noble bookstore.

The northern and western edges of Union Square
Park have become the home of an extremely popular
Greenmarket. Four days a week, more than one hundred
upstate farmers bring an impressive display of fresh produce, wine, flowers, preserves, pastries, and breads. By
attracting new consumers to the area, the Greenmarket
has helped pave the way for the commercial transformation of the square. Gradually, the failing discount businesses that once dominated the square have been replaced by chic restaurants, coffee shops, and major national chains, including Barnes and Noble, Toys R Us,
Seaman's, Staples, and Starbucks.

Directly in front of the band shell is the statue *Abraham Lincoln*, sculpted by Henry Kirke Brown and dedicated at Union Square Park in 1868. It is believed to be the first public statue of Lincoln erected in the country. Unlike Brown's masterful *George Washington* on the opposite end of the park, this statue was not well received after its unveiling. Brown's Lincoln, with his rumpled clothes and plain demeanor, may have accurately captured the historical man but it was deemed uninspiring because it failed to meet the public's expectations of the mythical president. The outpouring of public emotion following Lincoln's assassination on Good Friday 1865 raised the fallen president to an almost Christlike stature in the popular mind. In Brown's rendering, the solemn president holds a rolled copy of a speech—or perhaps the Emancipation Proclamation—in his left hand, which hangs calmly and unheroically at his side.

Union Square is a fitting spot for New York to honor Lincoln's memory. It was during the Civil War that Union Square became the central gathering place in the city—the Times Square of the nineteenth century. After the fall of Fort Sumter, President Lincoln's call for volunteers was answered by thousands of young men who flocked to enlist at recruiting tents that dotted the interior of the park. Nearly a quarter-million people gathered at Union Square on Saturday, April 20, 1861, to hear speakers denounce the Southern rebellion while the tattered American flag rescued from Fort Sumter waved from the statue *George Washington*, where it had been patriotically placed.

➤ **Exit the park by walking east of the Lincoln statue and down the ramp to Park Avenue.**

Across the street and a block to your north, at the corner of Seventeenth Street and Park Avenue, is the New York Film

Academy. The academy is housed in the last of the Tammany Hall headquarters, built in 1929 during the administration of Mayor Jimmy Walker. Walker, the last mayor to be elevated to power by Tammany Hall, embodied the flashy style of the affluent 1920s. The construction of this federal-style building was financed by Wall Street investments, but the stock market crash that ruined the investors later that year also helped bring about the downfall of Tammany Hall itself. In 1933, New Yorkers elected a Republican mayor, Fiorello La Guardia, who promised to destroy Tammany forever.

TAMMANY HALL

The Society of St. Tammany or Columbian Order was formed in 1788. The name Tammany is derived from the legendary Delaware Indian chief Tamanend, who was adopted as the club's patron saint. The organization enjoyed using pseudo-American Indian titles, such as "sachems" for council members, "braves" for its rank and file, and "wigwam" for its headquarters. It became a Jeffersonian political club under the influence of Aaron Burr in the 1790s and later a Jacksonian Democratic club under the leadership of Martin Van Buren.

The club formed a powerful grassroots alliance with immigrant voters, based on a system of graft in which local "bosses" would dispense financial assistance and protection to supporters in exchange for their vote. Fernando Wood first used the Tammany political machine to capture the mayor's office in the 1850s. In the 1860s, Tammany's "Grand Sachem," William Marcy "Boss" Tweed, used the organization autocratically to control patronage of the city's elected and appointed public offices, while embezzling millions from the city's coffers. The exposure of the Tweed ring in 1871 scandalized the nation.

In 1868, Tammany Hall moved to Fourteenth Street near Union Square (on ground now occupied by the Con Edison Building). The

The Tammany Hall Wigwam, East Fourteenth Street near Third Avenue, circa 1870. Built in 1868 under the direction of William Marcy "Boss" Tweed, the building was razed in 1911, when the Con Edison Building was constructed in its place. The clock tower was designed by Warren and Wetmore. Photograph courtesy of the New-York Historical Society.

impressive building—whose top was adorned with a statue of a fierce-looking American Indian, armed with a tomahawk and scalping knife—hosted the 1868 National Democratic Party Convention. Despite the downfall of Tweed a few years later, Tammany Hall continued to be a powerful force in city, state, and sometimes even national politics until the 1930s. Remaining a staunch defender of the working man and maintaining an entrenched patronage system, Tammany facilitated the long political career of Governor Alfred E. Smith (a presidential candidate in 1928) and Mayor Jimmy Walker, both the sons of Irish immigrants.

The 1932 judicial investigation into corruption charges against Tammany, launched by Governor Franklin D. Roosevelt and led by Judge Samuel Seabury, ended in the sensational downfall of the Walker administration. The corruption scandal that resulted forced Mayor Walker to flee to Europe to escape prosecution. During the twelve-year reign of Mayor Fiorello La Guardia, Tammany became all but extinct.

Perhaps the prevailing ethic of Tammany Hall was best summed up by George Washington Plunkitt, who once explained the extraordinary wealth he had acquired as a Tammany "sachem" by saying: "I seen my opportunities and I took 'em."

➤ Walk south toward Fifteenth Street, along the east side of Union Square.

The statue of the French general *Marquis de Lafayette* (1873) was done by Frédéric-Auguste Bartholdi, the same man who designed the Statue of Liberty. Lafayette served as a major general on the staff of George Washington. An inscription on the monument's pedestal quotes Lafayette's words: "As soon as I heard of American Independence my heart was enlisted." In 1824, at the invitation of Congress, Lafayette returned to America, where he was warmly embraced as the toast of New York society. Lafayette was the first foreigner ever bestowed with honorary American citizenship (the second being Winston Churchill).

➤ Walk to the corner of Fifteenth Street and Park Avenue.

On the northeast corner of Fifteenth Street is the old Union Square Saving Bank, designed by Henry Bacon in 1924. A landmarked building, it is now used as a concert hall. The Corinthian temple exterior of the bank is somewhat suggestive of Bacon's later masterpiece: the Lincoln Memorial in Washington, D.C.

To the southeast of the square is an infamous intersection once known as "Dead Man's Curve," where speeding trolley cars and horse-drawn carriages often mowed down careless pedestrians who thronged this shopping and theater district. Looming over Dead Man's Curve today are the four massive red towers of the Zeckendorf Towers (Davis, Brody and Associates, 1987), a mixed residential and business complex. The Towers stand on the former site of S. Klein's discount department store, which left its building abandoned in 1975 (thus betraying its nickname, "S. Klein-on-the-Square"). Neighborhood residents protested against the construction of this enormous complex, which partially blocks the view of the striking Con Edison clock tower that stands behind it to the east. But the luxury apartments offered by the Zeckendorf Towers have played a key role in the regentrification of Union Square.

On the south side of Fourteenth Street is a similar apartment complex completed in 1998, housing the Virgin Megastore and Circuit City at the street level. Adorning its facade is an elaborate $3 million dollar piece of artwork titled *Metronome*. Unveiled in September 1999, *Metronome* is a jumble of symbols that has been described by its creators, Andrew Gizel and Kristen Jones, as "an ode to the impossibility of knowing time." It features fifteen digital numbers that count off the time elapsing from midnight, a black and gold sphere that rotates in synchronization with the phases of the moon, and a five-foot opening that periodically belches blasts of steam. In a whimsical nod to its neighborhood surroundings, Gizel and Hones cast the disembodied hand that stretches forth from the top *Metronome* from Henry Kirke Brown's statue of George Washington across the street.

➤ **Cross Park Avenue and walk east on Fifteenth Street three blocks to Stuyvesant Square, passing the sights described below.**

At 109–111 East Fifteenth Street stands the oldest surviving clubhouse in the city: the Century Association Building, now the Century Center for Performing Arts, which was designed by Charles Gambrill and Henry Hobson Richardson in 1869. Formed in 1847, the Century Association (and Club) was founded as an intellectual society bringing together men "of all guilds," aspiring to cultivate "a taste for Letters and the Arts and social enjoyment" among New York's leading citizens. Though its members aspired for their club to become the American equivalent of the French Academy, in reality it remained more about socializing than about serious intellectual discussion. In the 1880s, William Watson Gilder, the first editor of *Century* magazine, borrowed his journal's name without permission from the Century Club, of which he was a member.

The headquarters of the Consolidated Edison power company towers above the southeast corner of Fourteenth Street and Irving Place. It stands on the site of its predecessor, the Manhattan Gas Light Company, which was located here from 1885 to 1910. Construction of this building began in 1911, and the main section was designed by Henry J. Hardenbergh, who was also responsible for the Dakota on Seventy-second and Central Park West. The building's most majestic feature is the Tower of Light (Warren and Wetmore, 1926), a massive clock tower that caps the building and is most impressive when brilliantly illuminated at nighttime.

➤ **Walk north on Rutherford Place to the Sixteenth Street entrance to Stuyvesant Square.**

STUYVESANT SQUARE

On arriving at Stuyvesant Square from Fifteenth Street, the first landmarks to grab your attention are the red-brick Friends Meeting House and Seminary to your left, which date from 1860. Part of a five-building complex that also includes the original schoolhouse, an elegant nineteenth-century townhouse (across Fifteenth Street), and a modern school building, the Friends Seminary dominates the southwest corner of the square. A doctrinal split in the Quaker community prompted the construction of this meetinghouse when this group seceded from another congregation a few blocks away at Gramercy Park. When the two groups reconciled in 1958, the Gramercy Park congregation abandoned their building to join this one.

St. George's Episcopal Church stands north across Sixteenth Street from the Friends Meeting House. Completed in 1856, this brownstone structure is one of the earliest examples of Romanesque revival architecture in America. The exterior by Otto Blesch had to be restored after the church was badly damaged in an 1865 fire. Leopold Eidlitz, who designed the original interior, rebuilt it according to Blesch's original plans. The two spires were never properly restored and finally were torn down in 1888. Next door, on the north side of the church, is St. George's Chapel (1911), a fine Gothic revival companion to the older building.

➤ **Enter the park.**

The four-acre twin parks of Stuyvesant Square are bifurcated by Second Avenue, which creates a noisy invasion of this otherwise pastoral setting. The extension of Second Avenue through the park was part of the original plan when the square was deeded to the city by Peter Gerard Stuyvesant in 1836, but no one could have foreseen the incredible volume of traffic that would later speed down this avenue. The cast-iron fence that surrounds each section of the park dates from 1850.

Like the other residential squares developed in the 1840s, Stuyvesant Square originally occupied the center of an upper-class neighborhood. Several excellent examples of early residences can still be found in the vicinity. One prime example facing the park from the north is the Sidney Webster House (1883) at 245 East Seventeenth Street. (Note its four-peaked front.) This modified French Renaissance–style townhouse is believed to be the last surviving residential building in New York designed by the great Richard Morris Hunt. This house and most other buildings around the west side of the square are protected as part of the Stuyvesant Square Historic District, designated in 1976.

Near the center of the Square's western wing is the bronze statue of the famous peg-legged Dutch governor, *Peter Stuyvesant* (1936), sculpted by Gertrude Vanderbilt Whitney, founder of the Whitney Museum. (Stuyvesant Square, and all the land from Twentieth to Fifth Street, was within the farm of Peter Stuyvesant in the 1650s.)

➤ **Cross Second Avenue to the eastern wing of the square.**

Across Second Avenue, in the far northeast corner of the square's east wing, stands a life-size bronze monument of the celebrated Czech composer Antonín Dvořák, done by Yugoslavian sculptor Ivan Meštrović. For nearly three decades this statue was tucked away in obscurity on the roof of Avery Fisher Hall at Lincoln Center, where a planned roof garden was never built. It was finally placed here by the New York Philharmonic in 1997. Dvořák lived on East Seventeenth Street (Dvořák Place), within sight of this statue, during his tenure as director of the National Conservatory of Music from 1892 to 1895. During this time, he composed the acclaimed symphony *From the New World*, colloquially "New World Symphony," his tribute to the music of America.

By the 1890s, Stuyvesant Square had become a small, wealthy enclave of American-born residents amid a growing immigrant population of Jews and Catholics who had moved up from the Lower East Side. "It is an aristocratic neighborhood," says an 1893 guidebook, "but the Square is mostly used by the East-Side tenement dwellers." Indeed, the proximity of the struggling immigrants of the Lower East Side to the wealthy residents of Stuyvesant Square and Gramercy Park formed a dynamic that was at times both creative and destructive.

For instance, St. George's Parish was dominated for decades by its senior warden, the banker J. P. Morgan— one of the world's most powerful men. The church faced a crisis in the 1890s because the neighborhood's rapidly dwindling Episcopalian population left its pews increasingly deserted. To reach out to the non-Protestant immigrants of the neighborhood, St. George's, with Morgan's approval, became a leader in the Social Gospel movement. It survived as an institution by de-emphasizing religious doctrine and offering a variety of secular programs to address social ills, both educational and recreational, enlisting thousands of young people from the nearby tenements.

The proximity of the classes elicited a mix of political ideas, movements, and forms of expression. William Dean Howells, one of the most influential literary figures in America, lived in a formerly elegant brownstone at 330 East Seventeenth Street, just east of the square, in the 1880s and 1890s. The leading light of American realism, Howells often drew inspiration for his fiction by perusing the tenement districts and pondering the injustices of capitalism through a genteel medium of social protest—the popular novel.

Just a few blocks away, Emma Goldman lived on the sixth floor of a tenement (still standing) at 210 East Thirteenth Street that housed the cramped headquarters of Goldman's fledgling anarchist movement. Goldman was a frequent stump speaker at Union Square, and in response to her antiwar stance and criticism of mandatory conscription laws during World War I, the U.S. government imprisoned her for two years and then deported her in 1919.

On Sunday, April 18, 1920, a neighborhood anarchist named Thomas W. Simpkin tried to assassinate J. P. Morgan Jr. outside St. George's. Incensed by anti-Communist remarks made by the younger Morgan, Simpkin attempted to ambush him as he left Sunday Mass. In a case of mistaken identity, Simpkin instead tragically shot and killed Dr. James Markee, the Morgan family doctor. Five months later, the bombing of the Morgan Bank on Wall Street was widely assumed to be another "anarchist attack" aimed at Morgan.

Dominating the east side of Stuyvesant Square is the Beth Israel Medical Center and the Hospital for Joint Diseases Orthopaedic Institute, a fully integrated member of Mount Sinai/New York University Health Organization. Beth Israel opened in 1891 on the Lower East Side, where it evolved from a neighborhood dispensary for Orthodox Jews. It moved to Stuyvesant Square in 1964 after it purchased Manhattan General Hospital.

➤ **Walk to the corner of Seventeenth Street and Second Avenue.**

On the northwest corner of Seventeenth Street and Second Avenue is the former Manhattan General Hospital Building, the most impressive of the several hospital buildings that border Stuyvesant Square. Completed in 1902 with money donated by J. P. Morgan, these stately headquarters, designed by Robert H. Richardson, originally housed the New York Lying-In Hospital. Once the largest maternity hospital in the United States, the Lying-In Hospital served the vast population of the impoverished Lower East Side and often allowed its bills to go uncollected. Because it was viewed in philanthropical circles as Morgan's personal charity, the hospital had difficulty finding other benefactors and inevitably turned to Morgan each year to make up its deficit. As a result, it became one of Morgan's most expensive philanthropical ventures. Today, this building houses luxury apartments and medical offices and is on the National Register of Historic Places.

Just a few blocks north, on the corner of Second Avenue and Twenty-second Street, once stood the Union Steam Works factory. Perhaps the fiercest battle of the New York City Draft Riots took place there in July 1863. Much of the neighborhood remains exactly as it appeared then.

➤ Walk north on Second Avenue and left onto Eighteenth Street. Then turn right onto Third Avenue and walk one block to Nineteenth Street. Turn left onto Nineteenth Street and continue to Irving Place.

NEW YORK CITY DRAFT RIOTS

The New York City Draft Riots were the largest and most destructive urban riots in American history, resulting in at least 105 deaths. Spanning four days, this series of riots was also the greatest uprising of Americans against their government, with the exception of the Southern Confederacy's secession. The riots resulted from the long-simmering anger of New York's working classes, especially Irish immigrants, who resented the Civil War draft laws and did not support Lincoln's decision to emancipate the Southern slaves.

An 1863 **Harper's** magazine depiction of the New York City Draft Riots along First Avenue. Image courtesy of the New-York Historical Society.

When the Emancipation Proclamation went into effect on January 1, 1863, many New York Democrats were furious. Led by Fernando Wood, who as mayor had advocated New York City's secession from the Union in 1861, New York's Peace Democrats virulently denounced Lincoln's emancipation policy and predicted that the city's labor market would become flooded with freed black workers. In March 1863, the passage of the National Conscription Act, which threatened to enlist tens of thousands of New York's working class by lottery, added fuel to their explosive antiwar rhetoric. A clause that allowed draft substitutes to be purchased for $300 was deemed particularly obnoxious by Peace Democrats, who perceived the law as promoting "a rich man's war, but a poor man's fight." The inflammatory rhetoric of Democratic leaders stoked working-class resentment.

On Saturday, July 11, 1863, the draft law went into effect. On Monday, July 13, working-class protestors marched on the draft house at Third Avenue and smashed the lottery wheel. By mid-morning a full-scale riot had broken out in several sections of the city. The rioters' path of destruction focused on symbols of the war effort, including draft houses, Republican leaders' homes and businesses, and African Americans. At least eleven black men

were lynched and mutilated. Rioters also torched the Colored Orphan Asylum on Fifth Avenue, leaving its 237 children to flee for
their lives. Wealthy individuals who might buy their way out of the
draft were also targets, and the rich neighborhoods around
Gramercy Park and Stuyvesant Square were a focal point of attacks on property.

A mob of thousands besieged the Union Steam Works, a former
wire factory that had been converted for wartime arms production. Owned by a prominent Republican, the Steam Works was a
popular symbol of the war effort as well as a strategic source of
arms. Twice the mob took control of the building and seized thousands of weapons. The Metropolitan Police were joined by the
Twelfth New York Infantry in the bloody effort to dislodge rioters
from the building. Howitzers were used by policemen to clear Second Avenue. In the end, rather than surrender the factory, the rioters burned the five-story brick building to the ground, killing ten
of their own who remained trapped inside.

The next day, July 15, five regiments of the Union Army, diverted directly from the battle of Gettysburg, began to arrive in
the city. The 152 New York Volunteers established their camp in
Stuyvesant Square, while the Eighth Regiment Artillery Troop en-
camped in Gramercy Park. By Thursday, July 16, order was restored. Rather than impose military rule in New York, President
Lincoln worked with the "War" Democrats of Tammany Hall to in-
dict and prosecute the rioters. Only sixty-seven people were eventually prosecuted for crimes related to these tragic events. For
years afterward, the Metropolitan Police continued to find and
confiscate weapons originally stolen from the Second Avenue
Union Steam Works during the riots.

At 146 East Nineteenth Street, you will see an oval plaque
that marks the former home of George Bellows, who lived
here from 1910 until his early death in 1925. A great realist
painter, Bellows's work was often classified as part of the

"Ashcan" school because he preferred to capture gritty scenes from everyday life. Like William Dean Howells, his subject matter was often drawn from frequent visits to the tenement districts. An avid socialist, Bellows frequently entertained leading radicals, including Emma Goldman, Eugene O'Neill, Max Eastman, and John Reed.

Directly across the street from Bellows lived Carl Van Vechten, in a home that used to stand at 151 East Nineteenth Street. A novelist and photographer, Van Vechten is most famous as the man who introduced New York white society to Harlem in the 1920s. Van Vechten's still-controversial 1926 novel *Nigger Heaven* helped popularize the Harlem Renaissance. His parties brought figures such as the poet Langston Hughes and jazz singer Bessie Smith in contact with the artists and wealthy patrons of the Gramercy Park neighborhood.

The entire block of East Nineteenth between Third Avenue and Irving Place is known as "Block Beautiful" and has achieved landmark status as part of the Gramercy Park Historic District. In the 1920s, architect Frederick J. Sterner renovated the facades of several of the townhouses, a fine blend of styles, some of which date from the 1840s.

➤   **Turn right at Irving Place and continue north one block to the front gates of Gramercy Park.**

GRAMERCY PARK

To a remarkable degree, the Gramercy Park neighborhood has remained true to the vision of its founder, Samuel Ruggles. This secluded enclave provides a striking contrast to the noisy commercial districts that surround it. When Ruggles took possession of Gramercy Seat in 1831, it was a

Gramercy Park West in the late nineteenth century. The contemporary block appears much as it did a century ago. Photo courtesy of the New-York Historical Society.

mixture of swampland and small hills. The name "Gramercy" some believe, is a corruption of an old Dutch phrase, *krom moerasje*, meaning "little crooked swamp." Others say it comes from the phrase *crommessie vly*, meaning "knife-shaped swamp." Whatever the case, Ruggles filled in the swamp in the 1830s with soil acquired from the leveling of the nearby Bowery Hill. When Ruggles drew up the deed to the park in 1831, he provided that five trustees, regularly elected by the neighborhood, be given the task of maintaining the grounds according to his precise specifications. Ruggles carefully laid out the pathways through the park and had fifty different trees and shrubs planted. The eight-foot iron fence has stood around it since it officially opened in 1844.

Gramercy Park was one of the first New York developments to impose building restrictions. Ruggles's deed prohibited the construction of any buildings on the square "save brick or stone dwelling[s]" and "any . . . trade or business dangerous or offensive to the neighboring inhabitants." He listed several examples of such businesses, which included any "slaughter house, smith shop," "brewery, distillery, public museum," or "circus." Ruggles's aspirations for his neighborhood were not based merely on a desire to turn a profit on his real estate investment. Open spaces where citizens could gather and reconnect to nature, Ruggles believed, were necessary to promote a feeling of community and a "civilized" temperament.

From the 1850s until the 1870s, Gramercy Park remained among the city's most fashionable neighborhoods. It lost status, however, after the Third Avenue Elevated Railroad was constructed close by in 1878. Though many left, its residents remained influential enough to persuade Governor David Hill to veto a measure that would have extended a cable-car line on Lexington Avenue through the park in 1890. In the years that followed, several more proposals to cut a road through the park were defeated. Since the 1940s, most of the townhouses on the square have been converted into apartments. By the 1980s, Gramercy Park once again had become a fashionable neighborhood, home to many celebrities. Gramercy Park is the only private park left in New York City today.

The earliest residential housing on the square exists along the southern and western rims.

➤ We like to begin our walk around the square at 1 Gramercy Park West in the northwest corner, so walk west half a block on East Twentieth and then a short block north on Gramercy Park North to begin in front of No. 1.

A solid row of red-brick townhouses, the residences occupying the west side of the park are the best-preserved section. Dr. Valentine Mott lived at 1 Gramercy Park, built in 1849, which he inhabited during the latter days of his life. A founder of both New York University Medical College and Bellevue Hospital, he was the most famous surgeon of his time. Dr. Mott died of shock after being told of President Lincoln's assassination by John Wilkes Booth in April 1865. He is buried in Green-Wood Cemetery in Brooklyn.

The buildings at 3 and 4 Gramercy Park West were designed by Alexander Jackson Davis. Probably the two finest houses on the square, their elaborate cast-iron porches are reminiscent of New Orleans' architecture. The two "mayoral lamps" that stand outside No. 4 were placed there by former mayor James Harper when he moved into this townhouse in the 1840s. These lamps were traditionally used to help citizens identify the mayor's home in an emergency and had formerly stood outside Harper's Rose Street home.

➤ **Walk south to Twentieth Street.**

At 10 Gramercy Park South was the former home of the painter Robert Henri. Considered the "father" of American realism, Henri led the movement away from romanticism in painting and trained such revolutionary painters as Edward Hopper and George Bellows. Henri encouraged his students to broaden their choice of subject matter. He held a popular weekly open house for local artists in his top-floor studio, which continues to be preserved by the Henri estate.

➤ **Walk east on Twentieth Street.**

Both 15 and 16 Gramercy Park South, completed in 1845, were among the original townhouses on the square. Today, No. 15 houses the National Arts Club. In the 1870s and 1880s, however, it was the home of 1874 New York governor and 1876 presidential candidate Samuel J. Tilden. Tilden's political success was built upon his role in bringing down the Tweed ring. Fearing for his life from disgruntled Tammany henchmen, Tilden built an underground tunnel from his house to Nineteenth Street as an escape route in case of an emergency. When Tilden died in 1886, he left behind a vast book collection and an estate exceeding $5 million, which he left to New York City specifically to be used for the building of a new public library and reading room. The New York Public Library's new headquarters opened in 1911, and his book collection was combined with the Astor and Lenox library collections to make up its original holdings.

The National Arts Club, founded in 1898, moved into Samuel Tilden's former home in 1906. The face of the building had been redesigned in 1884 by Calvert Vaux, who added the bow fronts and arched windows in Victorian Gothic style. The faces of Goethe, Dante, Franklin, and Milton can be seen in the decorative medallions adorning its facade. Founding club members include J. P. Morgan, Frederic Remington, Theodore Roosevelt, and Woodrow Wilson.

At 16 Gramercy Park South is the Players Club, founded by Edwin Booth in 1888. Widely considered to be the greatest actor of his generation, Booth came from a family of distinguished actors that included his unstable brother John Wilkes Booth. Devastated by Lincoln's assassination at his brother's hand, Booth vowed never to appear in public again and resigned from his starring role in a popular production of *Hamlet*. Friends and admirers, however, persuaded him to return to the stage nine months later, where he was greeted with an outpouring of sympathy and approval by New York society.

The acting profession was not highly regarded in nineteenth-century America. Perhaps because of his own family history, Edwin Booth felt this stigma most deeply and endeavored to raise the social standing of actors to "a higher social grade than the Bohemian level." He conceived of the Players Club as a genteel private society where actors could mix with those who were more cultivated. In 1887, Booth enlisted his friend Stanford White to remodel the facade of this building by adding the portico and balcony. Founding members included Mark Twain and General William T. Sherman. At the center of Gramercy Park stands a statue of Edwin Booth performing in the role of Hamlet (Edmond T. Quinn, 1917), erected by the Players Club in 1918.

At 19–20 Gramercy Park South is the former Sonnenberg mansion, a brick townhouse built in 1845 but altered many times since. When the Sonnenberg estate put the house up for sale in 1979, the *New Yorker*'s Brendan Gill called it "unquestionably the greatest house remaining in private hands in New York." Originally a four-story building, the fifth floor and mansard roof were added in the 1850s. In 1887 it was again remodeled, mostly on the interior, by the firm of McKim, Mead and White. (The work has traditionally been attributed to Stanford White, but recently discovered evidence suggests otherwise.) In 1931, publicity man Benjamin Sonnenberg purchased the house along with the fashionable apartment complex next door at No. 20. Sonnenberg installed connecting doors between the two buildings and turned No. 20's studio apartments into guest rooms for his mansion, which now totaled thirty-seven rooms. The expanded mansion remains a private home today.

➤ **Walk to the southeast corner of the square.**

At 144 East Twentieth Street, off the southeast corner of the square, is the Brotherhood Synagogue, formerly the Friends Meeting House, built in 1859. The Italianate architecture is almost identical to Henry Ward Beecher's

1849 Plymouth Church in Brooklyn Heights. Rescued from demolition by the Historical Landmarks Commission in the 1960s, it was purchased in 1975 by the Brotherhood Synagogue of West Thirteenth Street for $425,000. To the east side of the building is a Holocaust memorial.

The first cooperative apartment in New York City, 34 Gramercy Park East, was designed by architect George da Cunha. Opened in 1883, this gorgeous brick building with red terra-cotta ornamentation originally contained twenty-seven apartments, three per floor, offering seven to twelve rooms each. Abundant amenities were offered to attract a "better" class of residents, including a gourmet restaurant owned by Louis Sherry, conveniently located on the eighth floor. The original gaslights flank the entrance and the hydraulic elevators inside (the first in the city) still function. Another early cooperative apartment stands next door at No. 36 Gramercy Park East. Designed by James Riley Gordon in 1910, the building's elaborate white terra-cotta ornamentation has a whimsical medieval theme. Monks, gargoyles, and cherubs can be detected in the finely detailed facade, while the front entrance is guarded by two cast-stone knights in armor.

➤ **Walk to the northeast corner of Gramercy Park North and Lexington Avenue.**

In the nineteenth century, a number of prominent New Yorkers made their homes near the northern entrance to the park. At 1 Lexington Avenue lived the daring entrepreneur Cyrus West Field. Field conceived of and organized the massive project of laying the first undersea transatlantic cable, establishing telegraph communication between London and New York. After several disappointments, the

cable finally became operable in 1865, making Field a national hero. Field also built much of Manhattan's elevated
railroads in the 1870s.

Next door, at 9 Lexington Avenue, lived one of Field's
friends and strongest supporters in the Atlantic cable project, Peter Cooper. One of New York's most beloved citizens, Cooper was an inventor of extraordinary talents. He
created America's first steam locomotive, the "Tom
Thumb;" produced the first steel rails; and invented numerous household products, including glue and gelatin.
Never having had the benefit of a higher education himself,
he founded Cooper Union for the Advancement of Science
and Art, a visionary free university designed to provide
higher education for the working classes. Thanks chiefly to
his original endowment of nearly $1 million, Cooper Union
still operates tuition-free for its select group of qualified
students.

➤ **Continue west on Gramercy Park North.**

Architect Stanford White lived along here from 1901 to
1906. One of the greatest and most prolific architects of his
time, White designed lavish mansions, churches, clubhouses, and monuments that can be found all over New
York City. White was also a serious art collector who imported antiques from around the world, keeping to furnish
his home those he did not sell to clients. Despite his artistic
achievements, White is best remembered today not for his
architecture but for the scandalous circumstances of his
death. More on this later when we visit the site of his tragic
murder.

➤ **Continue west on Gramercy Park North to the corner of
East Twenty-first Street and Park Avenue.**

Calvary Church, once the prestigious parish of the Roosevelt, Vanderbilt, and Astor families, has now been assimilated into St. George's Parish of Stuyvesant Square. When this impressive brownstone church was completed in 1848, it heightened the attraction of the Gramercy Park area and prompted the sale of Samuel Ruggles's several still-vacant lots on the square. Its architect, James Renwick Jr., also designed Grace Church and St. Patrick's Cathedral. Both Edith Wharton and Eleanor Roosevelt were baptized at Calvary. The church is best viewed from across the street, where the empty base of one of the two original wooden steeples can be seen. The steeples were taken down after repeated lightning strikes.

> Walk north along Park Avenue to Twenty-third Street. Turn left (west) onto Twenty-Third Street and continue to Broadway. Walk north across Twenty-third.

Across from the southeast corner of the park is the Metropolitan Life Tower, one of the most beautiful on the skyline. When completed in 1909, it more than doubled the height of the Flatiron Building to the south of the park to become the world's tallest building. Its seven hundred-foot tower, designed by Napoleon Le Brun, with its four-sided clock was inspired by the Campanile in St. Mark's Square in Venice.

Coming to a rounded point to the south of the park is the radically designed Flatiron Building (Daniel H. Burnham, 1902), which has remained a favorite among art critics and the general public for a century. Originally named the Fuller Building after its developers, the Fuller Construction Company, the Flatiron acquired its nickname because its unusual triangular shape, which conforms with the intersection of Broadway and Fifth Avenue, was thought to resemble an old-fashioned flatiron. Measured at a then-whopping three hundred feet in height, the Flatiron Building was a revolutionary construction and an early steel skeleton–supported structure. Its limestone-and-terra-cotta facade has subtle French Renaissance detailing, and the rounded northern corner is only eight feet wide (making for some unusual interior offices). Photographer Edward Steichen, who captured the mesmerizing effect of the Flatiron Building in his famous series of photographs, compared its northern side to that of "the bow of a monster ocean steamer" plowing up the heart of Midtown Manhattan.

MADISON SQUARE PARK

Once the home of the most fashionable hotels and restaurants in New York, Madison Square is now bordered on all sides by massive office buildings. The neighborhood around Madison Square has been through many transformations. Like Union Square, it degenerated in the 1960s and 1970s into a meeting place for drug dealers and the homeless. It has just undergone a $5 million restoration project (half of which was donated by the surrounding businesses).

This site was first used by New Yorkers as a paupers' burial ground in the eighteenth century, before becoming a military parade ground soon after the American Revolution. In 1811, the Commissioner's Plan that laid out the grid pattern of Manhattan's streets designated the entire area between Twenty-third and Thirty-fourth Streets and Third and Seventh Avenues as a park. It was named in honor of President James Madison in 1814.

Madison's Square's first claim to fame was that it became the site of the earliest baseball games in the country. In the 1840s, the Knickerbocker Base Ball Club—the

Stanford White's Madison Square Garden in 1893. Built in 1889 at a cost of more than $3 million, it was New York's second tallest building. White scandalized "proper" New York society by placing Augustus Saint-Gauden's naked **Diana** atop his lavish creation. Photo courtesy of the New-York Historical Society.

nation's first baseball team—used a vacant lot at Twenty-seventh and Madison as its original playing field. In 1846, however, the residential development of Madison Square forced the club to move out of the city to Elysian Fields in Hoboken, New Jersey, where they held the first baseball game under modern rules.

From its official opening in 1847 until the 1870s, Madison Square was the center of a genteel, residential neighborhood. In 1859, Amos Enos constructed the enormous white marble Fifth Avenue Hotel, which occupied an entire block between Twenty-third and Twenty-fourth Streets, facing Madison Square. Dubbed "Enos's folly" during its construction, skeptics believed the hotel too far uptown to be successful. But Enos was vindicated when, within ten years, Madison Square became the most fashionable hotel district in the city (home to the Albemarle, the St. James, the Hoffman House, the Victoria, the Brunswick, and the Gilsey Hotels). In 1876, New York's finest restaurant, Delmonico's, moved from Fifth Avenue and Fourteenth Street to the northwest corner of Madison Square.

In 1873, Madison Square also became a center of popular entertainment and spectator sports. P. T. Barnum that year constructed the world's first three-ring circus arena, christened the Great Roman Hippodrome. It was widely rumored that participants in its raucous circus acts and sporting events—which included Roman-style chariot races—were killed on a regular basis. Despite Barnum's denials, the *New York Times* protested that "several people have been killed there." But "considering the popular thirst for excitement," the *Times* editorialized, "it is possible that several may not be reckoned too many [by Mr. Barnum]." In 1879, William Kissam Vanderbilt took control of Barnum's arena and rechristened it Madison Square Garden.

The most fashionable hotels abandoned the area in the 1890s, moving north along Central Park. When Metropolitan Life built its first headquarters on the southeast corner of the square in 1893, it marked the beginning of the square's transformation into a business district. Other office buildings soon followed. Today, some of the city's finest architectural achievements in commercial buildings can be seen bordering Madison Square.

Now turn your attention to the park itself. In its southwest corner stands a prominent bronze statue of William H. Seward, former New York governor and U.S. secretary of state. Seward is probably best known for having orchestrated the purchase of Alaska from Russia for $7 million, dubbed "Seward's folly" at the time. Soon after the unveiling of this statue in 1876, a rumor began that its sculptor, Randolph Rogers, originally cast the figure as a statue of Abraham Lincoln issuing the Emancipation Proclamation. When commissioned for the William Seward project, however, Rogers removed Lincoln's head, replaced it with Seward's, and transformed the document in the figure's left hand from the Emancipation Proclamation into the deed to Alaska!

There is some truth to this story. Rogers sculpted a nearly identical statue of Lincoln holding the Emancipation Proclamation a few years earlier, which stands today in Fairmont Park, Philadelphia. Although he did not make this statue from the exact same cast as the Lincoln statue (the poses are ever-so-slightly different), he may nonetheless be said to be guilty of self-plagiarism. Both statues are proportionately the same, wearing the same clothing, seated in the same chair, with a quill pen in the figure's right hand while displaying a document in the left.

➤ **Walk back toward the intersection of Twenty-third Street and Madison Avenue. Walk north along Madison Avenue towards Twenty-fifth Street.**

On the southeast corner of the square, across from the Metropolitan Life Tower, stands a statue of former New York senator Roscoe Conkling (created in 1893 by John Quincy Adams Ward). Like William Seward, Conkling was a powerful figure in the Republican Party for many years and an unsuccessful aspirant to the presidency. Conkling died from exposure a few days after being caught in the Great Blizzard of 1888. Stubbornly refusing to pay an exorbitant cab fare, Conkling attempted to walk in the driving snow from his downtown office to the Manhattan Club at Madison Square. He blindly stumbled into a snowdrift while crossing Union Square Park and remained trapped there for several hours. He never recovered from the effects of the ordeal and died a few weeks later.

Along the east side of Madison Square is a wealth of splendid architecture. Across from the Met Life Tower is the North Building of the Metropolitan Life Insurance Company (Harvey Wiley Corbett and D. Everett Waid, 1932). This Art Deco skyscraper has been praised for its elegant, angled setbacks and high-vaulted entrances. It stands on the former site of the Madison Avenue Presbyterian Church, designed by Stanford White in 1906. The white-marble church, which resembled a Greek temple, was demolished a mere thirteen years after its construction, due in large part to the dwindling residential population of the neighborhood. Many considered it White's most beautiful building.

Directly across East Twenty-fifth Street stands the Appellate Division of the New York State Supreme Court. Designed by James Brown in 1900, this classical-style masterpiece of white marble is bedecked with statuary. Standing atop the building's facade are the great lawgivers of history, including Zoroaster, Solon, Louis IX, Manu, and Justinian (facing East Twenty-fifth Street) and Confucius and Moses (facing the park). A statue of Mohammed originally stood next to Zoroaster, but it was removed and destroyed in 1955 at the request of the city's Muslim community, which pointed out that Islam forbids images of the Prophet. The front steps of the courthouse are flanked by statuary symbols of Wisdom and Force.

➤ **Return to the park and walk to the Admiral Farragut Monument.**

One of the finest memorials in the city, the *Admiral Farragut Monument* (1880) is a collaboration between Augustus

Saint-Gaudens and Stanford White. The bronze figure of Farragut was done by Saint-Gaudens while the base and relief sculpture were done by White. The hero of New Orleans and Mobile Bay, David Glasgow Farragut was a much-beloved Civil War figure. Appropriately defiant, Saint-Gaudens's Farragut stares ahead with the same fearlessness as the man who famously ordered at Mobile Bay, "Damn the torpedoes, full speed ahead!" White's relief depicts two female figures, symbolizing Loyalty and Courage, who look on in admiration as wild sea currents swirl around them.

A statue of the twenty-first president, Chester A. Arthur (1829–1886), stands in the northeast corner of the park (George Bissell, 1898). Known as the "Gentleman Boss," Arthur controlled thousands of political appointments as Collector of the Port of New York. Elected vice president in 1880, he ascended to the presidency in 1881 after the assassination of James Garfield. Though he had epitomized the corruption of machine politics, Arthur shocked the Republican Party machine when he championed civil-service reform as president. New York Republicans viewed this political turnabout as treachery to the system to which Arthur owed all of his political success. His former friend and patron Roscoe Conkling was particularly taken aback. During his presidency, Arthur kept secret that he was suffering from a fatal kidney disease, and he died soon after his term ended at his nearby brownstone home on East Twenty-fifth Street.

➤ **Walk to Twenty-sixth Street and Madison Avenue, the northeast corner of the park.**

On the southeast corner of Madison Avenue and Twenty-fifth Street used to stand a lavish six-story mansion of red brick and white marble with a handsome mansard roof.

Built by Leonard Jerome in 1859, the mansion was the most striking residential home ever to stand on Madison Square. In this home, the future mother of Winston Churchill, Jerome's daughter Jennie, spent much of her youth before she married Lord Randolph Churchill and moved to Britain. Sadly, the mansion was demolished in 1967 to make way for the characterless glass-and-steel skyscraper that stands on the site today.

Merchandise Mart (Emery Roth & Sons, 1973) makes little contribution to its physical surroundings except to completely block all southern sight lines to Cass Gilbert's much superior New York Life Insurance Building (1928) next door. Capped by a brilliant gilded pyramid, the latter limestone skyscraper is adorned with dozens of gargoyles that punctuate its many dramatic setbacks.

This lot has a storied past. On the site of the present-day New York Life Building once stood, successively, the original playing field of the Knickerbocker Base Ball Club, the Harlem Railroad Station, P. T. Barnum's Great Roman Hippodrome, the original Madison Square Garden, and Stanford White's second Madison Square Garden.

One of White's greatest achievements, the second Madison Square Garden (1891) was a $3 million Moorish-style building capped by an ornately decorated 249-foot tower. It housed an eight thousand-seat auditorium, a theater, a concert hall, a roof garden, and the city's largest restaurant. The most talked-about architectural feature of the building, however, was Augustus Saint-Gaudens's gilded *Diana*, perched atop the large tower. Diana's brazen nudity scandalized members of New York's genteel society, who felt it improper for a female nude to be displayed in such a public location. Soon after its unveiling, one popular magazine observed that Madison Square Park had suddenly become "thronged with club men armed with field glasses."

Ironically, it was here, at one of his most notable masterpieces, that Stanford White met his tragic demise. A frequenter of the Madison Square Garden's Roof Garden theater, White also kept an apartment for himself within the main tower (which was convenient for his legendary liaisons with showgirls who performed there). On the night of June 25, 1906, White attended a performance of *Mamzelle Champagne* at the Roof Garden theater, as did Harry K. Thaw and his wife, former showgirl Evelyn Nesbit. Thaw had become obsessed with his wife's sexual past and, in particular, her previous relationship with the notorious playboy White. During the performance of the musical, the *New York Times* reported, Thaw suddenly "passed between a number of tables, and, in full view of the players and of scores of persons, shot White through the head . . . after firing three shots and looking at White to make sure that he was stone dead, Thaw uttered a curse and added: 'You'll never go out with that woman again.'"

The story, revealed after Thaw's arrest, captured the public's attention. Details of White and Nesbit's kinky relationship came to light in the sensational murder trial that followed. At the verdict, Thaw was found innocent for reasons of insanity. Aspects of this sordid affair have been depicted in the films *Ragtime* and *The Girl in the Red Velvet Swing*. For many years after his death, White's architectural achievements were denigrated and his name regarded with embarrassment by New Yorkers, which may have aided in the destruction of many of his greatest buildings. Madison Square Garden met the wrecking ball in 1925.

Samuel Ruggles once predicted: "Our spaces will remain forever imperishable. Buildings, towers, palaces may molder and crumble beneath the touch of time, but space . . . glorious, open space will remain to bless the city forever." Time so far has proven him correct. Though the buildings around them have changed remarkably, these four city squares, carefully laid out in the 1840s, have survived as valued spaces that continue to enrich New York's urban landscape. These public spaces, through the generations, have remained imperishable.

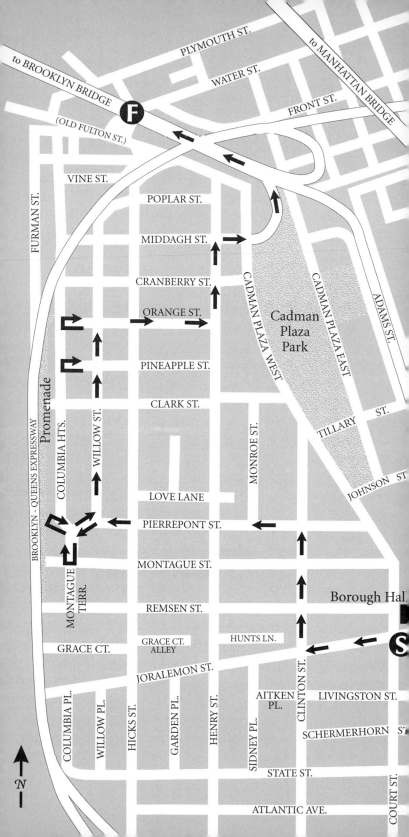

5 THE BROOKLYN BRIDGE

A Walk from Brooklyn Heights to City Hall

➢ Start: Begin at Brooklyn Borough Hall, which sits on a plaza between Court Street and Adams. To get there, take the A, C, or F train to the Jay Street Borough Hall stop; or the 2, 3, 4, or 5 to the Borough Hall stop; or the N or R train to Court Street (and walk a block to Borough Hall).

THIS WALK TAKES you through New York's first historic district, a neighborhood with more homes built before the Civil War than any other, and then across the most beautiful suspension bridge in the world.

We begin at what was the city hall of the City of Brooklyn until 1898 and finish at what has been the City Hall of New York City since 1812. Confused? Brooklyn and New York were separate cities until 1898, when they were consolidated into Greater New York—the current five boroughs. In that year, Brooklyn's 1849 City Hall was renamed Borough Hall, and a cupola was added to make it appear more like New York's City Hall. Borough Hall was originally designed in the spirit of "common-man" Jeffersonian democracy by Brooklyn carpenter and grocer Gamaliel King.

The idea of Brooklyn joining New York was contentious at the time, much as the idea of Staten Island seceding from New York City was contentious in the mid-1990s. Indeed, the consolidation referendum passed by only a few hundred votes in 1894. Many prominent Brooklyn citizens didn't want to merge what they saw as corrupt New York with pristine Brooklyn. After the consolidation referendum passed, a group of businessmen (including A. A. Low and Henry Pierrepont—two of the city's wealthiest landowners) and cultural and religious leaders formed the League of Loyal Citizens to oppose consolidation. Their vision of Brooklyn was of a white, prosperous, Protestant borough that wasn't teeming with Manhattan's immigrants.

League spokesperson St. Clair McKelway, editor of the *Brooklyn Eagle*, which sponsored an anticonsolidation song contest—"Up with the Flag of Brooklyn" won the $300 prize—wrote an editorial against consolidation in 1894:

> Brooklyn is a city of homes and churches. New York is a city of Tammany Hall and crime government. Rents are twice as cheap in Brooklyn as in New York and homes are to be bought for a quarter of the money. . . . Government here is by public opinion and for the public interest. If tied to New York, Brooklyn would be a Tammany suburb, to be kicked, looted and bossed as such.
>
> Vote against consolidation now and let the speculators wait till a better time, when New York will offer something like fair terms.

In spite of the League's opposition, of course, Brooklyn and New York were joined.

➤ **Walk across Court Street and look to the north, past Brooklyn's 1891 General Post Office, the Romanesque revival structure with tower.**

Looking up Montague Street in Brooklyn Heights in 1890, from near the water's edge toward what is today the Promenade over the cantilevered Brooklyn-Queens Expressway. The pedestrians are walking toward the ferry that would take them to Manhattan. Illustration courtesy of the New-York Historical Society.

The "park" stretching into the distance is Cadman Plaza, the eastern border of Brooklyn Heights. Brooklyn Heights was the city's first historic district, but you wouldn't know it from looking at most of the unattractive buildings that surround Cadman Plaza. It's hard to see the beauty of the neighborhood from this vantage point, which is actually good; if not for historic preservation, all of Brooklyn Heights might look like the Cadman Plaza high-rises.

HISTORIC PRESERVATION

Before the 1965 historic district law that preserved Brooklyn Heights's character, property owners and the city could and did destroy homes at will. In 1953 in Brooklyn Heights, construction for Robert Moses's Brooklyn-Queens Expressway razed parts of Columbia Heights, Middagh Street, and Poplar Street. Other losses over the years include the beautiful Brooklyn Savings Bank at Pierrepont and Clinton; the Church of the Restoration on Monroe; and many private homes on Henry, Monroe, Clinton, and Clark.

Cadman Plaza destroyed much of the eastern Heights, including the building in which Walt Whitman set the type for the first edition of the greatest book of poetry ever written in the United States—**Leaves of Grass.**

In the face of all the destruction, a group of neighborhood residents got together and formed the Community Conservation and Improvement Council (CCIC, pronounced "kick") in 1958. CCIC joined with the Brooklyn Heights Association in 1959 and proposed a historic zoning designation for the neighborhood, like that which had been granted to Boston's Beacon Hill. In January 1965 the U.S. Department of the Interior declared the Heights a historic district, and in April 1965 the New York City Landmarks Preservation Law passed. Brooklyn Heights was the first such neighborhood in New York, predating Greenwich Village.

Once a neighborhood is landmarked, its buildings can almost never be torn down or altered externally. The reason the Heights continues to look as it does is that a band of citizens fought to make it so.

➤ Walk to the first street south of (or behind) Borough Hall, which is Joralemon Street. Walk one block west on Joralemon to Clinton Street. Make a right and walk two blocks to Montague Street.

Spencer Memorial Church (1853) is on the southeast corner of Remsen and Clinton. Although built as the First Presbyterian Church of Brooklyn, its first minister was Ichabod Spencer; hence the name. Since Brooklyn Heights was self-consciously developed as an idyllic suburban enclave for wealthy New Yorkers and its promoters emphasized its "respectable" character, they saw to it that churches were erected wherever possible. Brooklyn was sometimes called the "borough of churches," as much for its proliferation of steeples as for the supposed bigotry of its earlier Protestant

"American" residents to newcomers. The church is now a group of co-op apartments.

Montague Street is the major shopping street in the Heights. During the late nineteenth century, Montague was also called "Bank Row" because of the number of banks here. The street also had a cable car running along its center beginning in 1887; this became an electrified trolley from 1909 to 1924. True Brooklyn trivia lovers know that the Brooklyn Dodgers baseball team was named after borough residents who had to dodge trolleys like this one while crossing streets.

In addition to banks, Montague was the original site of three of Brooklyn's greatest cultural institutions, all now demolished but rebuilt elsewhere in the borough. The 1864 Mercantile Library was on the north side of the block. It eventually merged with the Brooklyn Public Library, which moved to Grand Army Plaza in 1941. To the south was the 1872 Brooklyn Art Association, a forerunner to the Brooklyn Museum, which is now on Eastern Parkway just down from the Brooklyn Library. Finally, the Brooklyn Academy of Music had its opening night in 1861 on this block but now exists to the east, in the neighborhood of Fort Greene.

On the northwest corner of Montague and Clinton is the 1847 Church of St. Ann and the Holy Trinity. Go inside, if it is open, to look at the stained-glass windows by William Jay Bolton. Supposedly, Bolton left America for England after finishing these windows, never to do stained-glass again. Many years later one of his elderly surviving daughters, nearing the end of her life, discovered her father's past and journeyed to Brooklyn Heights to see the work. Seeing the windows inspired her to live another ten years.

➤ **Go one block further north on Clinton to Pierrepont Street.**

The 1880 Brooklyn Historical Society is on the southwest corner. The architect is George Post, who also designed the New York Stock Exchange Building. The society began in 1863 as the Long Island Historical Society and today houses one of the most extensive regional collections in the country. On the building's facade are busts of Christopher Columbus and Benjamin Franklin, and flanking the entranceway are heads of an Indian and a Viking. On the east side are numerous other heads and an inscription from Cicero translated as "History, the Witness of Time."

➤ **Make a left on Pierrepont and walk west toward the Promenade.**

At the northeast corner of Pierrepont and Monroe is the Church of the Savior (1844), now the First Unitarian Church, which has beautiful 1890 Tiffany windows. Continue on the south side of the street past 102 Pierrepont Street, former home of both Arthur Miller and Norman Mailer. Here, after World War II, Miller wrote *All My Sons* and Mailer wrote *The Naked and the Dead*. Between the First World War and the 1950s, Brooklyn Heights attracted a fair number of authors and artists who were looking for cheap rents. Many New Yorkers think of this as a high point for Brooklyn artistic life, but Heights residents often saw it as a sign of decline!

➤ **Continue walking along Pierrepont toward the Promenade but stop at Columbia Heights before proceeding down past the playground. To your right is Columbia Heights and to your left is Montague Terrace.**

Brooklyn Heights has examples of most major architectural styles present in America in the nineteenth century. To your right (north), the modern brown townhouse at 222

Columbia Heights was built to fit in with the others following landmark laws. Judge for yourself. Next door, at 218 and 220 Columbia Heights, are two examples of the Renaissance revival style, an opulent, Italianate design. The three townhouses at 21, 23, and 25 Pierrepont that you just passed on the right are also in this style. Note the continuous balcony-like balustrade that ties them together.

To your left, past Montague Street, is 5 Montague Terrace, where Thomas Wolfe lived from 1933 to 1934 and where he finished *Of Time and the River*. A friend described his place:

> The chief piece of furniture was an old table, work worn and ancient but still sturdy. It was marked by many cigarette burns and its surface was dented like a shelf after a hard battle. . . . At the right, as one entered, and opposite the windows, was one alcove containing a gas range and another with an electric refrigerator which bumped and hummed as refrigerators did then. Tom claimed that this sound stimulated him by its rhythm. On the old table and on this refrigerator he did most of his writing.

Immediately to your left is a playground and to the left of it are two of the three original mansions designed by Richard Upjohn in 1857. Farthest south, at 3 Pierrepont Place, is the former home of Abiel Abbott Low, a merchant who got rich trading with China and moved to the Heights in the mid–nineteenth century. His son Seth Low was the only person to be mayor of both Brooklyn (in 1884) and New York City (1901). He later became president of Columbia University. The next closest mansion, at No. 2, was the home of Alfred Tredway White, a wealthy merchant and philanthropist whose charitable motto was "Philanthropy plus 5 percent." White funded model tenements for the poor in Brooklyn.

The playground adjacent to 2 Montague Terrace is all that remains of the third of Upjohn's mansions. It was demolished in 1946 but was the home of Henry Pierrepont, whose family owned much of the surrounding land early in the nineteenth century.

Now walk straight ahead to the Promenade. As you stand and look out over the harbor to downtown Manhattan, you have a modern version of the view that merchants like A. A. Low had 150 years ago, when they wanted to look upon their business on South Street in New York. From here you can also see why the neighborhood is called the Heights. Many of the streets that end at the Promenade today once sloped down from the heights to the shoreline.

From here, in 1776, George Washington evacuated Long Island (Brooklyn), fleeing with his troops across to Manhattan under cover of fog and then northward to Harlem and out of New York, which was occupied by the British for the entire course of the Revolutionary War.

Finally, you have been listening to the roar of traffic. The Promenade is a cantilevered walkway over on the Brooklyn-Queens Expressway (BQE), which Robert Moses had built through the community in 1953. The building of the BQE and the destruction it wrought on much of the neighborhood were a primary cause for Heights residents to come together to protect their homes.

➤ **Double back along Pierrepont two blocks to Willow Street and make a left, walking north. Continue walking along Willow Street then left on Pineapple Street.**

There are examples of most of the architectural styles in the Heights along Willow Street.

The three Federal-style townhouses set back from the street at 155, 157, and 159 Willow, to your right, are some of the earliest in the Heights and were built in the 1820s. Note the arched dormered windows on top of two of the houses. At some point the owner of the house nearest Pierrepont Street extended the third floor upward and did away with the dormers. A plaque on the middle house says that it hid an underground storage space that was used to hide runaway slaves as they escaped northward to Canada from the South. You can see the glass brick that is the roof of this space if you look down at the sidewalk near the stairs of 157 Willow. Whether this spot was actually used as such is a matter of debate.

The carriage house at 151 Willow is an 1880 addition to the block, although it appears older. The stars on the front of the building actually cover iron tie-rods that go through the building and support the walls. Note the name posted on the tree inside the wrought-iron fence between 155 Willow and the carriage house: it's a redwood.

Continuing along, note the Gothic revival townhouses on your left, built in the 1830s and 1840s. The giveaway architectural signs are the large blocks that make up the outer walls and the Tudor arched windows. Further along on your right is 109 Willow, a Colonial revival building with exposed outside shutters.

Across the street is 108–112 Willow, a Queen Anne–style building constructed in the 1880s and mixing elements from across architectural history—terra-cotta, shingles, bay windows, gables, and a small tower. It is a bizarre style that somehow works.

When you reach the building at 101 Willow, at the southeast corner of Clark, you are at an excellent 1838 Greek revival home. Note the Greek Ionic portico over the front door and high basement. The current owner of this house actually had bricks from the back of the home moved to the front, where they would make it look appropriately aged.

Look to your right (east) down Clark to the St. George Hotel, which takes up most of the block between Hicks and

Henry. The St. George Hotel defined residence-hotel elegance in the latter half of the nineteenth century and in the early twentieth century. It was built in stages from 1885 to 1929 and had between twenty-six hundred and twenty-eight hundred rooms, making it the largest hotel in the United States for many years. That honor now goes to the five-thousand-plus-room Venetian in Las Vegas. Many New Yorkers had coming-out parties, weddings, and anniversaries in the hotel's giant ballroom. It was a favored hangout of the Brooklyn Dodgers. Today the St. George has been divided into apartments. Its saltwater swimming pool with its mirrored ceiling is gone, and in its place are racquetball courts.

The St. George was also the site of the largest fire ever in Brooklyn. Early Sunday morning, August 27, 1995, a man using a blowtorch to remove copper pipes to sell for scrap started a fire in the 51 Clark Street part of the hotel. The fire spread to several attached buildings and grew to eighteen alarms, bringing five hundred firefighters to the neighborhood.

Continue further north to the northeast corner of Willow and Clark, past the 1928 Leverich Towers Hotel, another grand Heights hotel (whose towers can best be seen when you are further away). It's now a lovingly restored Jehovah's Witness residence hall.

Continue left on Pineapple and walk back to Columbia Heights. The prison-like structure on the southeast corner of Pineapple and Columbia Heights is a Jehovah's Witness dormitory and library. The *AIA Guide* calls it an "early and sensitive design under new Landmarks Law." Others see it as an unsuccessful attempt to incorporate the three brick housefronts next door and reproduce their bay-window motif on its own facade.

Brooklyn Heights is the world headquarters of the Jehovah's Witnesses, a church that over the years has bought and renovated many of the Heights's buildings and also torn down many of the others. It's important to note that when the Jehovah's Witnesses bought many buildings in the neighborhood, it was not the desirable and unafford-able place to live that it is now.

➤ **Double back to Willow Street and walk north to the cor-ner of Orange and Willow Streets.**

Why is there a Cranberry, an Orange, and a Pineapple Street in Brooklyn Heights? The myth is that Mabel Mid-dagh Hicks, a descendant of two wealthy Brooklyn fami-lies, was upset at all the family names on the streets, so she put up her own, more colorful ones. The Board of Alder-men eventually let them remain. Is it true? We don't know.

Another great old Heights story, this one *not* true, con-cerns Mabel's relatives, the Hicks brothers—"Milk" and "Spitter" Hicks. The Hicks family did have a farm here, and they likely sold produce in Manhattan. Supposedly, the word *hick* to describe a country bumpkin comes from phrase "Here come the Hicks" uttered when Hicks family traveled to Manhattan to sell vegetables. It's a great story, but "Hick" is a seventeenth-century British abbreviation for "Richard."

➤ **Turn left and walk one block west on Orange to the cor-ner of Columbia Heights.**

The twelve-story building on the northeast corner is the Margaret Apartments, formerly the 1889 Hotel Margaret (97 Columbia Heights). The Jehovah's Witnesses were ren-ovating it when it burned down in 1980. The Landmarks Preservation Law required height restrictions on new con-struction, but the Witnesses made a successful argument for rebuilding the structure to its former height because that was the height of the building when they began renovations.

Betty Smith wrote *A Tree Grows in Brooklyn* here in 1943, and H. G. Wells often stayed here when visiting New York.

The cookie-cutter brick building on the southeast corner (107 Columbia Heights) was finished in 1959, before historic preservation laws went into effect. Note how it overwhelms its neighbors. The building at 124 Columbia Heights, on the river side of the street, sits atop what was 110 Columbia Heights. Washington Roebling, the chief engineer on the Brooklyn Bridge (more on him later), lived in this house for a few years after having a nervous breakdown (or suffering a severe case of the bends, depending on whom you ask) and watched his bridge go up through a telescope for months at a time.

The writer Hart Crane rented what he was convinced was Roebling's room in the building from 1924 to 1929. He wrote of the bridge: "And up at the right the Brooklyn Bridge, the most superb piece of construction in the modern world, I'm sure, with strings of light crossing it like glowing worms as the Ls and surface cars pass each other coming and going."

➤ Return to Orange Street and walk two and a half blocks east (just past Hicks Street) until you come to the large, Italianate 1849 Plymouth Church of the Pilgrims, designed by Joseph Wells.

Across the grass courtyard is a statue of the Reverend Henry Ward Beecher. Preacher Beecher was the subject of the "trial of the century" of the 1800s.

"TRIAL OF THE CENTURY"

There is a "trial of the century" at least once a decade—think of Sacco and Vanzetti, the Lindbergh-baby kidnapping, Julius and Ethel Rosenberg, Charles Manson, O. J. Simpson, and so on.

Henry Ward Beecher's 1874 trial for "alienation of affection"—he had an affair with a married parishioner—captured the attention of the city in the post-Civil War decade. Beecher's fame at the time was exceeded only by that of his sister Harriet Beecher Stowe, author of **Uncle Tom's Cabin,** which outsold all books except the Bible in 1850s.

Henry Beecher was America's leading abolitionist and spoke widely, using Christianity to condemn slavery. He was so popular that extra ferries, called "Beecher's Boats," were run on Sundays to bring attendees from Manhattan to hear him preach. By 1859, Beecher was making thousands yearly as a minister. Both Abraham Lincoln and Mark Twain came to hear this brilliant man speak. It is hard to impress on the modern reader the national stature of a preacher like Henry Ward Beecher in the nineteenth century—think Billy Graham, Jesse Jackson, and Norman Vincent Peale all rolled into one.

So it was quite a surprise when this man who advocated high moral standards in others was accused of having sex with a woman other than his wife. Beecher managed to hush up his affair with parishioner Elizabeth Tilton until it was brought into the open by Victoria Woodhull and her sister Tennessee Claflin, both noted equal rights advocates, spiritualists, investors, and feminists.

Woodhull had the radical idea that a woman's sexual needs are equal to a man's and that love (sex) should not be controlled by anyone but the parties involved. She called it "free love," noting, "I have an inalienable, constitutional and natural right to love whom I may, to love as long or as short a period as I can, to change that love every day if I please."

Woodhull and Claflin's Weekly newspaper declared Beecher a closet "free lover" and urged him to come out into the open. The twentieth-century equivalent would be the posters pasted up in New York that "outed" supposedly straight men and women as being gays and lesbians. In her argument, Woodhull cleverly drew a link between her struggle for "social freedom" and Beecher's for freedom from slavery:

"I propose . . . to ventilate one of the most stupendous scandals which has ever existed in any community. . . . I intend that this article shall burst like a bombshell into the ranks of this moralistic social camp.

I am engaged in officering, and in some sense conducting, a social revolution on the marriage question. This institution . . . has outlived its days of usefulness, and the most intelligent and really virtuous of our citizens have outgrown and are systematically unfaithful to it. It is obvious the human animal demands free love. . . .

The immense physical potency of Henry Ward Beecher is one of the greatest and noble endowments of this great and representative man. His only crime is not to openly admit his having frequently indulged in the practice of free love."

Woodhull, Claflin, and their publisher were almost immediately jailed for obscenity after publishing the charges. Other newspapers reprinted their article, but no one else was arrested. Woodhull's plight became a cause célèbre, and Beecher's six-month-long civil trial, brought by Elizabeth's husband, Theodore Tilton, became a fascinating entrée into sex, infidelity, and free love in Victorian America. The trial ended with a hung jury, and two inquiries by the church exonerated Beecher, although historical evidence has long since shown that he was clearly "guilty."

The last word should go to a contemporary paper, which wrote: "The trial was a fine illustration of the power of money and the tricks that can be played with the law." Indeed.

➢ **Continue east on Orange to Henry, then left one block north to Cranberry.**

About where Cranberry used to meet Fulton Street (now Cadman Plaza West) was the greatest landmark of all in Brooklyn Heights, now gone. Here Walt Whitman set the first edition of *Leaves of Grass*.

Harper's illustration showing the 1874 trial of preacher Henry Ward Beecher for "alienation of affection"–adultery. Beecher's courtroom drama was "the trial of the century" for his decade and involved everyone from Victoria Woodhull to Susan B. Anthony. Illustration from **Frank Leslie's**, April 17, 1875, in **John Grafton, New York in the Nineteenth Century** (New York: Dover), 1977.

On Cranberry behind Plymouth Church is the site of one of Walt Whitman's many homes in New York. As Whitman remembered it: "From 1824–28 our family lived in Brooklyn in Front, Cranberry, and Johnson Streets. In the latter my father built a nice house for a home, and afterwards another in Tillary St. We occupied them one after the other, but they were mortgaged, and we lost them." And we have lost them all too, including Whitman's printer's, another building in which he edited the *Brooklyn Daily Eagle*, and more.

We have come in an arc from Borough Hall through the Heights, returning to the northern end of Cadman Plaza. As you look up and around you, take stock of the neighborhood you have walked through and note how different Cadman Plaza is. The low townhouses and some of the other buildings are named for Whitman, but he wouldn't know them.

BROOKLYN WRITERS

Crowds of men and women attired in the usual costumes, how curious you are to me!

On the ferry-boats the hundreds and hundreds that cross, returning home, are more curious to me than you suppose,

And you that shall cross from shore to shore years hence are more to me, and more in my meditations, than you might suppose.

—WALT WHITMAN, "Crossing Brooklyn Ferry"

At three o'clock in the morning when the rest of the city is silent and dark, you can come suddenly on a little area as vivacious as a country fair. It is Sands Street, the place where sailors spend their evenings when they come here to port. At any hour of the night some excitement is going on in Sands Street. The sunburned sailors swagger up and down sidewalks with their girls. The bars are crowded and there are dancing music, and straight liquor at cheap prices.

—CARSON McCULLERS, "Brooklyn Is My Neighborhood"

On a summer's evening a stroll across the bridge, with cool winds singing through the steel shrouds, with stars moving about above and ships below, can be intoxicating, particularly if you are headed toward the roasting-pork, sweet-and-sour aromas of Chinatown.

—TRUMAN CAPOTE, "A House on the Heights"

➤ Continue north on Henry Street to Middagh Street. Cross Henry and walk on the sidewalk across from Middagh Street and follow it as it curves through the park, until you are walking under the car approach to the Brooklyn Bridge. Take the staircase on your left up to the walkway at the center of the Brooklyn Bridge.

When you come out on what bridge designer John Augustus Roebling called the "elevated pleasure walk," stop and look out at the bridge.

The granite and steel of the archetypal suspension bridge–the Brooklyn Bridge–with the panorama of Manhattan behind it. Photo courtesy of the New-York Historical Society.

Remember as you walk across to stay to the side of the path that is marked for pedestrians. The other side is for bicyclists, who will run you down if you stray onto "their" side.

The bridge is pregnant with aesthetic symbolism. You're looking at the most ancient material—stone— girded with what was in its time the most modern—steel. A suspension bridge brings together the two great forces in engineering, tension and compression. The steel cables are under nothing but tension as they strain to hold up the bridge. The granite towers are under nothing but compression as they strain to support the massive steel cables.

What exactly is a suspension bridge? Simply, it is one in which the roadway is hung, suspended—from cables. The cables take the load of the roadbed and transmit it to the towers and then to the ground. Anchorages underground on the Brooklyn and Manhattan shorelines hold down the ends of the four cables, each one composed of thousands of individual strands. The cables pass over massive towers and hold up the deck, which is hung by yet more steel cables called "suspenders." Even more diagonal cables, called "stays," hold the bridge rigid.

The Brooklyn Bridge is 1,595 feet long from tower to tower. It was the longest in the world from 1883 until the George Washington Bridge was completed between Manhattan and New Jersey in 1931. Today, the Brooklyn Bridge is a piker: it doesn't even make the top twenty suspension bridges in the world.

Suspension bridges made of rope, vine, leather, and wood have been around for thousands of years. But it wasn't until the early 1800s that wrought iron could be produced cheaply enough to make it a suitable substitute for wood, stone, and cast iron, thus making the modern suspension bridge possible. Even then, the iron was first made into a chain and lifted up all at once, a feat that was limited by the weight of the chain. It was the idea of "spinning" a cable one strand at a time, making the cables in place, that made possible the suspension bridges we have today.

Begin walking across the bridge, and remember to stay in the pedestrian path. After a few hundred feet, pause to think about the anchorages hidden beneath you.

Inside these massive stone structures, the cables are connected to a series of eyebars attached to metal plates that sit beneath tons of cement and rock. The lower ends of the eyebars are attached to the plates and the upper ends are attached to the cables. The sheer weight of the material on top (including your body right now) holds down the cables and resists their pull, just as if you were to stand on a string while a cat tried to pull it out from under your foot.

Stop when the walkway turns from cement to wood and consider the men who designed the Brooklyn Bridge—John Roebling and his son Washington Roebling.

TIMELINE

April 1867:	New York Bridge Company chartered by state legislature.
June 1869:	Surveying begins.
June 1869:	John Roebling dies.
October 1869–March 1870:	Brooklyn caisson built.
May 1870:	Brooklyn caisson towed into place and men begin working inside.
June 1870:	First stone laid on Brooklyn caisson.
March 1871:	Brooklyn tower foundation complete.
September 1871:	New York caisson towed into place.
July 1872:	New York tower foundation complete.
February 1873:	Brooklyn anchorage started.
May 1875:	New York anchorage started.
June 1875:	Brooklyn tower finished.
June 1876:	Cable making started.
July 1876:	New York tower finished and New York anchorage finished.
August 25, 1876:	E. F. Farrington's ride across cable in boatswain's chair.
October 1878:	Cable making finished.
December 1881:	Structure for bridge floor finished.
May 24, 1883:	Bridge opened.

John Augustus Roebling (1806–1869) grew up in Germany and finished his degree in engineering at the Royal Polytechnic Institute in Berlin in 1826. His senior thesis was on suspension bridges. While in Berlin studying engineering, Roebling also studied with G. W. F. Hegel. Whether he ever understood Hegel's *Phenomenology of Mind* we'll never know, but Roebling did understand Hegel's dictum that America "was the land of desire for all those who are weary of the historical lumber room of old Europe."

Like many young men of his generation, Roebling left Germany and came to the United States where, as he later said, "the numerous hindrances, restrictions, and obstacles which are set up by timid governments and hosts of functionaries against every endeavor in Germany are not to be found." He moved to a western Pennsylvania community called Saxonburg and started farming. But Roebling soon tired of life in the fields and began working on engineering projects for the state.

Roebling got the idea for wire rope—the thin strands of metal that could be compressed into cables—while on an engineering job. He noted that the three- to nine-inch-thick hemp ropes used to tow canal boats up inclined railways were expensive and dangerous. Roebling believed that rope made of metal would be stronger and cheaper. He was right. He returned to his farm and soon had most of the townsfolk working for him, making wire rope. In 1848 he moved his whole family to Trenton and founded a wire-rope company that existed as John A. Roebling's Sons until it was sold in 1953. It finally closed in 1973.

Roebling started his bridge-building career with an 1844 suspension-bridge aqueduct in Pittsburgh. He went on to build other aqueducts and even suspension-bridge canals! One canal still stands as a single-lane auto bridge near Port Jervis, New York. He even built a railroad bridge across Niagara Falls. Roebling was certainly the most famous bridge builder in the United States when the New York Bridge Company chose him as chief engineer for the Brooklyn Bridge project in 1867.

Roebling, unfortunately, was a firm believer in the curative properties of water. He was surveying land for the anchorages on a dock near the Brooklyn shore on June 28, 1869, when his foot was crushed against a piling by a dock-

An 1882 inspection of the truss work. Engineers and officials are standing on the nearly completed bridge roadway, viewing the steel truss work that surrounded the cable-car system. Photo courtesy of the New-York Historical Society.

ing ferry. He treated himself by pouring cold water over the wound and died a month later from tetanus. That left his son Washington Roebling, thirty-two, to take over.

Washington Roebling (1837–1926) had a civil engineering degree from Rensselaer Polytechnic Institute in Troy, New York. After graduating, he served in the Union Army with both artillery and cavalry units, fighting at Gettysburg, Chancellorsville, and other battlegrounds. He also built four suspension bridges, all of which were destroyed by the Confederate Army.

> Walk onto the bridge to the point where the walkway intersects the descending cable on your right. Reach out and touch the cable. Hold onto the suspenders (the twisted cables hanging vertically from the main cable). You are actually helping to hold up the roadbed when you do this, and you can tell your friends you held up the Brooklyn Bridge. Seriously.

Inside the galvanized iron wrapping of the cable from which the suspender hangs are exactly 5,434 wires squeezed together into a single 15 ¾ inch cable. They're not twisted like the suspenders but are perfectly straight. The thousands of strands are divided into nineteen bunches of 286 wires each. That's 14,370 miles of wire, weighing almost 7 million pounds.

➤ **Walk to the Brooklyn tower and look at the plaques illustrating the bridge-building process.**

From August 1876 to October 1878, after the towers were completed, Roebling's workers spun the cables back and forth across the river. The first strand came across on August 11, 1876. Two weeks later, Master Mechanic E. F. Farrington made the first crossing of the East River by the great bridge. He did it sitting in a boatswain's chair—nothing more than a flat board with a rope loop holding it to a pulley wheel. It took him twenty-two minutes to go from the Brooklyn to the New York side.

The Brooklyn Bridge is the first bridge that used steel cables rather than iron ones. The process began on the Brooklyn side. Huge drums of cable were brought to the bridge. One end of wire was attached to a traveling wheel. Using steam power, the strand was then pulled out of the drum and sent across the river. When the wheel reached the other side, the wire loop was pulled off and the wheel sent back empty to repeat the journey. After the 143d trip (making 286 strands), the wire was cut and the final end spliced to the first, making a single, continuous length of cable.

Under ideal conditions—a rarity—the cables traveled at five and a half feet a second, meaning a pair of wires could theoretically be laid in place in half an hour. But wind, ice, snow, and breakdowns slowed the process. Ten wires a day in each cable was considered good work, and

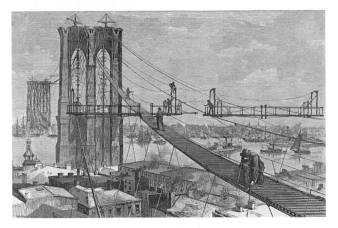

Illustration of wooden walkways that allowed access to the beginning of the cables and the almost-completed towers on the Brooklyn Bridge. Any visitor could go to the office of the chief engineer and request a pass to go onto the walkway. Imagine that in today's litigious society. Illustration from **Frank Leslie's**, June 16, 1877, in John Grafton, **New York in the Nineteenth Century** (New York: Dover), 1977.

the entire cable spinning, excluding the wrapping of the cables in the galvanized iron you touched, took eighteen months.

Look up at the height of the tower. For many months the cables could be reached by a footbridge running from anchorage to anchorage and open to anyone who asked the chief engineer for permission to walk across. Imagine a process like that in today's lawsuit-ridden America! "You want to climb on the girders? Go ahead, it's your life." Pedestrian access to the footbridge was eventually halted, not over liability but because pedestrians paralyzed by fear had to be rescued by workmen. This was clearly an unproductive use of workers' time.

Read the anachronistic plaque to Emily Warren Roebling on the Manhattan-facing side of the Brooklyn tower. Emily Roebling (1843–1903) was Washington's tireless go-between for communicating instructions to E. F. Farrington and others on the bridge. When Roebling became too ill in 1872 to continue personally supervising the work, Emily became his private secretary. He dictated specifications to her and she communicated information to assistant engineers. By 1879, she had spent seven years absorbed with the bridge.

BROOKLYN BRIDGE STATISTICS

Span: 1,595 ft.

Total bridge length: 3,455 ft.

Total bridge length plus approaches: 5,989 ft.

Height at mid-span: 135 ft.

Width: 85 ft.

Grade: 3.25 percent

Caissons: 168 x 102 ft. (Brooklyn); 172 x 102 ft. (New York)

Depth of base below high water: 44.5 ft. (Brooklyn); 78.5 ft. (New York)

Tower height above high-water mark: 276 ft.

Height of arches above roadway: 117 ft.

Anchorages: 129 x 119 ft. at base.

Cables

Number: 4

Length of each: 3,578.5 ft.

Number of wires in each: 5,434

Total length of wire in each: 3,515 miles

Weight of each: 870 tons

Number of vertical suspenders: 1,520

Number of diagonal stays: 400

Cost of land: $3.8 million

Construction: $11.7 million

Total: $15.5 million

Now that you've been standing on the tower for a few minutes, consider this: the Brooklyn tower rests on bedrock, but the Manhattan tower rests only on "hard pan" or "hard pack," closely packed rock and soil. Washington Roebling made the decision to stop digging beneath the high-water mark at 78.5 feet. But more on that when you reach the Manhattan tower.

Continue walking across the bridge until you reach what is about the midpoint, which is 135 feet above the high-water mark by order of the War Department, which had to ensure that ships made at the Brooklyn Navy Yard upriver could pass beneath.

A bridge is a constant invitation to the reckless. The first person to jump from the bridge was Robert Odlum, a Washington, D.C., swimming instructor. On May 19, 1885, he leaped, hoping to survive. Unfortunately, he didn't.

The most famous jumper of all was Steve Brodie, who on July 16, 1886, at age twenty-seven took bets that he could jump and live. He did—or at least he said he jumped. Witnesses claimed he was successful, and Brodie took his $200 winnings and opened a saloon on the Bowery. He had an oil painting of himself jumping painted on a wall and sat beneath it for years, telling his story to all comers. (See the "Immigrant New York" tour in chapter 2 for more about Brodie's saloon.)

Remember that the bridge was built before automobiles clogged our streets. It was used by horse carts, pedestrians, and a cable railway that ran on the two inside lanes. A steam engine on the Brooklyn side powered the cable car on its five-minute/five-cent trip. From 1 to 5 A.M. the steam power was shut off and locomotives did the work. The cable car was gradually electrified but didn't stop running until 1944. In 1818 an electric trolley line was laid on the middle lanes, leaving only the outside lane to horses.

➤ Continue on to the Manhattan tower. Enjoy the brass plaques with more construction information.

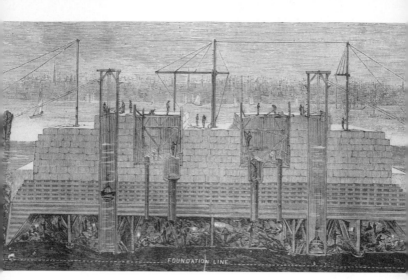

Cross section of the caisson and the beginning of one of the towers for the Brooklyn Bridge. The illustration clearly shows the men working on the riverbed inside the caisson, air locks and entry tubes, and clamshell excavators. Illustration courtesy of the New-York Historical Society.

The Manhattan tower is not standing on bedrock. How it got here is another story. Excavating and creating the foundations for the towers was the most innovative, difficult, and uncertain part of building the bridge. The problem was how to get a foundation onto an area 100 by 170 feet, 44.5 feet beneath the water on the Brooklyn side and 75 feet beneath it on the Manhattan side. The solution was caissons—essentially, huge bottomless wooden boxes, fifteen feet thick at the top and nine feet at the sides decreasing to less than a foot. The Brooklyn caisson was 168 by 102 feet and the Manhattan one was 172 by 102 feet. The caissons were built in shipyards north of the bridge site, launched like giant barges, and floated to the foundation site. Once there, they were anchored in place with pilings.

Compressed air was pumped into the caisson, keeping water out—except for a foot or so at the bottom. Shafts driven through the roof allowed things in and out. Dirt and rocks went out via a water shaft; an iron tube filled with water allowed access from riverbed to surface and contained a giant clamshell-shaped dredging claw. Men entered and left via an airshaft.

As the men dug and dynamited down inside the caisson, masonry was laid across it on top, sinking it further and further into the earth. The caissons were lit by sperm whale–oil candles, and the temperature inside was eighty degrees and humid. When the workers reached bedrock on the Brooklyn side and hardpan on the Manhattan side, they were pulled out and the caissons filled with concrete.

BUILDING THE BRIDGE

"Inside the caisson everything wore an unreal, weird appearance. There was a confused sensation in the head. . . . The pulse was at first accelerated, then sometimes fell below the normal rate. The voices sounded faint unnatural, and it became a great effort to speak. What with the flaming lights, the deep shadows, the confusing noise of the hammers, drills and chains, the half-naked forms flitting about, with here and there a Sisyphus rolling his stone, one might, if of a poetic temperament, get a realizing sense of Dante's inferno."

—MASTER MECHANIC E. F. FARRINGTON

"In a bare shed where we got ready, the men told me no one could do the work for long without getting the "bends.". . . When we went into the "air-lock" and they turned on one airlock after another of compressed air, the men put their hands to their ears and I soon imitated them for the pain was acute. . . .

When the air was fully compressed, the door of the airlock opened at a touch and we all went down to work with pick and shovel on the gravelly bottom. . . . The six of us were working naked to the waist in a small iron chamber with a temperature of about 80 degrees Fahrenheit: in five minutes the sweat was pouring from us, and all the while we were standing in icy water

that was only kept from rising by the terrific pressure. No wonder the headaches were blinding. The men didn't work for more
than ten minutes at a time, but I plugged on steadily, resolved
to prove myself and get constant employment."

—FRANK HARRIS, author of *My Life and Loves*

As a sixteen-year-old boy, Harris allegedly worked in the caisson
but quit after a few weeks. Some historians believe he never actually worked in them.

➤ Continue on, leaving the bridge and crossing Centre
Street, until you find yourself standing between the giant
Municipal Building to your right and the tiny City Hall (the
southern building in City Hall Park, not the northern one,
which is the Tweed Courthouse) to your left.

Take one final look at the bridge. When the bridge opened
on May 24, 1883, it was the biggest celebration since the
opening of the Erie Canal at the beginning of the century.
Tickets for seven thousand guests were issued; fifty thousand more attended; and the celebration began with an
hour of fireworks and bands on steamers beneath the
bridge. President Chester Arthur and the mayors of both
Brooklyn and New York attended and Emily Roebling led
them across. It was a glorious day for New York.

One week later, on Memorial Day, twelve pedestrians
were trampled to death on a narrow stairway like the one
you climbed at the Brooklyn end. The crowd thought the
bridge was falling and panicked running to get off. They
were wrong, but it was a tragic end to a masterful building
process.

If you can get close to City Hall when you read this, it
means that New York City has relaxed restrictions on people getting near the government. Finished in 1811, the

building is only the third city hall that New York has ever had. Construction costs came in under the $250,000 that was budgeted. Most of the building is marble, but the back wall was famously faced in brownstone because it faced northward and was out of sight of the rest of the city at the time.

From here you can walk north and east to our "Immigrant New York" walk (chapter 2) or down Broadway to the U.S. Custom House for our Lower Manhattan walk (chapter 1).

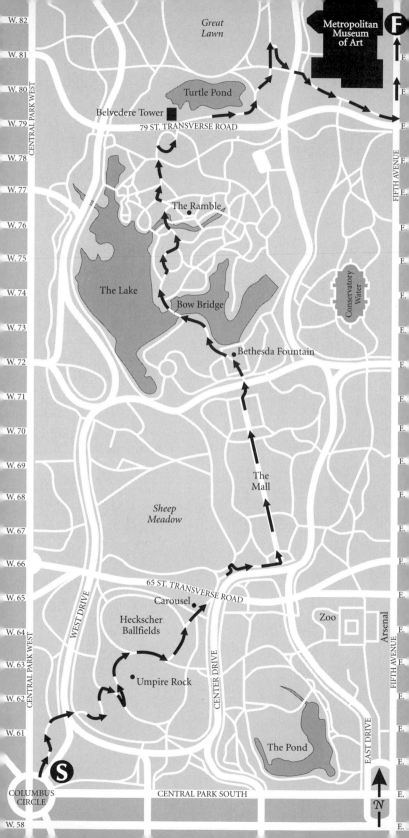

W. 82
W. 81
W. 80
W. 79
W. 78
W. 77
W. 76
W. 75
W. 74
W. 73
W. 72
W. 71
W. 70
W. 69
W. 68
W. 67
W. 66
W. 65
W. 64
W. 63
W. 62
W. 61
W. 58

CENTRAL PARK WEST

Great Lawn

Metropolitan Museum of Art

F

Turtle Pond

Belvedere Tower

79 ST. TRANSVERSE ROAD

The Ramble

The Lake

Bow Bridge

Bethesda Fountain

Conservatory Water

FIFTH AVENUE

The Mall

Sheep Meadow

65 ST. TRANSVERSE ROAD

Carousel

Heckscher Ballfields

Zoo

Arsenal

WEST DRIVE

CENTER DRIVE

EAST DRIVE

Umpire Rock

The Pond

S

COLUMBUS CIRCLE

CENTRAL PARK SOUTH

FIFTH AVENUE

N

E.
E.
E.
E.
E.
E.
E.
E.
E.
E.
E.
E.
E.
E.
E.
E.
E.
E.
E.
E.
E.
E.
E.

6 CENTRAL PARK
New York City's Largest Work of Art

➤ **Start: Columbus Circle at Fifty-ninth Street and Central Park West, in front of the Maine monument near the exit for the 1, 9, A, B, C, and D trains.**

YOU ARE ABOUT to enter the largest work of art in New York City, Central Park, a "natural" landscape that is at the same time a gigantic social institution. I say "natural" because almost everything inside was designed, planted, landscaped, and laid out by human hands. As park designer Frederick Law Olmsted said, "Every foot of the Park's surface, every tree and bush, as well as every arch, roadway and walk, has been placed where it is with a purpose."

The park is a nineteenth-century space that has entirely different meaning in the new millennium than it did when it was completed at the end of the Civil War. On this tour, we'll consider the park in its various forms—a natural environment, a recreational place, a commercial space, and a civic center. Each of these radically different perspectives provides a unique window through which we can view what many believe to be New York's greatest public space.

THE DESIGNERS: FREDERICK LAW OLMSTED AND CALVERT VAUX

The two men most responsible for the park's design are the American Frederick Law Olmsted (1822-1903) and the English immigrant Calvert Vaux (1824-1895). Olmsted, who was decidedly not a park designer before Central Park made him one, was responsible for the park's landscaping. Vaux (pronounced "vawx"), who was probably the first person to call himself a "landscape architect" as opposed to a "landscape artist," was responsible for many of the park's structures, helped by architect Jacob Wrey Mould.

Olmsted's pre-park experience included being a small farmer on Staten Island, an agricultural writer, a founder of the **Nation** magazine, and supervisor of a California gold mine. But he was best known for his writing on slavery in the South. Vaux had come to the United States to join a partnership with landscape designer Andrew Jackson Downing, who would have been the most likely candidate for park designer had he not drowned tragically before the project began.

Olmsted landed a job in 1857 as the supervisor of land clearance for the park through influential friends. He then teamed up with Vaux to design the winning Greensward Plan for the park. The city's request for proposal had specific design requirements, which Olmsted and Vaux met masterfully. A parade ground became the Sheep Meadow; a fire lookout tower became Belvedere Tower—"the castle"; a skating area became the Lake; and four cross-streets became the four sunken transverse roads that are hidden from view below ground level.

When their design was chosen as the winner, Olmsted was appointed architect in chief, while Vaux was made assistant to the architect in chief. After designing the park, Olmsted went on to become one of the best-known park designers in the country, designing in whole or in part New York's Prospect and Riverside Parks, Boston's Back Bay Fens, Philadelphia's Fairmont Park, Louisville's park system, Detroit's Belle Isle, Montreal's Mount

Royal, Buffalo's parks and parkways, Chicago's Riverside suburb, Oakland's Mountain View Cemetery, Washington, D.C.'s Capitol grounds, Stanford University's campus, and more.

Though Vaux designed Prospect and Fort Greene Parks in Brooklyn with Olmsted, their partnership ended in 1872. Vaux went on to design the Metropolitan Museum, the American Museum of Natural History, Frederic Church's Olana home along the Hudson River, and buildings for the Children's Aid Society. He was never as celebrated as Olmsted and became bitter in later life. He drowned off the current site of the Brooklyn Navy Yard in 1892, and it is entirely possible that he committed suicide.

New Yorkers, especially wealthy ones, gradually developed a desire for a city park in the mid–nineteenth century. Park boosters included writers such as William Cullen Bryant and Horace Greeley, real estate speculators such as James Beekman, and Mayor Fernando Wood. They compared New York unfavorably to European cities that had parks. Further, the wealthy wanted a place to ride their carriages away from the *hoi polloi* of the city streets. There were many competing arguments for the park: for example, that it would establish New York as the nation's cultural capital, provide a retreat for the wealthy, and be a social safety valve for the city's poor, who were crammed into tenement housing with no parks to the south.

Interestingly, the desire for a democratic park for all people was frightening to the middle classes and precipitated a debate over the use of public space by "respectable" and "disorderly" classes, as this editorial in the *New York Herald* of 1858 illustrates:

It is folly to expect in this country to have parks like those in old aristocratic countries. When we open a public park, Sam will air himself in it. He will take his friends. . . . He will knock down any better-dressed man who remonstrates with him. He will talk and sing, and fill his share of the bench and flirt with the nursery maids in his own coarse way. Now we have to ask what chance have William B. Astor and Edward Everett against this fellow citizen of theirs? Can they and he enjoy the same place? Is it not obvious that he will turn them out, and that the great Central Park will be nothing but a great beer garden for the lowest denizens of the city, of which we shall yet pray litanies to be delivered?

Furthermore, a democratic park did not mean treating those who currently lived in what would become parkland democratically. A lot of propaganda and boosterism demonized the pre-park inhabitants of the land to make it easier for the city to take their property. The *New York Times*, expressing anti–Irish Catholic bigotry typical of the nineteenth century, described park residents as "principally Irish families [in] rickety . . . little one storie shanties . . . inhabited by four or five persons, not including the pig and the goats," and other newspapers made much of the "vagabonds" and "scoundrels" living in the park.

More than 90 percent of those living on what would be parkland were either immigrants, largely Irish and German, or African Americans. In the latter case, Seneca Village, whose principal street was in the park across from West Eighty-fifth Street, was a well-established town with a school, three churches, and 250 residents. Indeed, a careful search of records shows that a far higher percentage of people living in the park actually owned their own land than did people in the city at large. Nonetheless, landowner, renter, and squatter alike were evicted in 1857 and 1858 to make way for construction.

We begin the tour by looking at the giant monument to the *Maine*, regilded now and shining in the sun. To the south of the park, Fifty-ninth Street is called Central Park South and is lined with a row of buildings that, when seen

When the city bought Central Park's 843 acres, it forced at least two thousand homeowners, renters, and squatters off the land. Nonetheless, people have built homes in the park many times since, especially during financial depressions. These are from the 1890s. Photo courtesy of the New-York Historical Society.

from the Sheep Meadow a few blocks north in the park, make for one of the classic New York panoramas.

The *Maine* memorial is to the American battleship that blew up, or was blown up, in Havana harbor in 1898, killing over 250 sailors and precipitating the Spanish-American War. William Randolph Hearst, whose *New York Journal* fervently supported the war, helped raise money for this monument. It was supposed to stand in Times Square but never made it. Instead, visitors come here to see "Columbia Triumphant" (the statue at the top) surrounded below and in front by Victory, Peace, Courage, and Fortitude; on the back stand Justice, Warrior, and History; and on the sides the Pacific Ocean (as an old man) and the Atlantic Ocean (as a young man).

➤ Facing the front of the monument, enter the park at the leftmost stone entrance, called Merchants Gate. (Most entrances are named, though few are labeled.) Take the

footpath farthest to your left and stay to your left past the first fork. Walk to your right as the path forks again and you will very quickly come to Greyshot Arch, one of over forty bridges designed by Vaux with Jacob Wrey Mould.

Walk under the sandstone balustrade and through the vaulted, red-brick archway. The passage is just over thirty feet wide, ten feet high, and eighty feet long. Continue along the path and take the left fork to come to Pine Bank Arch, two hundred feet beyond Greyshot Arch. Walk over this cast-iron beauty. The entire structure was rebuilt with a new wooden floor in 1984. Every single arch and every bridge in the park is different.

At the end of the arch, take a right and then a left to walk alongside Umpire Rock, the giant piece of Manhattan schist that supervises the Heckscher Ballfields and the Ballplayers House immediately to the north. Schist is what makes up the bedrock under Manhattan; geologically, it's a combination of mica, quartz, feldspar, and hornblende. If you look carefully at much of the schist that sticks up in the park, you'll see the pieces are smoother to the north side, where glaciers first thoroughly scraped parts, and rougher and more irregular to the south side. You can impress friends by telling them that major outcroppings are called *roche moutonée* (laying sheep) because the glacial cuttings supposedly make them look like sleeping sheep.

➤ **Follow the path as it curves to the right between Umpire Rock and Heckscher Ballfields.**

As you walk past the ball fields, they seem a perfectly natural part of the park, as do concrete playgrounds. But recreation had little to do with the original park, which didn't have a single playground but only provided three meadows for children's field sports. And to play on the meadows,

New York City's Largest Work of Art | CENTRAL PARK 187

kids had to have a certificate of good attendance and character from teachers—a difficult prospect for many nineteenth-century children who were working and not in school. Concrete and asphalt playgrounds came about at the turn of the twentieth century and in the decades afterward thanks to social reformers who believed that playgrounds would save children from gangs and, as they got older, unemployment. Further, adult baseball diamonds weren't a serious feature in the park until the 1920s! It is worth remembering what Olmsted and Vaux envisioned, in accordance with nineteenth-century sensibility:

> We want a ground to which people may easily go after their day's work is done, and where they may stroll for an hour, seeing, hearing, and feeling nothing of the bustle and jar of the streets, there they shall, in effect, find the city put far away from them. . . . We want depth of wood enough about it not only for comfort in hot weather, but to completely shut out the city from our landscapes.

Look to the south at the wall of buildings along Central Park South as you read those words. Also, think about the different ways in which people in a democratic society use a public park. Is a picnic acceptable? Music? Volleyball? Barbecuing? Dancing? What is "respectable" and what is "unacceptable" today?

WHO BUILT IT, HOW BIG IS IT, AND WHAT DID IT COST?

The park runs north-south from 110th Street (Central Park North) to Fifty-ninth Street (Central Park South) and east-west from Fifth Avenue to Central Park West (Eighth Avenue). It is just over 840 acres, which is about twice as large as feudal-relic Monaco and several times bigger than Governors Island in New York Harbor. The city paid the landowners of this rocky, swampy farmland almost $7.5 million for their land in the late 1850s. By contrast, the United States paid a few hundred thousand dollars less to Russia to buy Alaska only a few years later.

Construction began in 1858, and much of the landscaping south of Seventy-ninth Street was finished by December 1860. It took another five years to complete things up to 110th Street, but the park is never truly finished; it is a continuous work in progress. As far as historians can tell, Irish workers did almost all the labor and there were no black workers. The only women employed cleaned offices. The general rhythm of construction was, to begin with, about two thousand workers in early spring, expanding to thirty-five hundred by late summer and then cut back in the fall. A ten-hour day paid $1 for unskilled laborers who brought in millions of cubic yards of soil, planted hundreds of non-native trees, laid out six and a half miles of road, dug out a 106-acre reservoir, and built mile upon mile of trails and walkways.

➤ When you reach a four-way intersection as you seem to be curving away from the ball field, turn left and walk to a fork. Then turn right and you will come to the Carousel.

The Carousel in front of you was built in 1908 in Coney Island and moved to the park in 1951 to replace the park's original 1871 carousel, which burned down. The original was supposedly powered by a blind horse and a blind mule on a treadmill underneath it. The Carousel is a business that receives a contract from the city. For years Sal Napolitano ran it, but he was outbid by the Makkos Organization (formerly M & T Pretzel Company), an immigrant success story run by Greek immigrant Themis Makkos and his sons.

Commercial activities for children were allowed in the early park, and before the 1860s were over, the city had issued permits for boats at sixty cents an hour, carriages at twenty-five cents an hour, wheelchairs (with an attendant) for fifty cents an hour; and a goat cart and pony rides for ten cents each.

➢ **Take the path immediately to the east of the Carousel, which slopes uphill and northward. Continue north to the chain-link fence around the Sheep Meadow, the large grass field to your left.**

Originally landscaped to fulfill the function of a parade ground, the Sheep Meadow began hosting sheep in 1864. Olmsted required a particular breed of Southdown sheep whose gray-and-white coloring offset the grass. In choosing sheep for their ornamental use, Olmsted was following in the footsteps of William Gilpin, who wrote a book called *Forest Scenery*, which Olmsted loved. Gilpin wrote: "Sheep particularly are very ornamental in a park. Their color is just that dingy hue, which contrasts with the verdure of the ground; and the flakiness of their wool is rich and picturesque." The Sheep Meadow was fairly green until a series of concerts in the 1960s and 1970s killed much of the grass. It was replanted in 1979 and remains green by banning organized sports, concerts, and any activity when the grass is wet.

➢ **Turn around and walk back to the path along Center Drive (the roadway). Follow the traffic on the roadway east for less than two hundred feet until you come to the southern end of what a huge, inlaid-marble plaque on the ground asserts is Literary Walk. New Yorkers call it the Mall. The left hand of the statue Columbus (1892) points you in the right direction.**

The Mall is the formal promenade at the center of the naturalistic park. A wide, straight pathway bordered on both

People walking on the Mall beneath the overhanging branches of the double row of elms. The view is from the few statues at the southern end toward Bethesda Terrace in the north. Photo courtesy of the New-York Historical Society.

sides by double rows of overhanging elms runs northwest right up to Bethesda Terrace, the formal center of the park. Note the statues at the southern end. Surprisingly, Olmsted and Vaux did not intend statues anywhere but at Bethesda Terrace, which we'll come to shortly. All the rest were forced on them by the city, under pressure from civic, ethnic, and religious groups who wanted figures of their great men in the park.

You will see *Shakespeare* (1870) toward the Mall's eastern entrance, *Sir Walter Scott* (1871) on your immediate right, and *Robert Burns* (1880) on your immediate left.

➤ Walk north along the Mall until you come to the statue of Fitz-Green Halleck, on your right.

Halleck, who died in 1867, was one of the most famous poets in the country in the nineteenth century. His poems are now almost completely forgotten, which is why you'll be amazed to know that when this statue was unveiled in 1876, Rutherford B. Hayes, then president of the United States, his cabinet, and ten thousand others came for the unveiling ceremony. That today no one knows who he is speaks volumes about representing people in statues, an idea that is well past its heyday.

To drive the point further home: Can you name the most famous statue of a woman in the park? It's *Alice in Wonderland*. In fact, there are no statues in the park of women who were living, historical figures. All the statues of women are allegorical figures or characters from nursery rhymes. In all of the public spaces in Manhattan there are many statues of women, but again, these are invariably not of actual people. We can count, at present time, only four: Gertrude Stein, Golda Meir, Joan of Arc, and Eleanor Roosevelt.

➤ **Continue on along the Mall until you find yourself standing with a band shell on your right.**

Olmsted and Vaux installed a cast-iron bandstand to the *west* in 1859, but the current one is a historical anachronism. In 1923, retired banker Elkan Naumberg donated money to build it. This band shell has hosted Leonard Bernstein, Duke Ellington, Benny Goodman, Martin Luther King Jr, Fidel Castro, and Mayor Fiorello La Guardia selling war bonds during World War II. It was a very popular spot for ballroom dancing in the 1940s and 1950s, when the Goldman Band played here live. But as the popularity of ballroom dancing waned, so did the use of the band shell. The city wanted to tear it down in accordance with plans by the Central Park Conservancy (the nonprofit agency that actually runs the park), but Naumberg's great-grandson and others sued the city. The courts ruled that the city had to maintain it as a gift it had willingly accepted, whether or

After the theatre

ETHEL MERMAN
STAR OF "ANYTHING GOES"
By arrangement with Vinton Freedley

LEO REISMAN
AND HIS ORCHESTRA

CASINO IN *Central Park*

| LUNCHEON | DINNER |
| COCKTAILS | AFTER THEATRE |

Cocktail Dansant Saturdays & Sundays

NO COVER CHARGE FOR DINNER GUESTS AT ANY TIME
Reservations: RHinelander 4-3034

An early 1930s playbill from the Central Park Casino, in whose Joseph Urban-designed interior Mayor Jimmy Walker used to entertain friends. The casino was open only from 1929 to 1934, when Parks Commissioner Robert Moses had it torn down. The free concerts of Summer Stage now take place on the site. Image courtesy of the New-York Historical Society.

not it fit with the old-style benches that have been built around it.

Above the band shell on the hill is Rumsey Playfield, a desolate asphalt lot with a storied history that is now home to Summer Stage, the series of free concerts the park hosts every summer. The hill was originally the site of the Ladies Refreshment Pavilion, but in the late 1920s, Mayor "Gentleman" Jimmy Walker asked his friend Sidney Solomon to take over the space. Solomon hired Joseph Urban to re-design the interior, which included a black-glass ballroom. Walker and his mistress Betty Compton reviewed the plans, personally, and some financing even came from Arnold Rothstein (who had fixed the 1919 World Series).

The building opened as the Central Park Casino (with-out gambling) in 1929 and remained one of the most ele-gant places to eat in until Walker fled office under corrup-tion charges a few years later. In 1934, Robert Moses, then parks commissioner, demolished the casino with the argu-ment that only restaurants "within the reach of persons of average means" should be in the park. Interestingly, Moses then converted the sheepfold to the west of the Sheep Meadow into Tavern on the Green restaurant, which per-sons of average means have always found too expensive to afford.

THE HIRED CHAIR OUTRAGE

On June, 22 1901, the benches along part of the Mall were re-placed with new, green rocking chairs. When park visitors sat in them, uniformed attendants quickly walked up to demand five cents for a chair with arms and three cents for one without.

Entrepreneur Oscar Spate had secured a rocking-chair fran-chise from Tammany Hall. He hoped to make $250 a day here and in other city parks. Soon afterward, the angry public rioted, smashing and stealing chairs. A chastened Parks Commission withdrew Spate's franchise and replaced his chairs with ones marked "For the Exclusive Use of Women and Children, FREE."

➤ Continue north on the Mall. Walk down the steps under-neath Bethesda Terrace and come out at Bethesda Foun-tain. Directly ahead of you is the Lake and beyond it is the Ramble.

The Lake's boathouse in 1894, with the Ramble in the distance and to the left. The current Loeb Boathouse has replaced the one in the photo, but the Lake still boasts a gondola. Photo courtesy of the New-York Historical Society.

Bethesda Terrace was the only place Olmsted and Vaux wanted any statues, and they ended up with only one here. The Moorish building you walked underneath was designed by Jacob Wrey Mould, who had studied Islamic architecture and reproduced its style here. The ceiling was originally covered with thousands of tiles that are now being reinstalled, thanks to the Central Park Conservancy.

Bethesda Fountain is crowned by Emma Stebbins's *Angel of the Waters* (1873), the only sculpture in the park by a woman. Stebbins was the sister of the president of the Central Park Board of Commissioners. The park's fountain is a reference to the one in Jerusalem noted in the Gospel of John: "There is at Jerusalem by the sheep market a pool, which is called in the Hebrew tongue Bethesda." In the Bible, the sick would wait at the pool for an angel to stir up the waters and would then enter it to be cured. There is a historical debate as to whether Stebbins's angel is a man or a woman. Some see it as a proto-feminist statement celebrating women, while others argue that angels are sexless and that the statue merely reflects contemporary design.

Skaters enjoying the frozen Lake, with the Dakota apartment building in the distance. This late nineteenth-century view makes it clear how little there was around the Park in the 1880s. Photo courtesy of the New-York Historical Society.

➤ **Walk around to the left (west) of the fountain. Take the last path on your left, going up a few steps and roughly following the Lake keeping its shore on your right. In a few hundred feet you'll come to Bow Bridge, one of seven cast-iron bridges built in the park.**

If you look at Bow Bridge from ground level on the side, you will see it is roughly shaped like a bow. As you stand on the bridge and look to the west along Central Park West, you'll see the low-peaked, verdigrised roofs of the Dakota with a flagpole at the top, perhaps Manhattan's most famous apartment building. When it was built in the mid-1880s, there was very little this far north. Today, most people know it as the building where John Lennon lived, and where he was shot. To the left and right of the Dakota, respectively, are two of Central Park West's twin-towered apartment buildings, the Majestic and the San Remo.

The Lake beneath you was designed for skating and boating. The small, square gazebos along its shore are built on the sites of the original taxi-boat steps. You can fish in the lake, catch and release, and you are supposed to have a license.

➤ **Continue across Bow Bridge into the Ramble.**

The Ramble was designed as a small forest with meandering paths curving around it. Olmsted believed: "There can be no better place than the Ramble for the perfect realization of the wild garden."

➤ **Be careful with these directions; it's easy to get lost in here. Walk straight, passing an intersection on your right. Do not take this path but continue on to a fork. Turn right at the fork and go uphill. Turn left at the next intersection and then go up a few steps to reach the Rustic Shelter, a rebuilt cedar-log shelter that is meant to mimic English ideas of a Romantic landscape.**

CRIME AND THE PARK

No discussion of Central Park would be complete without a discussion of crime. For whatever reason, crimes that take place in the park have national resonance, while crimes that happen elsewhere in New York City usually don't. The social or cultural explanation is likely that so many Americans think of the park as a sanctuary in the city that crime here appears as more of an assault on the body politic than crime elsewhere.

Early arrests in the park were mainly for driving carriages too fast along the roads. The first robbery-murder in 1872 caused the **New York Times** to remark: "Murder has actually stained the turf of that green fairy land." In the 1880s the **Police Gazette** wrote: "Perils of the park include murderous attacks upon the chastity of pure-minded young females" (i.e., flashers). Homeless men—"tramps" in nineteenth-century vernacular—were another focus of the papers' ire. The **New York Tribune** wrote in the 1870s that "tramps and other unpleasant people [have] quit their winter quarters for the benches in the Park. . . . Ladies and children hesitate to venture into the Ramble without escorts."

Today the Park has its own police precinct, and it has the lowest rate of violent crimes of any precinct in the city. Nonetheless, the occasional horrific assault receives enormous media attention today. We never offer advice on where to go or not to go in New York. Use your judgment and go only where you feel comfortable.

➤ Walk around the left (north) side of the Rustic Shelter (as you face it from where you came up the steps) and to the path that runs behind it. Stay left on this path, and in a few steps you'll see the Gill (a small pool on your right). Bear right at the fork. (If you find yourself going down steps, back up and then bear right at the fork you missed.) In a few steps you'll come to another intersection, with a cement bridge with iron railings ahead of you.

The bridge is built over the Lost Waterfall, which was demolished and turned into a stream running downhill in the 1930s.

➤ Continue across the bridge, up a few steps, passing the Lookout, a cedar bench on your right. Take your first left. Walk past the first intersection on your right and then turn right at your second intersection. There will be a giant schist boulder immediately ahead of you as you approach this turn. Continue straight on this path, passing first an intersection on your left, then a second on your right, then a third crossing from left to right, and finally you will begin to slope uphill. There will be a meadow on your left. Continue uphill, where the path will begin to weave. Walk up some stone steps, keeping to your right.

Walk up another set of steps and continue uphill to Belvedere Tower, the "castle."

Vaux designed the castle to fulfill the function of a fire watchtower. It sits on top of 135-foot-high Vista Rock, through which, beneath your feet, is blasted a tunnel for the Seventy-ninth Street transverse road. If the castle is open, go inside and up the stairs to one of the lookouts. The original castle had no glass in its windows; instead, the structure was meant to deteriorate as the park grew and changed around it. The effect was to show people that the work of human hands is ephemeral while nature is eternal. Since 1920, the official weather-reading station for New York City has been atop the castle and in the fenced-in area behind it. Instruments on top measure wind direction and speed and minutes of sunshine. Those inside the fence measure air temperature, precipitation, and humidity.

To the north, immediately below the castle, is the redone Turtle Pond. To the left of the pond is the 1960 Delacorte Theater, where free "Shakespeare in the Park" plays are performed every summer. And the giant green ball fields stretching out ahead make up the Great Lawn. The lawn is built on the site of an 1840s reservoir that was drained in 1930.

Until the early 1990s, the Great Lawn was the site of the park's giant free concerts and gatherings, including Elton John's performance in 1980 (300,000 people), Simon and Garfunkel's in 1981 (500,000), an antinuclear rally in 1982 (750,000), Diana Ross's concert in 1983 (400,000), Paul Simon's in 1991 (600,000), a gathering led by Billy Graham in 1991 (250,000), and more. The Central Park Conservancy spent over $18 million renovating the Great Lawn, laying irrigation, drainage, soil, and Kentucky bluegrass and perennial rye to make it what it is today. No more large events will take place on it.

SENECA VILLAGE

The largest town in the land that would become Central Park was Seneca Village (the origins of the name are still being debated), which stretched from Seventy-ninth to Eighty-sixth Streets to the west of the Great Lawn. Its main street ran east-west into the parkland at what is today Eighty-fifth Street. In 1855, two years before all its residents were evicted, Seneca Village had 264 residents (about three-quarters black and the rest Irish), homes, gardens, three churches, cemeteries, a school, and a spring that still bubbles up in the park east of Eighty-second Street. All that is left today are the cornerstones of one of the churches.

How Seneca Village came to be is one of the most interesting stories in the park.

Beginning in 1825, John and Elizabeth Whitehead started selling parts of their farm to black New Yorkers. The first buyer was Andrew Williams, a twenty-five-year-old bootblack, who bought three lots for $125. Williams was followed by members of the African Methodist Episcopal (AME) Zion Church, "Mother Zion," from downtown. By 1829 there were nine houses on the side.

The building of the now-demolished old reservoir (not the new one that's still there), which was part of the Croton Aqueduct system at the center of the park from 1825 to 1832 displaced another black community known as York Hill, and many of its residents moved to Seneca Village. With increased European immigration to New York in the 1840s and 1850s, Seneca Village also became the home to German and Irish immigrants. The two most famous were George Washington Plunkitt and Richard Croker, both of whom went on to fame in the Tammany Hall Democratic machine.

Contrary to mid-nineteenth-century accounts that demonized residents of the park as "vagabonds" or "squatters," the tax and housing records of Seneca Village tell a different story. Assessors' maps show several two- and three-story buildings, one even with a wraparound porch on three sides.

Land ownership provided not only homes and income for black New Yorkers but voting rights. In 1821, New York revised its state constitution to allow universal white male suffrage but required free blacks to own $250 worth of property to vote. In 1855 there were twelve thousand black residents in New York but only one hundred black voters, and ten of these lived in Seneca Village. Indeed, black Seneca Village residents were far more likely to own property than whites elsewhere in the city.

About three-quarters of Seneca Village residents regularly attended one of its three churches. The African Methodist Union Church was established by black migrants from York Hill. All Angels' Church was built in 1849 by white the Reverend Thomas Peters, with money he raised and other funds he donated. It held a black and German congregation, including members of AME Zion Church from downtown, until AME Zion moved into Seneca Village in 1853. Peters described his congregation as "white, black and Indian, American, German and Irish practitioners in monogamy and those who troubled themselves about no gamy at all; gentle folk deteriorated and rough lovers of free and easy life, saints the most exalted and sinners most abandoned."

All Angels also housed Colored School No. 3, whose black teacher struck a blow for equality a century before Rosa Parks. In July 1854, teacher Elizabeth Jennings, twenty-four, boarded a Third Avenue streetcar downtown at Chatham and Pearl Streets on the way to church. The car did not have a sign saying "Colored People Allowed in This Car," as others did. When Jennings refused to get off, she was forcibly removed by the conductor and a policeman. Jennings sued the Third Avenue Railway Company and was represented at her 1855 trial by twenty-four-year-old future U.S. president Chester A. Arthur. A jury decided that, according to a state law, the railway company was "a common carrier, bound to carry all respectable people and that colored persons, if sober, well-behaved, and free from disease, had the same rights as others."

The third church was the oldest black church in New York but the last to erect a home in Seneca Village. AME Zion was founded in 1796 by black members of the John Street Methodist Episcopal

Church because no white church would ordain blacks. Its members have included Sojourner Truth, Harriet Tubman, Frederick Douglass, and Thomas Fortune, who founded the **Freeman,** the **Globe,** and the **Age.**

Alas, not even churches were enough to preserve the community when it came time to build the park. A city commission surveyed and assessed the value of all lots in and around the park. Those inside the park's future limits were taken from their owners by right of eminent domain, which means the government forcibly, but with pay, takes your land for what it declares is the common good. The city paid Andrew Williams, the first property owner, $2,335 for his two-story house and three lots. Williams argued to no avail that the value of the house alone was $1,400 and that he had been offered $3,500 for house and lots.

About this time, the **New-York Daily Times** introduced white New Yorkers to black residents of Seneca Village as a contrast to Irish residents elsewhere in the park's domain:

"West of the reservoir within the limits of the Central Park, lies a neat little settlement, known as "nigger village." The Ebon inhabitants after whom the village is called, present a pleasing contrast in their habits and the appearance of their dwellings to the Celtic occupants, in common with hogs and goats, of the shanties of the lower part of the Park. They have been notified to remove by the first of August. The policemen find it difficult to persuade them out of the idea which has possessed their simple minds, that the sole object of the authorities in making the Park is to procure their expulsion from the homes which they occupy. It is to be hoped that their removal will be effected with as much gentleness as possible."

How gently they went is unknown, but almost every property owner protested vehemently that the city was not paying fair market value for their land. Nonetheless, by 1857, Seneca Village was gone. Its residents scattered among many neighborhoods, and their history is unknown to most who walk through the park today.

➤ Return to the path immediately behind the castle. Go left (east) along the castle's back and follow the path down that runs between the Turtle Pond and the Seventy-ninth Street transverse. Go left at the first intersection to the statue of King Jagiello on horseback.

The statue, by Stanislaw Ostrowski, was originally to be placed in Kraków, but it was later used at the Polish pavilion at the 1939–40 World's Fair, and the Polish government in exile gave it to New York in 1945. Jagiello was actually a grand duke of Lithuania who married the Polish queen to unite the two lands.

➤ Go on the path to Jagiello's right, leading northward. Walk until you come to a four-way intersection. Ahead of you is the obelisk, and to your right is the Metropolitan Museum of Art. Walk north and up a flight of stone stairs to your right.

This two hundred-ton obelisk, also known as *Cleopatra's Needle*, was erected in the park in 1881 but was originally installed in Egypt, in the fourteenth century B.C., by Thutmosis III. Over the next twenty-five hundred years it was vandalized by those who carved on, burned, and eventually buried it. The United States was offered this needle in the nineteenth century, and the obelisk sailed from Egypt to New York in 1880, with William Vanderbilt paying the $100,000 shipping cost. It landed at West Ninety-sixth Street and was rolled along on top of cannonballs and giant timbers to railroad tracks. Then workers graded the road ahead of it while picking up a railroad track from behind and shifting it in front, over and over. All in all, the work took 112 days to get from Ninety-sixth Street to where it sits now. On January 22, 1881, the obelisk was pivoted into place, upright, in under five minutes.

Contrary to what is often written, the surface of the obelisk has been altered very little by pollution in New York. Most of the blackening was fire damage from the sacking of Heliopolis by the Persians thousands of years ago. And being buried for five hundred years caused salt to crystallize on the needle, making it more susceptible to freezing and thawing.

➤ **Retrace your steps back to the intersection and make a left through Greywacke Arch under East Drive. (Greywacke is a type of stone used in the arch, along with sandstone and brownstone.) After coming out of the arch, go right on the path and follow it around the Metropolitan Museum on Fifth Avenue.**

As you pass under East Drive, remember that it was built for elegant carriages, not cars. In fact, there was a New York City tradition of a formal carriage procession that entered the park at Fifth Avenue and Central Park South and proceeded up East Drive and then across Bethesda Terrace to the west side. Commercial wagons were banned from the park when it opened, and police would refuse entry to anyone not driving a "pleasure carriage" onto the drive for many years after the park opened.

Alas, the first auto was driven into the park in 1899 by Winslow E. Buzby, who tested the park commissioner's ban with what he called an "automobile victoria-phaeton." Buzby was given a summons and appeared before a magistrate, who ruled that under the city ordinance that said, "The drive shall be used only by persons in pleasure carriages, on bicycles, or on horseback," Buzby's car was a pleasure carriage.

In response, the park board changed the rules to ban "horseless carriages and motor wagons" but soon relented. In the first official drive, Park Commissioner Clausen and a friend drove into the park, but their car broke down and they had to walk out. Nonetheless, change was relentless, and the park's drives were asphalted beginning in 1912. Today the drive is open to commuter traffic during morning and afternoon rush hours and sometimes late at night.

Today, the Metropolitan Museum is one of the largest art museums in the world. If you're counting, it has almost three and a half million items ranging in age from prehistoric times to a few decades ago.

In 1872, Olmsted and Vaux, under pressure, allowed a museum on this spot because the view to it was then blocked by the walls of the reservoir that stood on the Great Lawn. The museum was built in many pieces. The first museum building, designed by Vaux and Jacob Wrey Mould in 1871 and opened in 1880, is almost completely hidden inside the many later accretions. The museum was closed on Sundays until 1891, when forced to open due to a combination of protests by workers, who wanted to visit on their only day off, and the city, which threatened to withhold funds. Go inside; the "suggested donation" is only that—suggested.

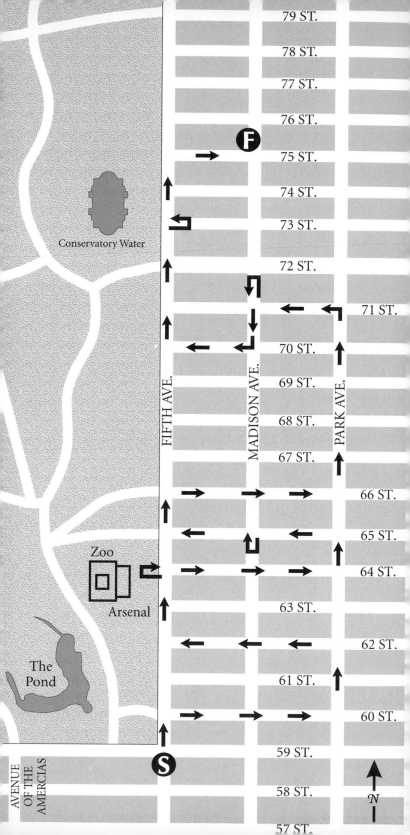

7 THE UPPER EAST SIDE

Manhattan's "Gold Coast"

➤ Start: The statue of William Tecumseh Sherman at Fifty-ninth Street and Fifth Avenue. Trains: N/R to Sixtieth Street; 4/5 to Fifty-ninth and Lexington.

THE UPPER EAST SIDE can be justifiably considered New York's "Gold Coast," and Fifth Avenue its "Millionaires' Row." It is in this neighborhood that Lady Caroline Astor countenanced the four hundred most important New Yorkers (those who would attend her illustrious parties); it is on these streets that J. P. Morgan had built—"damning the expense"—his famous Metropolitan Club; and it is here that the longest single uninterrupted set of mansions once stood. If ever there were a competition for wealth and power in one neighborhood, the Upper East Side would win hands down. Yet, despite its undeniable standing as an area of prominence and renown, the Upper East Side has a broader appeal. The neighborhood maintains a diversity to its history that is often overlooked amid the goings-on of Manhattan's *haute bourgeoisie*. This diversity can be observed not only in the eclecticism of its buildings but, as we shall see, in the many layers of development in its past. In short, it is more than the home turf to New York's rich and famous.

Traditionally, the Upper East Side is thought of as that area spanning Fifty-ninth Street to Ninety-sixth Street south to north and Central Park to the East River west to east. In the present tour, you will walk on a lower slice of this, from Fifty-ninth Street up to Seventy-fifth, weaving your way through Fifth, Madison, and Park Avenues. Much of the area you will see is now part of the Upper East Side Historic District, which runs from Fifty-ninth Street to Seventy-eighth (sometimes as far east as Third Avenue) and was designated in 1981. There are several other historic districts in the neighborhood as you head farther north. (Carnegie Hill, established in the 1980s and 1990s, is perhaps the most serene.)

Although the Upper East Side is New York's most expensive address, in the 1850s this area was mostly farmland, with the land that would become Central Park inhabited by a few thousand residents in towns and shanties. New York's richest families lived only as far north as Twenty-sixth Street, and the grid system laid down north of Fourteenth Street in 1811 had only just begun to take hold. With the acceleration of commercialization and immigration, however, New York's aristocracy was pushed increasingly farther north.

Perhaps the strongest reason for the development of the neighborhood, and Fifth Avenue in particular, was the clearing of land for Central Park, which began in 1857. The park's completion in 1865 set off a frenzy of mansion development that utterly transformed the landscape of residential living.

As the twentieth century progressed and living conditions changed, many of these one-family homes were replaced by luxury apartment buildings. Today, the Upper

East Side contains a mixture of modest brownstone row-houses, opulent townhouses, mansions, and impressive apartment houses. Some of the finest American examples of urban residential architecture can be found on these streets. You will see a rich variety of these over the course of the tour.

But to repeat, the streets of the neighborhood boast more than lovely homes. They embody a history of social and economic change that has produced fantastic mobility in both the population and its institutions. As you walk, you will see abundant examples—whether a social club, armory, synagogue, or former park for the working class. Ultimately, the Upper East Side is like all other New York City neighborhoods, in that it is an area that has evolved dramatically over the past two centuries.

We begin at the gilded statue of General William Tecumseh Sherman, best known for his bloody march through the South in the fall of 1864 where, as the Union's commander in the West, he burned large portions of Georgia and South Carolina. Sherman himself showed little remorse at Georgia's fate. As he famously put it: "War is cruelty and you cannot refine it."

The award-winning statue was cast by the well-known New York sculptor Augustus Saint-Gaudens and presented in 1900 at the Paris Exposition. It was erected in the present location in 1903. The base is Charles McKim's, of McKim, Mead and White. Walking before Sherman, waving an olive branch, is the figure of Victory; the pine branch on the granite pedestal signifies Georgia, and the horses stomping on the pines are a painful reminder of the destruction of Sherman's March. The statue was regilded in the late 1980s to considerable complaint, as Sherman's bloody history was now seen as unseemly.

Karl Bitter's statue **Pomona** (financed by Joseph Pulitzer) as it appeared before the Sherry Netherland, Savoy, and Pierre Hotels were built. Across Fifth Avenue stand the precursors to those great hotels: the hulking dark turreted building is William Hume's 1892 New Netherland Hotel; to its right stands Ralph Townsend's 1892 Hotel Savoy; and to the very far right is a piece of Alfred Zucker's 1895 Bolkenhayn apartment house. Second from the left is the Metropolitan Club. Photo courtesy of the New-York Historical Society.

➤ **Walk south to Pulitzer Fountain, located in the small plaza across Fifty-ninth Street, in front of the Plaza Hotel.**

The fountain was erected in 1916 with a $50,000 gift from Joseph Pulitzer, who hoped to outdo his newspaper-magnate rival William Randolph Hearst, who had financed the Spanish-American War's *Maine* monument at Central Park's Broadway entrance.

The statue on top is Pomona, the Greek goddess of abundance. *Pomona* was finished by Karl Bitter, protégé of the architect Richard Morris Hunt. The day he finished the clay model in 1915, Bitter was tragically killed crossing the street as he left the Metropolitan Opera (then on Forty-seventh Street), and his apprentices were left to complete the statue.

➤ **Facing west, admire the Plaza Hotel.**

The Plaza, which dates from 1907, is one of New York City's great luxury hotels. Frank Lloyd Wright, who hated New York, would stay only here when he passed through. Other luminaries who made this their temporary residence have included the Beatles, Mark Twain, Groucho Marx, and Eleanor Roosevelt. The first guest to sign the register of the Plaza was Alfred Gwynne Vanderbilt, who later lost his life in the sinking of the *Lusitania*.

The French Renaissance building was designed by Henry Hardenbergh (the same person responsible for the Dakota and the Art Student's League). Its two majestic elevations overlook both Central Park and Fifth Avenue. A shallow pond that the wealthy used for ice-skating once occupied the site. The Oak Bar and adjoining Oak Room inside are two of the most grand and imposing spaces in New York. Back in the day, George M. Cohan was a perennial luncheon guest. Regulars also included Gloria Swanson and Rita Hayworth.

Donald Trump bought the hotel in 1988 but today holds onto only a small stake.

➤ **Turn around, now face east, and have a look at the two hotels across Fifth Avenue on Fifty-ninth and Sixty-first Streets, the Sherry Netherland and the Pierre, respectively.**

Along with the Savoy, replaced in the late 1960s by the banal General Motors building, the Sherry Netherland, Pierre, and Plaza formed a quadrumvirate of powerhouse hotels at the Fifth Avenue approach to Central Park. After all, if one had money where better to reside? In fact, many did reside in these buildings—*full time*. In the 1930s and 1940s, the great majority of residents at these hotels were

View of the grand hotels clustered around Central Park Southeast in 1939. They are, from left to right, the Pierre, the Sherry Netherland, the Savoy, and the Plaza. The Savoy was torn down for the 1968 General Motors Building. Photo courtesy of the New-York Historical Society.

year-round occupants. The Sherry Netherland advertised itself as "more than a place to live—a new way of living." Only in the last twenty-five years have the numbers flip-flopped, making the hotels' occupants predominantly overnight guests.

The Sherry Netherland, distinguished by its French Gothic pinnacle, holds in its lobby sculpture panels salvaged from Commodore William Vanderbilt's mansion, the largest mansion of those that used to dot Fifth Avenue. It contained a whopping 137 rooms. Bergdorf Goodman, across the plaza on Fifty-eighth Street, succeeded the mansion when it was torn down in 1928. The Sherry Netherland has 165 apartments that were converted to cooperatives in 1954. On Fifth Avenue, north of the entrance, Diane von Furstenberg commissioned architect Michael

Graves in 1984 to design an upscale salon, which shortly thereafter was taken over by Geoffrey Beene.

The Pierre, founded by the noted chef Charles Pierre (whose restaurant was located at 230 Park Avenue), has its own illustrious history. In 1932, Dashiell Hammett stayed here while working on *The Thin Man*; he wasn't able to meet the bill he ran up, so he donned a disguise to avoid paying his tab.

The Pierre had a rocky beginning and went into bankruptcy in 1932, only several years after its construction (even with luxury hotels, the depression took its toll). J. Paul Getty bought it six years later for $2.5 million. The Four Seasons Chain is the most recent owner (from 1986).

Both the Sherry Netherland and the Pierre were designed by Schultze and Weaver, the same architects responsible for the best-known hotel in New York, the Waldorf Astoria.

➤ **Cross the avenue and walk up to Sixtieth Street and Fifth Avenue.**

As you walk from Fifty-ninth to Sixtieth Street, have a look at the cast-iron sidewalk clock—one of the few left in the city—on the east side of Fifth Avenue. Also see New York's only example of the work of great postmodernist Michael Graves, in his facade for Geoffrey Beene's store.

J. Pierrepont Morgan formed the Metropolitan Club, here on the northeast corner of Fifth Avenue and Sixtieth Street, in anger. Some of his close comrades and fellow captains of industry were unable to win entrance into the other elite clubs of the time, principally the Union Club. Morgan, the great New York City banker, had proposed membership at the Union for John King, president of the Erie Railroad, whose "career and character have won him the universal respect of all who know him." It was said, however, that King's table manners were not up to snuff, and he was promptly denied membership.

Morgan's retribution was to get New York's most famous architect, Stanford White, to build "the largest, most imposing, and most luxurious of the clubhouses of New York" (or so noted the man who was then dean of architectural criticism, Montgomery Schuyler). The Italian palace facade is similar in style to that of the University Club on Forty-fourth Street and Fifth Avenue. Morgan, it is said, summoned White with the words "Damn the expense."

In its temerity to challenge the Union Club, the Metropolitan Club was dressed in an all-marble facade. One lure to new Metropolitan members was a dining room sequestered from the all-male enclaves and set aside for female guests. The Ladies Restaurant overlooked the courtyard. Joining Morgan in his new venture were Cornelius Vanderbilt and Robert Goelet.

Never to be outdone, the Metropolitan Club erected a thirty-five- by sixty-foot courtyard, set off by an entryway of paired Doric columns and wrought-iron gates, at the 1 East Sixtieth Street entrance. The Metropolitan at the time was unrivaled in size—the main building measured 90 feet on Fifth Avenue by 150 feet on Sixtieth Street.

➤ **Walk east on Sixtieth Street toward Madison Avenue.**

Across from the Metropolitan Club stands the Harmonie Club at 4 East Sixtieth Street. The club was formed in 1852 by the German Jewish community as the *Harmonie Gesellschaft* (Harmony Society) and distinguished by having German as its official language and by hanging the kaiser's portrait in its hall. It was the first men's club in the city to admit women at dinner and the first eventually to have women as members.

The club dates back to a period when the chasm between first-wave German Jews and second-wave Eastern Europeans was massive. Many Harmonie denizens, in their eagerness to assimilate, had little desire to associate with their impoverished and "unAmerican" brethren from the East. This disturbing trend was partially offset by several far-sighted, if high-handed, German Jews such as Lillian Wald and Jacob Schiff. (See chapter 2 on the Lower East Side for further details.) While Harmonie's descendants today may hail from both central *and* eastern Europe, classwise they still have more in common with their German predecessors.

The Copacabana was at 14 East Sixtieth Street. This club was a venue for New York's stage and sports celebrities as well as your average New Yorker. Ask many a New Yorker of a certain generation and learn of high school proms, college balls, and first (and sometimes last) dates that took place here.

May 1957 saw one of the more notorious events ever to occur at the Copa. With Sammy Davis Jr. on the stage and Yankee Billy Martin celebrating his twenty-ninth birthday with fellow players Mickey Mantle, Yogi Berra, and Hank Bauer, a brawl broke out between the Yankee players and a New Jersey bowling team. Police charges were ultimately dropped, but the Yankees owner blamed Martin and traded him that July to Kansas City. He would not return until the 1970s, when he became the Yankees' manager.

Four years later, in October 1961, New York City detectives Eddie Egan and Sonny Grosso were having drinks after work at the club. They noticed a "little man in a silk suit, with a diamond stickpin in his tie, flashing a huge bankroll." Egan and Grosso decided to follow the man. The chase was to last eighteen months, turning into *The French Connection*. In the end there were nine arrests, and

112 pounds of heroin were secured ($32 million worth in 1960s dollars).

The film's justly famous car-chase scene was filmed over five weeks underneath the Bensonhurst Elevated Railway—twenty-six blocks of Brooklyn's Stillwell Line from Bay Fiftieth Street Station along Stillwell Avenue, into Eighty-sixth Street, and finally into New Utrecht Avenue, ending at Sixty-second Street Station. The chase was filmed at full speed, with real pedestrians and traffic!

Next door to the Copacabana, at 14 East Sixtieth, was "Hotel 14." A lovely 1907 residential hotel turned into commercial offices in the 1970s; the British newspaper the *Financial Times* has top-floor offices. When the building was still a hotel, the first Israeli delegation to the United Nations stayed here, in 1948.

➤ **Look at Madison Avenue, New York City's narrowest avenue, which is named for America's fourth president (who sadly died in 1836, the year of its opening).**

Madison Avenue has a curious history, having gone from a predominantly residential thoroughfare to an outstanding commercial zone. You can get a taste of its former identity from several lovely brownstone vestiges along the avenue. Because of zoning, many of the fashionable stores are now housed in these very townhouses or brownstones.

Of the three avenues that dominate this tour, Madison was the first to emerge, fully formed, when it became an early nineteenth-century roadway. Fifth Avenue, as we noted, took off with Central Park's development in the latter part of the nineteenth century, and Park Avenue as the present day boulevard developed only in the early part of the 1900s. Of the three, however, Madison turned headfirst toward the commercial, becoming in the early postwar period the advertising capital of the world. No longer the center of advertising, Madison has reinvented itself (at least in this part of the Upper East Side) as "Boutique Row."

If you want to get a feel for the avenue's narrowness, take a detour south to Fifty-sixth Street. Here, at 550 Madison Avenue, you will find the Sony (formerly AT&T) building, a landmark postmodern skyscraper designed by Philip Johnson, which provides a staggering sense of the avenue's compressed quality. Johnson's hulk literally overpowers the street.

➤ **Cross Madison Avenue and continue walking east toward Park Avenue, on the north side of Sixtieth Street.**

The Grolier Club is located at 47 East Sixtieth Street. In contrast with the business-titan appeal of the Metropolitan down the road, here is a club for book lovers. Named for the sixteenth-century bibliophile Jean Grolier de Servières, the club was founded for "the literary study and promotion of the arts pertaining to the production of books." Bertram Goodhue, best known for his St. Bartholomew's Church next to the Waldorf Astoria, designed the club in 1916. The original Grolier Club is on 29 East Thirty-second Street.

On the northwest corner of Sixtieth Street and Park Avenue stands Christ Church, built in 1931 by noted church architect Ralph Adams Cram. Sign of the times: this church has an impressive Web site, www.christchurch-nyc.org! (Those interested in furthering their study of New York Methodism can venture downtown to 44 John Street, where the John Street United Methodist Church, America's oldest Methodist society, still stands.)

From dirt road to railroad to road of riches, Park Avenue has gone through several prominent permutations, reflective of social and economic changes wrought over two centuries. In the first half of the nineteenth century, when only two major thoroughfares existed in Upper

The Park Avenue Rails, 1899. The view is from the Forty-sixth Street Bridge, overlooking the New York, New Haven and Hartford Railroad Yards. Prior to the 1907 track electrification, the tracks along Park Avenue were open to the sky. Photo courtesy of the New-York Historical Society.

Manhattan (Boston Post Road, now Third Avenue, and Bloomingdale Road, now Broadway), Park Avenue was indeed a dirt road, employed as the thoroughfare to the village of Harlem. In the 1830s, the road was filled with railroad track and became known as Fourth Avenue. New Yorkers still refer to Park south of Grand Central as Fourth Avenue, although the name has been officially changed to Park Avenue South.

The idea of the New York and Harlem Railroad was to attract commuters and shoppers away from the riverboats normally used for the trip downtown. The line ran along the Bowery and then Fourth Avenue. The first occupants of Park Avenue were hospital institutions and educational establishments that took advantage of the inexpensive space adjacent to the railroad lines. Hunter College and the Armory to the north, which you will view later, are the last occupants remaining from that period.

Park Avenue in 1936, looking south from Forty-eighth Street. Now known as the Helmsley Building, this office tower was originally built as the New York Central Building by architects Warren and Wetmore in 1929. Photo courtesy of the New-York Historical Society.

With the New York Central Railroad's transition from steam to electric in 1907, the railroad lines were put underground and Park Avenue became, as its name implies, a beautifully landscaped boulevard with dignified apartment houses.

In the post–World War II period, the major changes on the avenue have actually transpired south of Fifty-ninth Street. Most of the former apartment buildings and hotels in this part were either torn down or reclad in glass and steel as the area was transformed to conform to the modernist standards prevailing in the 1950s. The change itself was prompted by several decades' respite in financial and commercial office construction downtown and the attendant move of such offices to the Park Avenue environs.

Although this tour is headed uptown, enjoy some of the bona fide classics of 1950s commercial architecture a tad south such as the Lever House and the Seagram Building.

(Detour down to Fifty-third and Fifty-second Streets, respectively.) For Frank Lloyd Wright fans, the master's "other" Manhattan building (the first being the Guggenheim) stands on Fifty-sixth Street—believe it or not, the Mercedes Benz showroom. Built in 1955, four years before the showroom went in, it is still in use.

> ➤ Look across the street from Christ Church on the southeast corner of Sixtieth and Park.

You're looking at 515 Park Avenue, the latest luxury condos by William Zeckendorf and his brother. They are, at press time, the most expensive per-square-foot apartment building in New York City, charging an average of $3,000 per foot. The brick and limestone forty-four-story building boasts eight floor-through duplexes with servants' quarters. The $4,000 monthly condo fees won't be optional, but a $25,000 climate-controlled wine cellar is. Goldman Sachs head, turned Senator, John Corzine of New Jersey bought an apartment here but never moved in. Has Zeckendorf outtrumped Trump?

> ➤ Walk north along Park Avenue to Sixty-second Street.

The Colony Club (northwest corner of Sixty-second and Park) was formed in 1903 by Florence "Daisy" Jaffray Harriman. It was (with the Cosmopolitan) New York's most important all-women's social club and the first in the United States to build its own clubhouse.

When the club moved into these facilities in 1915, the brass window fixtures had been ordered from France and the chandeliers from Germany, though World War I had already begun. The delay in deliveries turned out to be so long that some members were said to be in favor of joining the peace expedition and going after their needed elite accessories. Who says the rich are pawns for the war machine?

The original Colony Club building on Thirtieth and Madison, still standing, was designed by Stanford White. Honorary club members once included the wives of J. P. Morgan and Stanford White.

➤ **Walk west on Sixty-second Street to Madison Avenue.**

The low building on the northeast corner of Sixty-second and Madison was originally the famed Louis Sherry's restaurant. It was often heard that if you were to take tea there, "you are sure to see a certain number of Our Best People." Louis Sherry's downtown restaurant and apartment hotel was earlier on Thirty-seventh Street and Fifth Avenue in 1890 (in 1898 at Forty-fifth and Fifth) and was a competitor of the famed Delmonico's. Sherry made his money as a first-class "confectionaire," providing sweets to the rich. His lavender boxes and tins were a standard item in the staterooms of the ocean liners that left New York weekly.

Louis Sherry's restaurant was better known in some circles for the antics that went on at its premises. One particularly outrageous affair was the 1903 dinner for the New York Horseback Riding Club, sponsored by Chicago millionaire Cornelius Billings, at which diners ate on—you guessed it—horseback. The tab? A mere $50,000.

Although there is no plaque, across Madison Avenue on the west side stood the home that Theodore Roosevelt lived in from 1895 to 1897, during his tenure as police commissioner of New York. Appointed under the reform administration of Mayor William Strong, his official title was "President of the Police Board." As commissioner, he forced the resignation of the chief of the uniformed police, who had justified recently amassing $300,000 as the result of successful stock picks. Roosevelt adopted the practice of prowling the streets at night, dressed in a black cape, looking for policemen shirking their duty. While these strolls made for good public relations, his popularity suffered when he insisted on enforcing the Sunday blue laws, closing saloons. New Yorkers were happy to see him move on when, in 1897, he accepted President William McKinley's appointment as assistant secretary of the navy. He became McKinley's vice president after the 1900 election.

The youngest person ever to succeed to the presidency (after the assassination of McKinley in 1901), Roosevelt also had his childhood home (a re-creation now, but with original furnishings) in Manhattan, on East Twentieth Street. Go and visit; there's a lovely museum too.

➤ **Continue walking west on Sixty-second Street to Fifth Avenue.**

The fabulous beaux-arts townhouse at 11 East Sixty-second Street is known as the Fabbri Mansion. It was commissioned and built in 1900 for William Vanderbilt's eldest daughter, Margaret Louisa Vanderbilt Shepard, who then presented it to her daughter Edith and her son-in-law. The name Fabbri is for Edith's husband—note the F's designed into the wrought-iron balconies. Some of the many splendid trappings of this extraordinary building include a wholly original nineteenth-century interior, with 1890s mahogany paneling in a twenty-five- by forty-one-foot dining room and walk-in safes and coal bins untouched for generations.

Despite the fact that the block between Fifth and Madison was the heart of New York prestige (if the Social Register is any guide), the Fabbris left after only a year, preferring the more bucolic qualities of Carnegie Hill to the north. The house was recently purchased as the residence for the permanent representative of Japan to the United Nations, for the whopping sticker price of $30 million—the highest ever for a townhouse in New York.

Just a few doors from the Fabbri Mansion, at 5 East Sixty-second Street, is the Fifth Avenue Synagogue. Check out the mid-1950s cat's-eye windows, with elliptical stained glass. The architect, Percival Goodman, ingeniously dealt with the synagogue's narrow lot by finding a solution in the traditional Sephardic layout, which calls for a *bimah* and ark in a clear central area, with facing sections of worshipers. This centralized plan, in contrast to the more common layout where rabbi and cantor face the audience from the front, allows congregants to better *hear* the service.

New York City is one of those classic urban spaces where a prominent place of worship can be sandwiched next to other buildings (rather than being, say, prominently displayed on a street corner).

One of the most famous congregants is the irrepressible Abe Hirschfeld, who has set up an organization to register as many Kohanim and Levites as possible throughout the world. It is his attempt to organize so-called Jewish royalty. Hirschfeld, former owner of the *New York Post*, as we go to press is serving time for hiring a hit man to kill his business partner.

Architect Percival Goodman is the brother of the great social critic Paul Goodman. They cowrote the late 1940s tract *Communitas*, attributing the breakdown of the city to postwar consumerism and other modern maladies. In all, Goodman has designed more than fifty synagogues.

The Knickerbocker Club is located on the southeast corner of Fifth Avenue and Sixty-second Street. One of the most exclusive clubs in New York, it was founded in 1871 as a reaction to the eased entry requirements at other clubs. It was Washington Irving who coined the word *knickerbocker* to refer to New York's most socially prominent families—

more specifically, to describe any New Yorker who could trace his or her family to the original Dutch settlers. The word derived from Irving's 1809 comic history of the Dutch regime in New York, *A History of New York*, authored by the imaginary "Dietrich Knickerbocker," who was supposed to be an eccentric Dutch American scholar. The book became part of New York folklore and the historical fiction part of the vernacular.

Club founders include Alexander Hamilton's grandson, John Jacob Astor, and Moses Lazarus, father to Emma, author of *The New Colossus*, the poem said to be—though not really—carved on the Statue of Liberty—"Give me your tired, your poor. . . ." (Long after being written in 1883, Lazurus's poem was affixed to the *inside* of the statue's base.) Today the club still boasts some eight hundred members. As a club, it is one of the last bastions of old New York society; as a building, it's lovely, exceptionally well proportioned with marble trim from basement to roof balustrade. The same architectural team that designed the Georgian Colony Club—Delano and Aldrich—handled the equally Georgian Knickerbocker Club.

➤ **Walk north along Fifth Avenue one block to Sixty-third Street.**

Directly across from the Knickerbocker Club stand what replaced many of the imposing mansions that once dotted the length of Fifth Avenue—apartment buildings. But these, as you shall see, are not ordinary apartment buildings. It would be more fitting to label them "apartment houses," a term reminiscent of the grandeur and style of these early progenitors. It took some time before the new edifices were accepted as equivalent in stature to what came before. Certainly, their size and luxury helped make the transition smoother.

The apartment house 810 Fifth greets you with a grand iron marquee. Like many apartment buildings of the time, it was laid out with just one apartment per floor (it has remained such), at an average size of five thousand square feet. The aristocratic life was not difficult to come by with four bedrooms, four servants' rooms, living and dining rooms, and library. Those in search of an apartment in New York City today might gag, however, at the 1913 asking price; the thirteen-room apartments ranged from $72,000 to a whopping $96,000. One would be lucky to get a studio in Manhattan for that amount in 2002 (Manhattan, Kansas, that is).

This building has had many noted residents over the years, but perhaps the best known to New Yorkers was former senator Nelson Rockefeller. In fact, Rockefeller was so charmed by the building's locale that he lived here with both his first and second wives.

Architectural historian Andrew Alpern tells the story of how, in 1963, Richard Nixon purchased the fifth-floor apartment at 810 Fifth Avenue, shortly after Nelson and his second wife, Happy, moved into their new apartment. Steadfastly denying that his relocation to New York from the West Coast was politically motivated, Nixon averred: "I'm going to New York for the purpose of practicing law and not for practicing politics." Five years later, Rockefeller and Nixon were dueling Republican candidates for the nomination. During the political battle, they used different elevators to get to their respective apartments. Nixon might have been better off sticking to the law.

After Nixon's aborted second term, he decided to move back to New York, this time just down the way from his previous abode. Having lived at 810 in the 1960s, Nixon felt it might be easy to return to his former block. The co-op board of 817, however, disagreed—not because of Nixon's politics or because he was now out of a steady job, for they even claimed they believed him when he said he wasn't a crook! The co-op board rejected him on the grounds that they did not want to draw attention to themselves—from the media and potential protestors. The Secret Service presence would also have been rather noisome. To paraphrase Phil Ochs: "Richard Nixon, find yourself another co-op to be part of."

Nixon did—well, sort of. Shortly after his rejection, he purchased a twelve-room townhouse at 142 East Sixty-fifth Street for $750,000. He sold it in 1982 for $2.6 million. The townhouse had three bedrooms, seven baths, a study, two living rooms, two kitchens, two fireplaces, a paneled library, and an elevator. His yard backed onto the home of noted historian Arthur Schlesinger Jr. When asked about his new neighbor, Schlesinger said: "He's a very lucky man, living out his days in luxury when he ought to be in the federal penitentiary."

➤ **Continue walking to the northeast corner of Fifth Avenue and Sixty-third Street, to 820 Fifth Avenue.**

This apartment building, like many on the East Side known simply by its number, was renowned in the 1920s as the residence of Governor Alfred E. Smith. The first Catholic to run for U.S. president, Smith came up short in his race against Herbert Hoover in 1928. Perhaps as a consolation prize, Smith cashed in and became the well-paid head of the Empire State Development Corporation (the company that was soon to build the legendary skyscraper on Thirty-fourth Street).

Richard Nixon has company here. Ronald Perelman, owner of Revlon, was turned down by 820's co-op board.

➤ **Cross the avenue and walk up to Sixty-fourth Street. Head into Central Park for a moment.**

Directly in front of you is the Arsenal (1848–51). It has the distinction of being the only structure in Central Park that actually predates the park's development. When built, it housed the majority of New York State's ammunition during the war with Mexico. It was deliberately housed four miles from City Hall, a safety measure, since highly explosive arms and ammunition were stored in the relatively modest brick building. During the Civil War, the arsenal was a bunkhouse for Union troops. It later became, in turn, New York City's Museum of Natural History; park headquarters for Manhattan and Richmond (today's Staten Island); a police station; a weather observatory; and, since 1934, home to the city's Headquarters for Parks and the Central Park Conservancy.

Check out the eagle over the door and the pyramids made of cannonballs on the facade. The Arsenal also has eight crenellated octagonal towers.

If small children are involved in your walk, consider a quick stroll behind the Arsenal to Central Park's Children's Zoo.

➤ **Return to Fifth Avenue and cross to the southeast corner of Sixty-fourth Street.**

The 1896 building at 2 East Sixty-fourth Street is a fine example of one of the few remaining mansions on Millionaires' Row. Long since converted to condos, it was built as the city residence of coal magnate Edward J. Berwind (who also built "The Elms" at Newport). Berwind is perhaps best known for his fueling of U.S. steamships throughout World War I.

Berwind was also for a time head of the Interborough Rapid Transit (IRT). He is said to have belonged to some forty clubs and societies. The building was occupied for a number of years by the Institute of Aeronautical Sciences.

➤ **Walk East on Sixty-fourth toward Park Avenue.**

New India House stands at 3 East Sixty-fourth Street. Built in 1903 as a private residence for Mrs. Astor's daughter Carrie, and designed by Warren and Wetmore, the firm responsible for Grand Central Terminal, this is an ideal example of beaux-arts townhouse style. Check out the brilliantly detailed mansard roof; the small windows, offering minimal air and light, denote the prior status of those rooms as servants' quarters.

Since 1950 the building has been the headquarters of the Indian Consulate and delegation to the United Nations.

Donald Trump's ex-wife number two, Ivana, lives at 10 East Sixty-fourth Street. In her modest way (she at least learned something from the Donald), she wanted to build a $500,000 indoor swimming pool in her backyard. While appreciative of her nautical needs, the Landmarks Preservation Commission (LPC) thought twice about the pool's viability on a landmarked block. Across from Ivana's are several new townhouses that are conforming well with the requirements of the Landmarks Commission.

It is worth noting here the serious questions raised in the area of landmarking. Buildings that are landmarked (or in the case of the Upper East Side, whole streets) cannot be touched (usually only the exterior but sometimes the interior as well) without the express, written consent of the Landmarks Preservation Commission. While absolutely vital in a culture prone to destruction and ambivalence (witness the hundreds of extraordinary structures demolished in the era prior to the LPC's existence), landmarking is not without contradictions. Simply put, landmarking a street freezes it in time. It makes an aesthetic and social decision that how we value a street today is how it should be valued decades into the future. Undoubtedly this has the advantage of preserving "beauty" at the expense of greed. But definitions of beauty and importance are enmeshed in notions of power and culture. How to decide?

The famous Wildenstein Gallery is found at 19 East Sixty-fourth Street. Founded in Paris in 1875 by Nathan Wildenstein (1852–1934), who chose to leave his native Alsace in the wake of the Franco-Prussian War in order to remain a French citizen, this is one of the premier art galleries in the city. Raphael's *Madonna and Child* (ca. 1504) and Van Gogh's *Entrance to the Public Garden at Arles* (1888) are but two of the thousands of works sold over the years by Wildenstein to major museums and collectors. Jocelyn, the ex-wife of the current gallery owner, was christened by New York's tabloids the "bride of Wildenstein" for her interesting plastic surgery during the Wildensteins' very public divorce trial.

The structure was built in 1932 by Horace Trumbauer with Julian Abele, one of the few black architects working in a major firm at that time. Just a little farther north is one of Abele's early works, New York's graduate Institute of Fine Arts, the mansion at 1 East Seventy-eighth Street on Fifth Avenue, completed in 1912. Originally it was the residence of James B. Duke. It is thus no coincidence that Abele is the lead architect of the Duke University campus in North Carolina.

➤ **Crossing Madison Avenue, be certain not to miss the Verona on the southeast corner at 32 East Sixty-fourth Street.**

The Verona is the precedent-setting building for luxury apartment houses. Compare this Venetian Renaissance opulence with the cool, staid apartment edifices you just passed on Fifth Avenue. The Verona, built in 1908, originally housed only twenty apartments (two per floor), each with eleven rooms and three baths. Mike Wallace lived here for many years; Kitty Carlisle Hart still lives here; Charles Evans Hughes, Supreme Court justice and Republican nominee for president in 1916, lived here from 1917 to 1921. Perhaps the Verona's most distinctive feature is its monumental, eight-foot-high metal cornice that projects seven feet from the main structure. A stellar building.

As you reach Park Avenue, gaze across to the 1922 Central Presbyterian Church. This congregation began as the Norfolk Street Baptist Church on the Lower East Side and is now Riverside Church near Columbia University. The congregation's claim to fame, however, was the affiliation of John D. Rockefeller; the grand man himself taught Sunday school classes when the congregation was the Fifth Avenue Baptist Church.

Step inside to have a peek at the wonderful old manually operated passenger elevators.

➤ **Walk north along Park Avenue to Sixty-fifth Street.**

New York's flamboyant and notorious ninety-seventh mayor (from 1925 to 1932), Jimmy Walker, moved into a suite at 610 Park Avenue in 1928, soon after leaving his wife, Janet, for showgirl Betty Compton. The building was the Mayfair Hotel at the time. He lived here until 1932 when amid accusations of corruption, he was forced to resign his office. He immediately left for Europe, married Betty Compton, and lived broad for the next three years. Walker's penchant for frequenting nightclubs and enjoying the company of celebrities earned him the nicknames "Beau James" and the "Night Mayor." (See chapter 6 on Central Park for Gentleman Jimmy's role in the park's casino.)

Jimmy Walker was also known as a talented songwriter, who composed such legendary hits such as "Will You Love

Me in December as You Do in May?" In the first two years of his administration, Walker indulged himself with several vacations overseas, spending 143 days out of office, and was fond of saying, "I refuse to live by the clock." Walker ultimately returned to New York City, where his onetime political nemesis, Fiorello La Guardia, appointed him municipal arbiter to the garment industry in 1940.

Lillian Hellman lived at 630 Park from 1970 until her death in 1984. Hellman was a well-known playwright, whose works include *The Little Foxes* and *Toys in the Attic*. She has been labeled a Stalinist apologist for her long-standing defense of the former Soviet regime but was singularly courageous in her refusal to give names of associates in the theater world during the harrowing McCarthy period. Hellman also had a well-known and long-standing relationship with Dashiell Hammett until his death in 1961.

➤ **Walk east on Sixty-fifth Street toward Madison Avenue.**

Sara Roosevelt, mother of Franklin Delano Roosevelt, commissioned architect Charles Adams Pratt to design the buildings (which appear to be a single building) at 47–49 East Sixty-fifth Street in 1907, shortly after FDR married Eleanor. The house was meant to be a wedding present. The buildings have a single entranceway and interconnecting doors linking the two homes. Eleanor, however, was not fond of Sara's penchant for bursting into her home (as she often did). Franklin and Eleanor lived here from the fall of 1908 until he was elected to the state legislature in 1910. They continued to live here on and off for the next twenty years. It was in the fourth-floor bedroom that FDR convalesced from polio in 1921–22. After Sara's death in 1941, the building was purchased for use by Hunter College.

Take a brief detour and stand on Madison Avenue between Sixty-fourth and Sixty-fifth Streets and face the east side of Madison Avenue. Have a look at the two rowhouse vestiges at 741 and 743 Madison. Madison Avenue's development preceded Fifth Avenue's by more than a decade; from the early 1880s, downtown residents began building the rowhouses and small manors that emerged on Madison. Several residents, Richard Morris Hunt and Charles Tiffany, for example, were quite well known.

The first known storefront on Madison emerged in 1904, but it was well into the 1920s that Madison Avenue remained primarily residential. Heavy automobile traffic and city decrees ordering house owners to remove all stoops beyond the building line sped the conversion from residential to retail avenue.

➤ **Continue walking on Sixty-fifth Street toward Fifth Avenue.**

One of Manhattan's few significant modernist townhouses (1941) can be found at 17 East Sixty-fifth Street. The building has two separate wings, one on the street and one in the rear. It was built originally for Sherman Fairchild, the founder of the Fairchild Camera and Instrument Corporation and of Fairchild Engine and Airplane Corporation. He was a pioneer in the fields of photography, aviation, and sound engineering. Fairchild became known as one of the preeminent venture capitalists in the country (and was so recognized by cover stories in, among other magazines, *Time* and *Business Week*, the former calling him "the epitome of the new scientist-businessman-inventor").

The former residence of Mrs. Astor's son-in-law is at 16 East Sixty-fifth Street. Built in 1917 for James Van Alen, who in 1919 sold the house and moved to Europe in protest over the impending Prohibition, the building has been controlled by the Kościuszko (pronounced Kos-ts-iush-ko) Foundation since 1945. The foundation supports Polish ed-

Temple Fmanu-El, formed in 1845, is New York City's first Reform congregation. This is their third building, built in 1927. This Art Deco limestone synagogue seats twenty-five hundred people and is considered to be the largest Reform temple in the world. Photo courtesy of the New-York Historical Society.

ucational and humanities programs and is named in honor
of Tadeusz Kościuszko, who designed the fortress at West
Point and who was instrumental in the American victory in
Saratoga, New York, during the American Revolution.
Kościuszko Bridge spans Brooklyn and Queens.

Temple Emanu-El, at 840 Fifth Avenue on the corner of
Sixty-fifth Street, is the largest Reform synagogue in the
world (edging out the Dohany synagogue in Budapest). It
joined in 1927 with Temple Beth-El (formerly on Sixty-
seventh and Fifth Avenue). On this site once stood Richard
Morris Hunt's double-size mansion for *the* Mrs. Astor—
Caroline Schermerhorn Astor. Alongside hers was the

234 THE UPPER EAST SIDE | Manhattan's "Gold Coast"

home of her son, John Jacob Astor. Both masterpieces came down to make way for the synagogue. Temple Emanu-El previously had its building (from 1862) on Forty-third Street and Fifth Avenue, near to where the New York Public Library now stands. Members of the congregation helped found and support Mount Sinai Hospital, the Educational Alliance, and the Federation of Jewish Charities.

Built in the Byzantine/Romanesque style and reflecting the mixture of western European and Near Eastern forms, the synagogue is particularly expressive of the Jewish diaspora. Temple Emanu-El's main sanctuary rises to 103 feet (St. Patrick's Cathedral, by contrast, is 108 feet high) and holds twenty-five hundred persons. The auditorium is 150 feet long (St. Patrick's nave is 144 feet) and 77 feet wide (St. Patrick's is 48 feet). The side walls, running parallel east-west, are some of the largest load-bearing masonry walls anywhere, supporting huge transverse steel beams. For a people not known for their ecclesiastical architecture, this is pretty heady stuff. Do step inside, entering at 1 East Sixty-fifth Street. The rose window, stained glass, mosaics, and marble and granite podium are otherworldly. Believer or not, you will be transported.

➤ **Walk north on Fifth Avenue one block to Sixty-sixth Street, then east toward Park Avenue.**

Until the mid–nineteenth century, the area between East Sixty-sixth and Sixty-eighth Streets and from Fifth Avenue to Third Avenue was a city park that modified the relentless grid system of the streets in the neighborhood and provided sorely needed public space. Hamilton Park, as it was called, served, on a much smaller scale, many of the same purposes of Central Park today. The area was described in 1807 as "the most elevated of any land on this island south of Harlem [which] commands a superb view of the East River, and the variegated landscape in the vicinity of Hellgate [the narrow strait that connects the East River and Long Island Sound]." Twenty-six lots around the square in 1807 went up for sale with the city's stipulation that the buyers themselves should maintain the square. It was hoped this would preserve the serenity of the neighborhood. Sadly, Hamilton Park was destroyed in 1869, and streets run through it.

At 3 East Sixty-sixth Street was the last home of President Ulysses S. Grant (elected in 1868 and 1872, the latter year over New York's newspaper reformer Horace Greeley), who lived here from 1881 to 1885. He was forced to declare bankruptcy after a disastrous presidency that was marred by scandal, and he retired here to spend his last years and write his personal memoirs. Though he was battling cancer, Grant held on long enough to complete the memoirs, garnering not only favorable reviews but half a million dollars for his family.

Grant is indeed buried in Grant's Tomb. He and his wife are actually lying on polished black sarcophagi at ground level in what is the largest mausoleum in the United States. Later, take a trip uptown (to 122d and Riverside) to see this lovely copy of Mausoleus's tomb at Halicarnassus, one of the seven wonders of the ancient world.

The Lotos Club, dedicated to literature and the fine arts, is directly adjacent to the Grant home, at 5 East Sixty-sixth Street. Built in 1900 as the city residence of William J. Schieffelin, a grandson of John Jay, the club moved here in 1947. Former sites were at Irving Place, Twenty-first Street, Forty-sixth Street, and Fifty-seventh Street. Women were admitted in 1976. The Lotos is one of the oldest literary and arts clubs in the country (founded in 1870). Check out its wooden doors and elegant stonework detail.

Schieffelin was a reformer who is best known for his fierce opposition to Tammany Hall–style corruption in the city. The architect for the house was Richard Howland Hunt, eldest son of Richard Morris Hunt. Richard Howland Hunt carried on the work of the central wing of the Metropolitan Museum of Art after his father's death and, with his brother, Joseph Howland Hunt, continued his father's practice into the 1920s.

Just down the block, at No. 9, is the 1909 Charles and Louise Flagg Scribner House. This townhouse is now Permanent Mission of the Republic of Poland to the United States.

Scribner, the son of the founder of the Scribner company and, by 1879, the president of that firm, married the sister of architect Ernest Flagg, whose housing you can see on "The Other Boroughs: A Driving Tour" (chapter 10). For his sister and brother-in-law, Flagg designed this brick and marble townhouse. The main entry is through an arch designed to allow automobile access; an elevator took the car down to the basement. The facade was restored in 1994.

Be certain to note the lavishly detailed French Gothic cooperative apartment building on the northeast corner of Madison Avenue and Sixty-sixth Street. Check out the windows (twelve panes over twelve panes—see what a difference fenestration makes). When built in 1908, by architects Harde and Short, at the extraordinary cost of $1 million, the building dominated the Madison Avenue brownstones, and its distinctive round-corner tower was unusually prominent. The building was divided into only two apartments with twelve and thirteen rooms respectively—on each floor. The corner tower was occupied by bedrooms; only a handful survive intact. Originally built with no stores, shops were added in 1929. By the 1970s, the owner of the building had allowed it to deteriorate to the point that the tenants went on a rent strike.

Boris Karloff lived here in the early 1940s while per-forming in the Broadway production of *Arsenic and Old Lace*, which ran for 1,444 performances from 1941 to 1944. Architects Harde and Short went on to design Alwyn Court at Fifty-eighth Street and Seventh Avenue, accord-ing to a similarly sumptuous French plan. By the 1910s, however, the fashion for flamboyant design had passed, and subsequent buildings were in the more reserved Renais-sance and Georgian styles (e.g., the Verona on Sixty-fourth and Madison).

➤ **On reaching Park Avenue, cross and walk north along the east side of Park to the Armory.**

The Seventh Regiment Armory, built by Charles Clinton in 1877–79, is the only serious holdover from when the New York Central Railroad came barreling down Fourth Avenue. The socially prominent Seventh Regiment was formed in 1806 and in 1824 became the first regiment to adopt the term *National Guard*. In 1874 the city leased this site to the regiment, which raised the money to build a monumental new armory. The building became a proto-type for the later medieval-inspired armories throughout New York City. The Seventh Regiment Armory, an ex-travagantly turreted red brick and brownstone structure, is a triumph of nineteenth-century architecture and engi-neering. Built in 1877–81, the Park Avenue colossus de-fined the armory as a building type and became the proto-type for armory buildings for the next fifty years.

The wealth and importance of the Seventh Regiment are evident in the decoration of the Armory's interiors, no-tably in the different first-floor regiment rooms, used by of-ficers and the second-floor company rooms. Louis Tiffany, Stanford White, and the Herter Brothers all were responsi-ble for parts of the interior. The drill room, a massive two hundred by three hundred feet and one hundred feet high, is one of the largest unobstructed spaces in New York.

All ten original companies of the regiment commissioned the foremost New York design firms for their second-floor rooms. Most of the rooms were decorated with Renaissance-style woodwork, often with a large fireplace and an ornamented piano alcove. To round things out were ceiling and wall decorations, mirrors, ornate gas and electric chandeliers, ironwork, cast-iron radiators, stained-glass window screens, clocks, armor, decorative hardware, and parquet floors.

And yes, the building is still a living, breathing armory. You will often see National guardsmen mingling here amid Sunday-afternoon antique enthusiasts.

➤ **Continue to walk north on Park Avenue to Sixty-eighth Street. Cross Park to the southwest corner of Park Avenue and Sixty-eighth Street.**

Prior to the 1903 covering up of Park Avenue's train tracks, the avenue served as the structural divider between swanky Fifth Avenue and the poverty of Yorkville, east of Lexington Avenue. A quote from the 1880 *American Architect and Building News* describes one of the Upper East Side squatter areas (East Sixty-seventh and Sixty-eighth Streets) as follows: "The condition of the district is extremely bad, the ground soaked with filth, and the huts unusually crowded and close. It appears that the effluvium which hangs about the place is so offensive that the officers of the neighboring foundling asylum are obliged to keep their windows closed. Mount Sinai Hospital, also, which is situated on high ground nearby, is so invaded by the pestilential atmosphere that erysipelas, dysentery, and diphtheritic troubles are constantly prevalent in the wards nearest the foul village." Times certainly have changed.

The 1920 Delano and Aldrich townhouse at 60 East Sixty-eighth Street was originally the home of Harold Pratt, son of Charles Pratt, whose refining company was famous in its time for Astral Oil. The company eventually merged with the Standard Oil Trust. Harold Pratt was also the founder of the fine arts and design school—Pratt Institute—in Brooklyn.

At present, the building houses the prestigious Council on Foreign Relations (better known as "the Council"), a club for those in elite policy circles (with very strict entry requirements). The Council publishes the bimonthly *Foreign Affairs* magazine. Henry Kissinger can walk from here to his home by the river (River House).

Across the avenue at Sixty-eighth Street is Hunter College of the City University of New York (CUNY). Founded as the Normal College for Women in 1868, a teacher-training institution, in 1914 it was renamed for its first president, Thomas Hunter. By the late 1930s, Hunter was one of the largest women's colleges in the country. (It became co-ed in 1965.) Hunter is considered one of the top schools in the CUNY system. The Clinton administration's Health and Human Services Secretary Donna Shalala was president of Hunter from 1980 to 1987.

➤ **Continue walking north on Park Avenue to Seventy-first Street.**

Here, on the west side of Park between Sixty-eighth and Sixty-ninth Streets, is a splendid block of Georgian buildings: all four built as private homes between 1909 to 1926 and now serving diplomatic or cultural institutions. These include the Spanish Institute, the Italian Cultural Institute, the Italian Consulate, and the Center for Inter-American Relations. The last of these was the former Soviet mission, where Nikita Khrushchev once stood on the balcony and addressed students across the way at Hunter College (the same week as his infamous United Nations "We shall bury you" speech).

These buildings were saved from the wrecking ball in the 1960s by the Marquesa de Cuevas, a Rockefeller who rescued the houses with her magnanimity and handed them over to the organizations that now occupy them.

On the northeast corner of Sixty-ninth Street and Park Avenue, at 701 Park, is the prestigious Union Club. Founded in 1836 by men from the top echelons of New York City's upper crust, it is New York's oldest social club and the infamous one that kept out J. P. Morgan's comrades. Many of the younger clubs in the city are descendants from the Union. One in particular, the Union League Club on Thirty-eighth and Park, was founded by Republicans who left the Union Club in 1863, incensed by its failure to expel Confederate sympathizers. Morgan, we now see, was not alone.

The Asia Society, on the northeast corner of Park and Seventieth Street, was founded in 1956 by John D. Rockefeller III to foster understanding between Asians and Americans (and to have a repository for his massive Asian art collection). Asia House on East Sixty-fourth Street was the first home of the institution. In 1981, the Asia Society moved to this location on Park Avenue, a red sandstone (courtesy of Rajasthan, India) and polished granite (from Oklahoma) building. The combination of stone further illustrates the cooperation between Asia and America. The society currently mounts about four major exhibitions per year, thematically focusing on a country, culture, or medium. Its bookstore has one of the largest selections of books relating to Asia. Under its current expansion, the Society will be able permanently to display the entire Rockefeller collection.

➤ **Walk west on Seventy-first Street one block to Madison Avenue.**

The radio- and television-broadcasting pioneer David Sarnoff lived in the six-story, thirty-room townhouse at 44 East Seventy-first Street for many years, until death in 1971. Sarnoff rose from a $5.50-a-week office boy to chairman of RCA Corporation and later NBC. (See our "Immigrant New York" walk in chapter 2 for information on Sarnoff and the Educational Alliance.) On April 14, 1912, Sarnoff was working at the Marconi station atop Wanamaker's department store on Eighth Street when he picked up a message relayed from ships at sea: "S.S. *Titanic* ran into iceberg, sinking fast." For the next seventy-two hours, the story goes, he remained at his post, giving the world the first authentic news of the disaster.

➤ **Walk one block north on Madison Avenue to Seventy-second Street.**

The Gertrude Rhinelander House, now Polo Ralph Lauren, stands at 867 Madison, on the southeast corner of Seventy-second Street. The Rhinelanders where heavily involved in the colonial-era sugar business. They owned the Rhinelander Sugar House, which was behind the current site of the Municipal Building downtown. During the British occupation of New York City from 1776 to 1783, their warehouse was a brutal prison for American soldiers.

The Rhinelanders parlayed their sugar fortune into vast swathes of land in the then-uninhabited Upper East Side. Alas, Gertrude Rhinelander never had the good fortune to reside here—her husband (a former police commissioner who can be found in the novel *Ragtime*) died while it was being built, and she couldn't afford to keep the home.

➤ **Turn around and walk back down to Seventieth and then west to Fifth Avenue.**

The Frick Collection is located at 1 East Seventieth Street. This Indiana limestone building by Carrere & Hastings, designers of the New York Public Library, is the former home of the art collector, coal magnate, and union buster Henry Clay Frick. He is infamous for helping instigate the crackdown on the Homestead strikers at the Carnegie Steel Plant in Pennsylvania in 1892. Apart from his strike-smashing tendencies, Frick knew his art and was fearful that the Pittsburgh fumes would tarnish his prized works.

The addition on Seventieth Street (finished in 1977) is based on the Grand Trianon at Versailles. In the 1930s, at the time of Frick's wife's passing (Frick himself died in 1919), John Russell Pope turned the building into a museum. The central court with fountain is one of New York City's finest public spaces.

The gallery itself is full of superior works that range from the Renaissance to the nineteenth century (but, according to the gallery's charter, nothing travels). There are several Vermeer, Rembrandt, Titian, Bellini, and other old masters.

➤ **Cross Fifth Avenue and locate the Richard Morris Hunt Memorial directly opposite the Frick between Seventieth and Seventy-first Streets.**

This memorial commemorates one of America's most influential architects. Richard Morris Hunt (1827–95) is known for the base of the Statue of Liberty; the Fifth Avenue facade of the Metropolitan Museum of Art; New York City's "first" apartment house, which stood at 142 East Eighteenth Street (1869–1957); and numerous mansions. To honor Hunt, a founder of the Municipal Art Society and the AIA, colleagues erected this monument in 1898. Daniel Chester French, of Lincoln Memorial fame, sculpted the two female figures (the left representing Art and the right Architecture), as well as the bronze bust of Hunt. Hunt was the first American to be trained at the famed École des Beaux Arts in Paris. He is perhaps best known for his work at the World's Columbian Exposition of 1893 in Chicago (the "White City")—an array of buildings designed in classical style, turning America toward visions of European splendor. A replica of one of these buildings is being held in the hands of the female figure on the right.

One of Hunt's greatest works was the Lenox Library, which stood on the current site of the Frick Gallery until it was destroyed in 1912. In 1895 the library merged with the Tilden Trust and the Astor Library to form the New York Public Library.

➤ **Walk north along Fifth Avenue to Seventy-third Street.**

Arnold Rothstein—the infamous gambler and underworld mobster who allegedly fixed the notorious Black Sox 1919 World Series—lived at 912 Fifth Avenue (between Seventy-second and Seventy-third Streets) with his wife during the last few years of his life. A favorite of writers, Rothstein was Meyer Wolfsheim in *The Great Gatsby* and Nathan Detroit in *Guys and Dolls*. He was murdered at age forty-six on Election Day in November 1928 at the Park Central Hotel. True to form, Rothstein had bet heavily on the election—had he lived, he would have collected $570,000. His murder remains officially unsolved.

➤ **At Seventy-third Street, take a brief detour to 11 East Seventy-third.**

244 THE UPPER EAST SIDE | Manhattan's "Gold Coast"

After his house on East Fifty-fifth Street burned down in 1900, Joseph Pulitzer had Stanford White build him a large, new, fireproof home here, at 11 East Seventy-third Street. Borrowing from seventeenth-century Venetian architecture (White was a master for interpreting historical styles), the architect built one of New York's finest urban mansions.

As an owner and publisher, Pulitzer made the *St. Louis Post-Dispatch* a phenomenally successful newspaper, later purchasing the *New York World*. His notorious methods of popularizing the paper included the use of illustrations, news stunts, crusades against corruption, and cartoons, as well as aggressive news coverage.

Pulitzer was so sensitive to noise that he had a sound-proof wing, set on ball bearings, added to the rear of his home in 1904. He lived there until his death in 1911, after which the building was eventually converted to apartments.

➤ **Return to Fifth Avenue and continue north two blocks to East Seventy-fifth Street.**

The mansion at 1 East Seventy-fifth Street is the 1909 Edward S. Harkness House, built by James Gamble Rogers. This elegant five-story neo-Renaissance mansion of Tennessee marble is now home to the Commonwealth Fund. It is said that the beautiful wrought-iron fence surrounding the mansion on both sides was a gift by the emperor of Japan, in gratitude for the fuel Standard Oil provided to the Japanese Navy during the 1904–5 Russo-Japanese War.

Harkness, the son of one of the six original partners in Standard Oil, not only invested his inheritance but, more important, gave most of it away, possibly some $130 million. The noted philanthropist gave much of his largesse to

Fifth Avenue and Fifty-second Street in 1885. The corner mansion, designed by Richard Morris Hunt, was home to William K. Vanderbilt, the grandson of Cornelius Vanderbilt. Photo courtesy of the New-York Historical Society.

the Commonwealth Fund to improve children's health and rural hospitals, to the Columbia-Presbyterian Hospital, and to the Metropolitan Museum of Art.

Harkness was also a well-known patron of Yale University. In fact, he was so fond of his architect, James Rogers, that he had him build ten of the residential colleges at Yale. Boola boola!

➤ **Walk along Seventy-fifth Street to Madison Avenue.**

Across Madison Avenue is the imposing, and perhaps out-of-place, Whitney Museum of American Art. Designed by Bauhaus architect Marcel Breuer and built between 1963 to 1966, the Whitney houses the twentieth-century art collection of Gertrude Vanderbilt Whitney (1875–1942).

Gertrude was the great-granddaughter of Cornelius Vanderbilt, a Staten Island farmer who ran ferries to Manhattan in the early nineteenth century. His business expanded into steamships (giving Cornelius the nickname "Commodore") and, later, to a vast network of railroads (discussed earlier along Park Avenue). Gertrude, the daughter of Cornelius Vanderbilt II, grew up in the manor we began our tour with—the 137-room mansion at Fifth Avenue and Fifty-seventh Street, now the site of Bergdorf Goodman. Her marriage to Harry Whitney took place at The Breakers, the Vanderbilts' 70-room Newport summer cottage.

Whitney was a sculptor and patron of American art and bought and exhibited painters such as John Sloan, Edward Hopper, and Stuart Davis early in their careers. By 1929 her collection contained hundreds of twentieth-century master works. At that time she approached the Metropolitan Museum of Art to see if they had interest in permanently exhibiting her collection; the Met declined her offer. Whitney instead decided to exhibit her collection on its own merits and set up a museum that placed primacy on latter-day artists.

As you have seen on your walk, the Upper East Side is more than an area with attractive mansions and town-houses, although it certainly has more of these than any other part of New York City. Like other neighborhoods, the Upper East Side has changed from fields and hills to apartments and restaurants. As we've noted, it moved from mansions to apartment buildings on Fifth Avenue; from residential to commercial development on Madison Avenue; from dirt road to railroad to boulevard on Park Avenue. Although the neighborhood seems "stable," that word is fraught with all sorts of baggage. There is no telling what the Upper East Side will look like fifty or one hundred years from now, or even if many people will remember that it used to be known as the silk-stocking district.

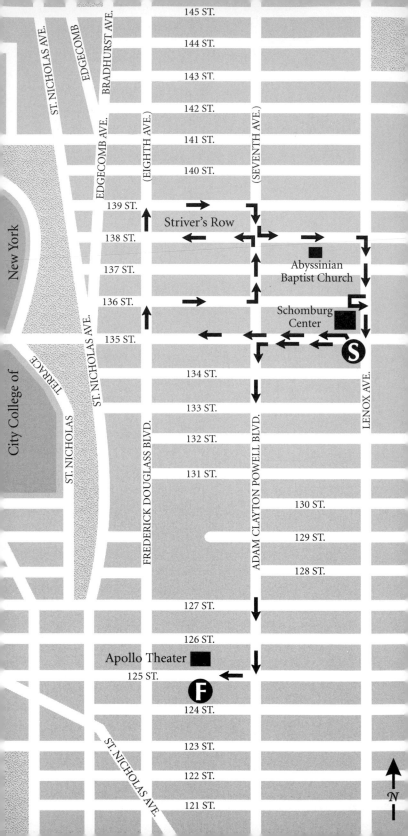

8 HISTORIC HARLEM

African American Capital of the Twentieth Century

➤ Start: The corner of 135th Street and Lenox Avenue, at the 2/3 subway stop.

"THERE IS SO much to see in Harlem," said the poet Langston Hughes. Some seventy years later, this still rings true. Bounded by the Harlem River, 110th Street, St. Nicholas Avenue, and Fifth Avenue, Harlem is home to some of the most beautiful architecture, interesting topography, and diverse history in the city. This tour could easily look at Harlem as an Italian, Jewish, elite Protestant, or Latino community. But Harlem is best known as the African American capital city. Concentrating on Central Harlem, this tour serves as an introduction to the African American history and culture of this neighborhood.

In 1658, a group of Dutch farmers settled in an area of northern Manhattan whose landscape reminded them of the Holland town of Haarlem. Their new settlement, which they christened "Nieuw Haarlem," was a distant nine miles away from New York City, which was then clustered around the southern tip of Manhattan Island. During the eighteeth century, elite New Yorkers began to establish country estates and working farms in Harlem. (The name was Anglicized after Dutch rule ceded to British in 1664.) One such estate was owned by Alexander Hamilton, who gave his name to the neighborhood Hamilton Heights, which was once his land. His home, Hamilton Grange, still stands as a monument to this area's colonial past.

Eventually, the gentlemen farmers overworked the land, and during the antebellum period Harlem became home to poor farmers and Irish squatters. But the late nineteenth century would again see Harlem emerge as an elite enclave, as advances in transportation, including the extension of elevated railroads, prompted real estate developers to look toward the unimproved lands of northern Manhattan. Charming brownstones were constructed for wealthy white Protestants and German Jews from downtown. Harlem became a genteel suburb, a haven from the over-crowded city.

The extension of the subway line up Lenox Avenue in 1904 encouraged another wave of speculative building in Harlem, especially above 130th Street. This boom included many apartment buildings. Some new immigrants, up-wardly mobile Jews and Italians, did take advantage of the housing opportunities in Harlem; in fact, vestiges of a thriving Italian community are still evident today in East Harlem. But real estate developers overspeculated and overbuilt. They simply could not fill their properties.

The depressed real estate market coincided with a major influx of African Americans to New York City. Southern blacks, fleeing racial violence and seeking eco-nomic opportunity, began migrating en masse to north-ern cities in the beginning of the twentieth century. At the same time, African Americans were being squeezed out of their neighborhoods on the west side of Midtown Manhattan. For years, white real estate developers, pres-sured by white Harlemites, had refused to rent or sell to blacks. But empty buildings and the urging of black entrepreneurs eventually convinced them to change their policies. In the first decade of the twentieth century, the Harlem housing market was opened to blacks. When their efforts to stem the tide of black in-migration failed, most white Harlemites moved out.

By the 1920s, Harlem, especially above 125th Street, was the undisputed capital of Afro-America, home to its political institutions and cultural life. During that decade, Harlem's nightlife became legendary, as did a tremendous outpouring of African American arts and letters, known as the Harlem Renaissance. The Great Depression of the 1930s, however, brought hard times to Harlem, including high unemployment and a race riot in 1935. During the subsequent decades, many middle-class blacks moved out of the neighborhood. Harlem's economy was further sapped during the postwar period, as local and federal government policies diverted money from the area. The neighborhood began a steady decline that it only recently has started to reverse. In 1920, black leader James Weldon Johnson wrote: "Will Harlem become merely a famous ghetto, or will it be a center of intellectual, cultural, and economic forces exerting an influence throughout the world—especially upon Negroe [sic] peoples?" Harlem has been all these things. A walk through the neighborhood shows its diverse and exciting history.

A note on street names: after the civil rights movement of the 1960s, the names of many of Harlem's streets were changed to honor prominent African Americans. Eighth Avenue became Frederick Douglass Boulevard; Seventh Avenue was renamed Adam Clayton Powell, Jr., Boulevard; and Sixth Avenue, originally named Lenox Avenue, became Malcolm X Boulevard, while 125th Street was renamed after Martin Luther King, Jr.

➢ We begin our tour on the northwest corner of 135th Street and Lenox Avenue. Walk west toward Adam Clayton Powell, Jr., Boulevard.

Notice the row of tenement houses (Nos. 107–145) on the north side of the street. Although these apartments were constructed in 1905 to house middle-class and ambitious working-class whites, the real estate depression of the early twentieth century meant that many apartments remained vacant. The owner refused to rent to African Americans, who were beginning to occupy buildings east of Lenox Avenue.

When St. Philip's Episcopal Church, a black congregation from the Tenderloin, decided to move to Harlem in 1911, it purchased these tenements. The Reverend Hutchens Bishop, the pastor of St. Philip's, recognized that his parishioners would have difficulty in the restricted housing market of Harlem. Bishop, a light-skinned man, managed to purchase this real estate because the developers who sold it to him thought he was white. As a result of this transaction, the color line west of Lenox Avenue was broken, paving the way for the development of Black Harlem.

St. Philip's, located at 210–216 West 134th Street, is still a prominent congregation and major real estate owner in Harlem. In recent years, St. Philip's has raised more than $30 million to construct and renovate low-income housing in the neighborhood.

➢ Walk west to the southwest corner of 135th Street and Adam Clayton Powell, Jr., Boulevard, an intersection that served as the institutional hub of Harlem during the 1920s and 1930s.

In the 1920s and 1930s, within a stone's throw one could find the headquarters of the NAACP (National Associa-

Speculative building at 25-53 West 133rd Street. These three-story brown-stones, built around 1877, were part of the great Harlem land rush that foresaw the connection of Harlem to Lower Manhattan via the newly developed elevated rail lines. Photo courtesy of the New-York Historical Society.

tion for the Advancement of Colored People), the National Urban League, and the Universal Negro Improvement Association, all sites we will see later in the tour. Also close by were the offices of the major black newspapers—the conservative *Amsterdam News* and the more militant *New York Age*—the New York Public Library, and the YMCA (Young Men's Christian Association). By 1920, Harlem had become New York's primary African American neighborhood, and most black political and social institutions had moved here by that decade.

The YMCA is located at 181 West 135th Street. Founded in 1851 to provide moral and spiritual guidance to young male migrants from rural areas, the YMCA's membership and outreach efforts were restricted to white men until 1867. A "colored men's branch" of the Y opened on West Fifty-third Street in 1900, to serve the needs of migrants from the South. It moved to this location in 1919. So great were the demands on the services of this YMCA that an annex was built across the street in 1932.

This particular branch of the Y also served as a hotel for black visitors to New York City who were denied access to the segregated hotels elsewhere. Among its guests were Ralph Ellison, Langston Hughes, and James Baldwin. During the Harlem Renaissance, the literati met here to exchange ideas. The YMCA's Little Theater program started the careers of actors such as Sidney Poitier, Eartha Kitt, Cicely Tyson, and Danny Glover. Other patrons of the Y who would go on to prominence include Jackie Robinson, Richard Wright, Paul Robeson, Jesse Owens, Bill "Bojangles" Robinson, and Willie Mays.

Although the building is empty now, at 2294 ½ Adam Clayton Powell, Jr. Boulevard, on the southwest corner of 135th Street, was Ed Small's Paradise, one of Harlem's most popular jazz clubs and restaurants from the 1920s to the 1940s. Those who could afford the prices at the "Hottest Spot in Harlem" would be treated to music, elaborate floor shows, and singing waiters. The small dance floor at Small's Paradise got so crowded that each patron was said to have a dime's worth of floor space for dancing. A young Malcolm Little, after losing his job as a waiter here, began a downward spiral into criminality that eventually landed him in jail. There he converted to Islam and changed his name to Malcolm X. In the 1960s, basketball star Wilt Chamberlain reopened the restaurant as Big Wilt's Small's Paradise.

➤ **Cross Adam Clayton Powell, Jr., Boulevard to the northwest corner and continue west on 135th Street one block.**

As you walk west, and just after you cross 135th Street, notice the Big Apple plaque on the side of 2300 Adam Clayton Powell, Jr., Boulevard. Beginning in the 1930s, this building housed the Big Apple Restaurant and Jazz Club. In recognition of its status as a center of jazz, musicians dubbed New York the "Big Apple." The phrase stuck as a moniker for the city as well as for this club, although research has also turned up references to the city as the Big Apple in horse-racing columns two decades earlier.

To your left, across the street, you will see what was 220 West 135th Street, the former home of Florence Mills, one of the most popular singers and dancers of the 1920s. An international star, Mills performed on Broadway as well as in productions abroad. Hoping that her success would make "people think better of other colored folk," Mills passed over an offer to perform in the Ziegfeld Follies in order to participate in an all-black revue. Mills was a true pioneer, paving the way for other black women entertainers such as Josephine Baker. She died of appendicitis in 1927, at the age of thirty-one. Her funeral was the largest in Harlem's history: more than 5,000 mourners filled Harlem's Mother Zion AME Church for her funeral service and more than 150,000 followed the funeral cortege through the streets of Harlem. At the cemetery, a low-flying plane released a flock of blackbirds as a final goodbye.

Right next door is 224 West 135th Street, the former headquarters of the NAACP, now Flo's Beauty Salon. The interracial NAACP, formed in 1909, has historically fought, through judicial and legislative channels, for voting rights, integration, and equal educational and economic opportunity for African Americans. *The Crisis*, the monthly publication of the NAACP, had a circulation of more than one hundred thousand by 1920. Edited by civil rights leader W. E. B. Du Bois from 1909 to 1934, *The Crisis* was one of many important periodicals produced in Harlem in the early twentieth century.

The NAACP's Legal Defense and Education Fund, established in 1939, would go on to try the landmark *Brown*

Florence Mills (1895–1927), one of the most popular singers and dancers of the 1920s, best known for her role in **Blackbirds** at the Alhambra Theatre and later in Paris and London. She died suddenly in the fall of 1927 of appendicitis. Her funeral was one of the most spectacular in Harlem's history, with more than five thousand in attendance and one hundred thousand lining the streets. Photo courtesy of the Schomberg Center for Research in Black Culture, New York Public Library.

vs. Board of Education case of 1954. Legal Director Thurgood Marshall's argument before the Supreme Court led to nationwide school integration and sparked the legal phase of the civil rights movement. In 1965, Marshall became the first African American justice to be appointed to the United States Supreme Court.

➤ **Turn right on Frederick Douglass Boulevard and walk one block. Turn right on 136th Street, walking back to Adam Clayton Powell, Jr., Boulevard, on the north side of the street.**

Unfortunately, one of the most important building sites on this block, 267 West 136th Street, is now a parking lot. During the 1920s, this was a boarding house occupied entirely by members of the vanguard wing of the Harlem Renaissance. Zora Neale Hurston, Langston Hughes, painters Bruce Nugent and Aaron Douglas, and novelist Wallace Thurman—the de facto leader of this radical group—all called "267 House" their home. Far more interested in exploring bohemian themes in his work than African American ones, Thurman resisted the notion that African American artists had to represent their race in their art. He mocked the Harlem Renaissance leaders who believed that civil rights would be gained through African American cultural production. Thurman and Hurston called these types "the Niggerati." While none of the niggerati lived at 267 House, the radical residents of the house self-deprecatingly called their boarding home "Niggerati Manor."

HARLEM RENAISSANCE

The 1920s was a golden age for Harlem. By then the preeminent African American community, Harlem provided entertainments unrivaled elsewhere. Harlem was arguably the center of black political life as well. Some of the most important black newspapers and periodicals were produced here, and the most prominent African American leaders in the country worked and lived in Harlem. All these factors contributed to making Harlem ripe for the explosion of African American art and literature known as the Harlem Renaissance.

The Harlem Renaissance was not a spontaneous burst of artistic expression. In many ways it was a political movement. Black intellectuals such as W. E. B. Du Bois, Charles Johnson, and Alain Locke promoted the notion that African Americans could gain equality and respect through arts and letters. They believed that when they saw the cultural contribution of African Americans, white Americans would naturally see blacks as their equals. The stakes were particularly high in the 1920s, a nadir in American race relations. Lynching was epidemic; economic and educational opportunities remained closed to African Americans; and the summer of 1919 saw so many bloody race riots across the country that it became known as the "Red Summer." Although these incidents were called riots, they were essentially sanctioned and generally unprovoked violence by whites against blacks.

Part of the reason for the volume of literary and artistic output during the Harlem Renaissance was the sponsorship available. Civil rights organizations joined black and white philanthropists in encouraging and funding artistic endeavors. **The Crisis** and **Opportunity,** the magazines of the NAACP and Urban League, sponsored literary contests; black leaders such as Alain Locke and Jesse Fauset sought wealthy patrons; the YMCA and the New York Public Library served as gathering places for writers and artists; and relaxation and intellectual stimulation could be found at the parties and salons of A'Lelia Walker Robinson.

Some of the central writers of the Harlem Renaissance included Langston Hughes, Claude MacKay, Zora Neale Hurston, Nella Larsen, Countee Cullen (the only native New Yorker in the bunch), and Wallace Thurman, the leader of the movement's avant-garde wing. Important visual artists were involved as well, including sculptor Augusta Savage, photographer James Van-DerZee, and painters Bruce Nugent and Aaron Douglas (who created many of the book jackets of the period). Yet, while the writers and artists were black, the publishers and patrons were almost entirely white. This dichotomy led many to argue that the Harlem Renaissance did not produce a "true" black form of expression;

rather, it catered to a white audience and a "white" view of black aesthetic forms.

This was not the only point of debate in the Harlem Renaissance. Far from a monolithic movement, the Renaissance fostered great discussion over the role and responsibility of the black artist and produced a wide diversity of artistic and literary expression. While Cullen and MacKay explored African American themes through traditional European literary forms, Hughes and Hurston referenced black folk expressions in their work. Meanwhile, Thurman and Nugent, both homosexual, explored bohemian themes in their art and ignored issues of race as much as they could. Alain Locke strongly disagreed with them, believing that black artists should create a uniquely black art, drawing on African models rather than European ones. Du Bois held that African Americans had a responsibility to be propagandists for their race, but he eschewed "folk" forms. In terms of music, for example, Du Bois believed that African Americans should record classical works but that jazz music, reliant on Southern black folk expressions, was not elevated enough to lift up the race. Debates of this sort did not end with the Harlem Renaissance. The question of black artists' responsibility—to their race or solely to themselves and their art—still troubles black artists and entertainers today.

While African American artists and writers have continued to produce works of excellence, the patronage and sponsorship behind the Renaissance dried up during the economic depression of the 1930s. But the Harlem Renaissance produced some of the most respected and enduring American art and literature of the twentieth century.

> **Continue east on 136th Street.**

For a brief period in the 1930s, 239 West 136th Street was the headquarters of the Brotherhood of Sleeping Car Porters (BSCP). At the time, virtually all railroad porters

were black men, for whom these jobs were high-status positions leading to a middle-class lifestyle. The BSCP, led by
A. Philip Randolph, was the nation's first African American labor union. Its most significant and prolonged campaign was its struggle (won finally in 1937) to gain official
recognition from the Pullman Company.

➤ **Cross to the north side of 136th Street and continue walking east.**

At 204 West 136th is the Manhattan branch of the National
Urban League (although the sign on the building may be
hard to see and lies on a newer concrete annex). Founded in
1911, the league has sponsored community improvement
programs and civil rights initiatives. During the Harlem
Renaissance, the Urban League's publication, *Opportunity:
A Journal of Negro Life* featured the works of writers such
as Zora Neale Hurston, along with other issues of interest
to African Americans.

➤ **Walk north along Adam Clayton Powell, Jr., Boulevard
and turn left onto 138th Street.**

The area bounded by 138th and 139th Streets and Adam
Clayton Powell, Jr., and Frederick Douglass Boulevards
comprises the St. Nicholas Historic District. Originally
known as the King Model Houses, these brownstones and
apartment buildings were the project of real estate developer David H. King. In 1890, King bought this large plot of
land from the Equitable Life Assurance Company and
commissioned three prominent architectural firms to design affordable, attractive homes for white middle-class
New Yorkers. The resulting blocks are some of the loveli-
est residential streets in the city. The alleys between and behind the buildings are a rarity in New York. Garbage and

delivery vehicles are diverted to the alleys, leaving the streets relatively free of congestion, noise, and dirt.

Due to the economic depression of the 1890s, King was able to sell only nine units of the 146 rowhouses and three apartment buildings. In 1895, Equitable foreclosed on the mortgage and took over the buildings. In the 1920s, after restricting them to whites for years, Equitable began to sell the buildings to African Americans. While some black professionals purchased homes on these blocks, most of the owners were members of the black working class, including laundresses, railroad porters, hairdressers, domestic servants, and elevator operators. They converted most of the homes into rooming houses. During this period, these streets became known as "Strivers' Row," reflecting the ambition of those who managed to reside here. As you walk west on 138th Street, notice the signs on the gateposts asking you to "Walk Your Horses."

➤ **Continue west on 138th Street to Frederick Douglass Boulevard. Walk north, stopping at the southeast corner of 139th Street.**

You are standing at the eastern edge of the neighborhood known as Sugar Hill. If Strivers' Row was for those who were working hard to make it, Sugar Hill was for those who had succeeded. The exquisite rowhouses and apartment buildings of this area were originally occupied by white professionals, but as the boundaries of Black Harlem pushed outward, whites fled and wealthy blacks moved in. "Sugar," slang for money, was found in abundance in this neighborhood, giving it its nickname in the 1920s. Wealthy denizens included Lena Horne, black socialite A'Lelia Walker Robinson, and NAACP officers W. E. B. Du Bois, Walter White, Thurgood Marshall, and Roy Wilkins. In the 1980s, the rap band the Sugarhill Gang made their neighborhood a household name when they released "Rapper's Delight," the first rap song to cross over to the pop charts. Sugar Hill is part of the neighborhood known as Hamilton Heights, which was once the country estate of Alexander Hamilton.

Looking west and up the hill from the corner, you will notice the impressive Gothic building with the white trim. This is Shepard Hall, the main building of the City College of New York (CCNY), one of the nineteen colleges that make up the City University of New York system. Established in 1847 as the Free Academy, CCNY has historically provided educational opportunities for immigrant workers and their children. In the period after World War I, CCNY gained a reputation for academic excellence and for a time was known as the "People's Harvard." City College has graduated eight Nobel laureates, more than any other public college in the United States. Its famous alumni include Upton Sinclair, Felix Frankfurter, Ira Gershwin, A. Philip Randolph, Jonas Salk, Ed Koch, and Colin Powell.

When CCNY moved to this location in 1902, the city was in the process of building the subway system. The Manhattan schist that they excavated, the bedrock of Manhattan Island, was used to construct Shepard Hall and other CCNY buildings.

➤ **Continue walking east on the north side of 139th Street, looking at the darker brown buildings.**

This side of the street was designed by Stanford White, perhaps the best-known architect of the late nineteenth century. (See our Four Squares walk in chapter 4 for White's interesting life and famous murder.)

➤ **Take a right on Adam Clayton Powell, Jr., Boulevard and walk south to 138th Street.**

On the southeast corner (formerly 2341–2359 Adam Clayton Powell, Jr., Boulevard) of the intersection is the original Renaissance Theater, Ballroom, and Casino, known locally as "the Renny." From the 1920s to the 1950s, the Renny was one of the most popular nightclubs in Harlem. It was also the home of the Rennies, the nation's first all-black professional basketball team, founded in 1923. Like most sports, professional basketball was segregated in the early part of the twentieth century. The Rennies were known during the 1930s as the best team in the world. When they stopped playing in 1940, they had an astounding record of 2,558 wins and only 592 losses.

➤ **Continue walking east, on the south side of 138th Street, one block to Lenox Avenue.**

You will pass Abyssinian Baptist Church (136–142 West 138th Street), one of the oldest and largest Protestant churches in the United States. In 1808 a group of free blacks protesting segregated seating in the First Baptist Church of New York City formed Abyssinian with a group of Ethiopian merchants. Their first church was on present-day Worth Street in Lower Manhattan. Eventually they moved to Waverly Place in Greenwich Village and then to West Fortieth Street. The Reverend Adam Clayton Powell Sr., who became pastor of Abyssinian in 1908, raised money to move the church to this location in 1920.

By 1937, when Powell turned the pulpit over to his son Adam Clayton Powell Jr., the congregation had a membership of seven thousand, making it the largest Protestant congregation in the country. Powell Sr. was active in civil rights activities as well as spiritual guidance. His son continued in this tradition, serving as pastor of Abyssinian as well as becoming the first African American congressman, representing Harlem in the U.S. House of Representatives from 1944 to 1970. His successors, Samuel DeWitt Proctor and Calvin O. Butts III, the current pastor of Abyssinian, have also involved themselves and their church in political activism and community service. Abyssinian continues to be one of the most influential American churches, serving thousands of members and alumni and taking an active role in Harlem's development through its business arm, the Abyssinian Development Corporation (ADC). One of the ADC's many properties is the Renaissance Ballroom, which it plans to renovate and reopen as a reception hall.

BLACK MANHATTAN

Before there was an English presence in New York, there was an African one. Dutch settlers brought African slaves to New Amsterdam as early as 1644. Both the free-black and slave populations grew. As late as 1760 the city was home to the highest number of blacks in any urban area and had the highest or second-highest ratio of slave to free in all the colonies. People of African descent comprised at least 15 percent of the city's population before the Revolutionary War.

While slaves lived with their masters, free blacks lived in small enclaves on the outskirts of town. As the center of population moved up Manhattan Island, African Americans were pushed out of their neighborhoods and forced to the periphery, where one "Little Africa" after another was formed. Certain streets in these districts were predominantly African American, but blacks in these neighborhoods were surrounded by nonblack neighbors, mainly working-class immigrant families.

Interracial violence was frequent and tended to accelerate African American movement throughout the city, from the Wall Street area, to Greenwich Village, to the neighborhood in the West Thirties known as the Tenderloin and the San Juan Hill neighborhood in the West Fifties. A race riot in the Tenderloin in 1900 was one factor among many that led African Americans to look for new housing options. El and subway construction as well as the building of Penn Station, completed in 1911, also pushed many blacks out of their homes in the Tenderloin. Added to this was a significant increase in the black population of New York City in the late nineteenth and early twentieth centuries.

The mechanization of agriculture led to massive unemployment for Southern blacks. Seeking economic opportunity in the North and fleeing antiblack violence in the South, African Americans began the trek northward. Joining the Southern migrants, particularly during the 1920s, were forty thousand black immigrants from the West Indies. The black population of New York City, about 60,000 in 1900, had jumped to over 320,000 by 1930.

Meanwhile, the speculative real estate boom of the early twentieth century led to many an empty apartment building in Harlem. Harlem real estate developers had intended to construct a white middle-class residential community. But white middle-class tenants failed to materialize. At first, landlords and real estate developers banded together with white Harlemites to block African Americans from moving into Harlem. But the landlords' greed eventually trumped their racism. Not only did they want to fill their empty units, but they recognized that they could get well above market value if they opened their buildings to African Americans. Because their housing opportunities were limited in New York, blacks were often forced to pay higher rents than whites. African Americans moved into Harlem, and whites immediately began to move out. By 1920, 70 percent of New York City's blacks lived in Harlem.

While landlords charged exorbitant rents to African Americans, generally 10 percent above market value, blacks enjoyed far better housing in Harlem than ever before. African Americans took in lodgers, lived with extended family and friends, and had monthly parties to pay the rent. Along with the black real estate agents who managed white-owned buildings and the black churches who bought tenements to house their parishioners, African American Harlemites would create the largest urban black community in the United States.

In the 1920s, 120 West 138th Street was the site of Liberty Hall, the Harlem headquarters of Marcus Garvey's Universal Negro Improvement Association (UNIA). Garvey was a flamboyant, charismatic, and extremely popular figure who arrived in New York from Jamaica in 1917. Important for many reasons, Garvey also reminds us of the central and assertive role played by West Indian immigrants in Harlem life. Initially influenced by the self-help doctrines and racial accommodationist stance of Booker T. Washington, Garvey became a proponent of black pride and pan-Africanism. The UNIA, an international organization, had a huge national membership, appealing, unlike other civil rights organizations, to the Southern migrants and Caribbean immigrants who made up the black working class. The Harlem branch of the UNIA, the country's largest, had more than forty thousand members.

Garvey's political activities and stance made him enemies among other black leaders, including A. Philip Randolph, James Weldon Johnson, and W. E. B. Du Bois. Du Bois particularly took issue with Garvey's image and separatist stance. But in the end, Garvey was defeated by the white power structure. Arrested on trumped-up charges of mail fraud in 1923, Garvey was convicted in 1927. His subsequent deportation to Jamaica effectively ended his activities in the United States. But Garvey left a strong legacy behind and would eventually prove a major influence on the black nationalist movements of the 1960s and 1970s.

Lenox Avenue was the site of all the major parades through Harlem in the early decades of the twentieth century, including the frequent and colorful pageants orchestrated by the UNIA. In July 1917, W. E. B. Du Bois, James Weldon Johnson, and other NAACP officers led ten thousand people down Lenox Avenue in a solemn protest march. Three weeks before, in East St. Louis, Illinois, nearly two hundred African Americans had died and six

Silent Protest parade on Fifth Avenue, July 28, 1917, in response to the East St. Louis race riot. In front row are James Weldon Johnson (far right), W. E. B. Du Bois (second from right), Rev. Hutchens Chew Bishop, rector of St. Philip's Episcopal Church (Harlem), and realtor John E. Nail. Photo courtesy of the Schomberg Center for Research in Black Culture, New York Public Library.

thousand were burned out of their homes in the worst race riot in American history. The Harlem protesters walked in silence, bearing signs proclaiming "Thou Shalt Not Kill" and "Mr. President, Why Not Make America Safe for Democracy?"

The hypocrisy on the part of the federal government—fighting a war abroad in the name of liberty and freedom while refusing to address civil rights at home—led many African Americans to question whether they should participate in World War I. The black leadership was unsure as well. President Woodrow Wilson appealed to them to encourage African Americans to support the war, promising attention to civil rights issues in exchange. In the end, black Americans did fight in the war. Indeed, the 369th Regiment, an all-black unit from Harlem, became the most highly decorated American unit and the only one awarded the French croix de guerre. The 369th, known as the "Harlem Hellfighters," returned home triumphantly in February 1919 to a parade through Manhattan. When they crossed 110th Street and turned onto Lenox Avenue, the parade became a party as they were greeted by friends, family, and great cheers in Harlem.

The federal government reneged on its promise to address civil rights issues, but black participation in World War I did contribute to a more assertive, more militant stance among African Americans. Black soldiers found that they had received better treatment abroad than they did at home, and many refused to adhere any longer to the "wait-and-see" attitude promoted by nineteenth-century black leader Booker T. Washington. The "New Negro," scholar Alain Locke noted in his 1925 essay of that name, would take a much more immediatist stance. The ramifications of this position would be seen in the artistic outpouring of the 1920s and in the protest movements of the subsequent decades.

➤ Walk south on Lenox Avenue three blocks toward 135th Street. At 136th Street, take a slight detour west to the Countee Cullen Branch of the New York Public Library at 104 West 136th. (Look for the library flag hanging from the building on the south side of the street.)

The library stands on the site of the former home of Madame C. J. Walker, the richest self-made woman in early twentieth-century America. Born in the South, Walker made her fortune developing and selling hair straighteners, skin lighteners, and other beauty products for African American women. In 1916, already a wealthy woman, she moved to New York and built a home, beauty salon, and school here. Walker was also involved in politics and civil rights activism. She led a delegation of women to see Pres-

A'Lelia Walker Robinson (1866-1931) was the daughter of Madame C. J. Walker, who became the wealthiest self-made woman in early twentieth-century America through her beauty parlor products business. Robinson was known for her lavish lifestyle and elaborate parties and regularly hosted salons for literary figures of the Harlem Renaissance. In 1927 she converted one floor of her home into the "Dark Tower," a coffee house where artists were quickly outnumbered by wealthy and prominent New Yorkers. Photo courtesy of the Schomberg Center for Research in Black Culture, New York Public Library.

ident Woodrow Wilson to protest segregation in the military and gave significant sums of money to charities and civil rights organizations.

Her daughter A'Lelia Walker Robinson was known for her lavish lifestyle and elaborate parties. She hosted salons for literary figures of the Harlem Renaissance and fetes for diverse guests. Perhaps her most legendary party was when she served African Americans caviar and champagne while whites, seated at a separate table, received chit'lins and bathtub gin. In 1927 she converted one floor of this home into the "Dark Tower," a coffeehouse where artists could gather around inexpensive refreshments and exchange ideas. But the bohemian types for whom the place was originally intended could barely fit in the room, so full was it of wealthy and prominent New Yorkers, and the prices were well out of reach for any but the latter.

Despite the failure of the Dark Tower, Robinson was central to the cultural life of Harlem. Langston Hughes claimed that, more than any other event, her death in 1931 marked the end of the Harlem Renaissance.

➤ **Walk back to Lenox Avenue and continue south to 135th Street.**

On the northwest corner of 135th and Lenox, you will find the New York Public Library's Schomburg Center for Research in Black Culture, the premier research library for black history and culture. Arturo Schomburg, a Puerto Rican black, spent his life amassing a huge collection of books, pamphlets, manuscripts, and visual materials pertaining to the African and African American past. He began this endeavor in response to an elementary school teacher who claimed blacks had produced nothing worth studying. Schomburg proved him wrong. When the New York Public Library purchased Schomburg's collection in 1926, it consisted of five thousand items. It now has over 5 million. Schomburg himself played a major role in the Harlem Renaissance, sponsoring readings and literary salons as well as serving as curator of his collection for the New York Public Library.

You are standing on an important speakers' corner for soapbox orators of the early twentieth century. Legend has it that Marcus Garvey, on arriving in Harlem, stole the soapbox here from A. Philip Randolph. Both men were frequently seen and heard at this corner, which was also the first view of Harlem for most Southern migrants. From Penn Station, they took the IRT to 135th and Lenox and exited the subway into another world.

Southern blacks expressed awe at this black city within the city. If they craved a reminder from home, they could stop at the stand of Pig Foot Mary, located on the southeast corner. Born Lillian Harris, Pig Foot Mary sold Southern-style comfort food, such as pig's feet and chit'lins. Starting with $3 and a folding table on the street, Harris eventually made enough money to become a major real estate investor and Harlem philanthropist.

➤ **Walk west along 135th Street one block. Turn left on Adam Clayton Powell, Jr., Boulevard and walk to 125th Street.**

This was the stretch for strollers on Sunday afternoons and the "Great Black Way," named for the concentration of theaters and nightclubs along it. The block of 133rd Street between Adam Clayton Powell, Jr., Boulevard and Lenox Avenue was known during the 1920s, 1930s, and 1940s as "Jungle Alley." Here, downtown whites attracted to Harlem nightlife could live out their exoticized fantasies of black culture. Although adventurous and wealthy whites visited Harlem, there was not a great fostering of intercultural understanding in Harlem's nightclubs. Many, such as the Cotton Club and Connie's Inn (both since demolished), refused service to blacks, including the entertainers who performed on their stages. But most of the clubs along Jungle Alley catered to a mixed clientele, and unlike the Cotton Club and Connie's, some of the Jungle Alley spots were owned by black proprietors. Nevertheless, they all provided a white-inspired view of primitive, exotic Black

America. Scantily clad women would gyrate on stage to heavy percussion amid jungle decor. These scenes bore little resemblance to the reality displayed at neighborhood joints such as Small's Paradise and the Renny.

Williams Christian Methodist Church, located at 2225 on the east side of Adam Clayton Powell, Jr., Boulevard, is the former site of the Lafayette Theater. Opened in 1912, the Lafayette was one of the few integrated theaters in New York City. While the theater presented the same minstrel-style, all-black revues popular elsewhere, it did provide, in the early twentieth century, one of the few venues where blacks could perform in serious roles as well. During the 1930s, this was the Harlem headquarters of the Federal Theater Project of the New Deal's Works Progress Administration. Its most notorious production was the "Voodoo *Macbeth*." Directed by Orson Welles and featuring an all-black cast, this rendition integrated African elements into the Shakespeare classic.

Look south toward 125th Street on Adam Clayton Powell, Jr., Boulevard. The sculpture on the median in the center of the boulevard symbolizes the "Tree of Hope." The tree, which sat in front of the Lafayette, was rumored to have magical powers, bringing employment to out-of-work actors who rubbed its bark. The old oak did become a gathering place for actors; casting agents in search of entertainers could find them in droves in front of the Lafayette, so in a sense the tree fulfilled its magic promises. The original Tree of Hope was cut down in 1934; this interpretive sculpture was erected in 1972. A piece of the original remains a fixture on the stage of the Apollo Theater, participants in Wednesday's amateur nights rub its bark for luck before going out on stage.

➤ **Turn right on 125th Street and walk west toward the Apollo Theater.**

Lafayette Theater, also known as the "House Beautiful," was one of the few integrated theaters in New York. As early as 1912, African American theatergoers were allowed to sit in orchestra seats instead of only in the balcony. The theater seated two thousand and presented such Broadway hits as **Madame X** and **Dr. Jekyll and Mr. Hyde**. The photo shows opening night of a production of Shakespeare's **Macbeth** that was arranged and staged by Orson Welles. Photo courtesy of the Schomberg Center for Research in Black Culture, New York Public Library.

You are in Harlem's central commercial district. In the early twentieth century, black-owned businesses were found around 135th Street, but on 125th, all the stores were white-owned. The owners resisted the development of Harlem as a black neighborhood and most refused to hire black workers through the 1930s, though their clientele was almost entirely black. Even today, few of the businesses on 125th Street are owned by African Americans. In the 1960s, banks and insurance companies "red-lined" the area, refusing to lend money to individuals and companies interested in opening a business in Harlem. In light of this trend, it is not surprising that many community leaders were pleased at the influx of major corporate interests to 125th Street during the 1990s. Joining the ubiquitous fast-food restaurants in recent years are Pathmark (the first large supermarket to open in Harlem), Starbucks, Old Navy, and Harlem USA, a mall and movie multiplex backed by basketball star Magic Johnson. Some fear the impact this corporate invasion will have on Harlem, but many welcome the lower prices, job opportunities, and confidence in the neighborhood's future.

The tall white building on the southwest corner of 125th Street and Adam Clayton Powell, Jr., Boulevard is the landmarked Hotel Theresa, now an office building. When it opened in 1913, the hotel catered to a white-only clientele. In 1937 it was purchased by a black entrepreneur who overturned these segregationist policies. Posh hotels downtown refused service to blacks, and the Theresa became known as the "Waldorf of Harlem." In 1960, Fidel Castro, visiting the United Nations, stayed here to show his solidarity with black Americans. The Hotel Theresa also housed political organizations. A. Philip Randolph's 1941 March on Washington movement was coordinated here; this movement successfully pushed President Franklin Roosevelt to integrate defense industries during World War II. During the 1960s, after his break from the Nation of Islam, Malcolm X established the Organization of Afro-American Unity at the Theresa. On the corner outside the building, crowds would gather to hear the civil rights leader give his speeches.

As you continue west on 125th Street, you will pass the old Blumstein's Department Store at 230 West 125th Street, now subdivided into smaller stores at ground level. In the early twentieth century, Blumstein's, like most of the stores on the block, refused to hire black workers in any but the most lowly positions, despite the fact that its clientele was almost entirely African American. This position was particularly galling during the Great Depression, when Harlem's unemployment rate was substantially higher than in the rest of the city. In 1934, Adam Clayton Powell Jr. and other black leaders targeted Blumstein's in a boycott and picketing campaign. Taking as their slogan "Don't buy where you can't work," the protesters eventually forced the largest department store in Harlem to hire black clerks. In time, Blumstein's would be the first department store to have a black Santa Claus.

Stop at the Apollo Theater at 253 West 125th Street. The burlesque house that opened here in 1914 initially refused admission to blacks. In 1934 the former owners of the Lafayette Theater bought the Apollo and integrated it. It has since become the premier showcase of black talent in the United States. Virtually every black American entertainer of note has performed on its stage. During the 1930s and 1940s, black Harlemites and white visitors to Harlem could enjoy performances by dancer Bill "Bojangles" Robinson; singers Bessie Smith, Billie Holiday, and Ethel Waters; and revues from cabarets at the Cotton Club and the Ubangi Club. Famous bandleaders such as Duke Ellington took the stage of the Apollo backed by chorus girls in elaborate costumes.

While the music continued throughout the 1960s, including performances by Stevie Wonder and Diana Ross, the Apollo experienced a decline as big acts began to perform elsewhere. But in recent years, funded in part by the public Harlem Urban Development Corporation, the Apollo has been renovated and again claims its place in the spotlight. Wednesday amateur nights, an Apollo tradition since the 1930s, have been televised nationally since the early 1990s. Talents discovered here have included such greats as Ella Fitzgerald, Sarah Vaughan, and James Brown. Poor audience reception at amateur night at the Apollo does not, however, guarantee a failed career. Multiple-Grammy-winner Lauryn Hill was booed off the stage by the notoriously tough Apollo audience.

From here, you can walk two blocks east to the 2/3 station at 125th and Lenox; one block west to the A/B/C/D station at 125th St. and St. Nicholas Avenue; or walk east to Adam Clayton Powell, Jr., Boulevard, take a left, and walk to 135th Street, where we began the tour.

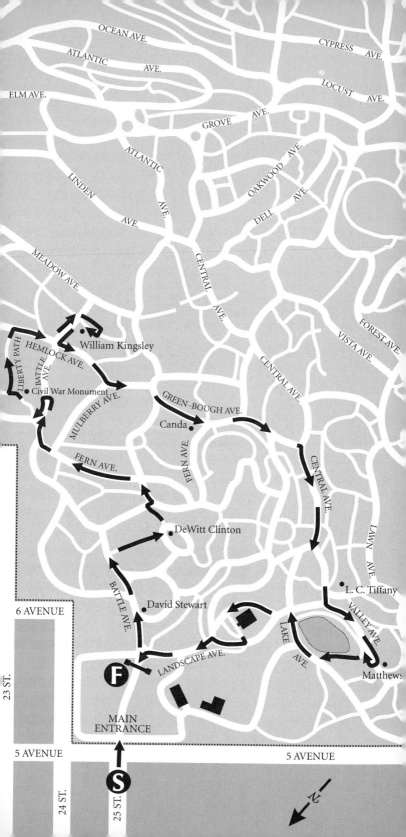

OCEAN AVE.

CYPRESS   AVE.

ATLANTIC   AVE.

LOCUST   AVE.

ELM AVE.

GROVE   AVE.

ATLANTIC

OAKWOOD AVE.

LINDEN

AVE.

AVE.

DELL   AVE.

MEADOW AVE.

CENTRAL   AVE.

FOREST AVE.

VISTA AVE.

William Kingsley

LIBERTY PATH

HEMLOCK AVE.

BATTLE AVE.

CENTRAL AVE.

Civil War Monument

MULBERRY AVE.

GREEN-BOUGH AVE.

Canda

CENTRAL AVE.

FERN AVE.

FERN AVE.

DeWitt Clinton

LAWN AVE.

L. C. Tiffany

6 AVENUE

BATTLE AVE.

David Stewart

VALLEY AVE.

23 ST.

F

LANDSCAPE AVE.

LAKE AVE.

Matthews

MAIN
ENTRANCE

5 AVENUE

5 AVENUE

24 ST.

S

25 ST.

N

9 GREEN-WOOD CEMETERY

A Garden Cemetery Revisited

➤ Start: The N/R subway stop at Twenty-fifth Street and Fourth Avenue in Brooklyn. Walk uphill to cemetery gates and enter.

When Green-Wood Cemetery was chartered on April 18, 1838, New York City was already the commercial and financial center of America and, with a population of more than three hundred thousand, its largest city. Manhattan churchyard cemeteries were rapidly filling and the island was quickly running out of available space. But newly incorporated Brooklyn had fewer than sixteen thousand residents and an abundance of unused land.

Our story begins when Henry Evelyn Pierrepont (1808–1888), scion of one of Brooklyn's most prominent families, visited Cambridge, Massachusetts, to study the newly opened Mount Auburn Cemetery, the first planned, nondenominational, rural cemetery in America. He then toured Europe, looking for a cemetery model to bring to Manhattan. Pierrepont returned from Europe with an image of a sprawling garden cemetery for Manhattan. His idea was dismissed as a waste of valuable real estate. He turned to Brooklyn and saw the opportunity to create a city like the great cities of Europe—with wide promenades, public squares, and a grand cemetery. Many of his contemporaries could not grasp Pierrepont's vision of the great American city on the East River. In fact, when the City of Brooklyn began to lay out its streets in 1835, it made no provisions for a cemetery site. Seeing the need for action, Pierrepont gathered a number of citizens who petitioned the New York state legislature for a charter of two hundred acres of land for a rural cemetery. The Hills of Gowanus, where you now stand, were selected as the site. Within a year, the Green-Wood Corporation, organized by Pierrepont plus other prominent Brooklynites, purchased nearly two hundred acres of grazing land at $750 per acre, for a total of $134,650, from the Wyckoff, Ibbotson, Dean, Sackett, Schermerhorn, Bennett, and Bergen families.

David Bates Douglass (1790–1849) was hired the next month to transform this grazing pasture into a cemetery. Douglass had served in the War of 1812 and had been a professor of mathematics and engineering at the United States Military Academy. Before working on Green-Wood, he had also been the chief engineer for the Croton Aqueduct System. Among other things he designed the High Bridge, which remains the oldest bridge still standing in the city, to transport Croton's water across the Harlem River to Manhattan.

One of Douglass's first tasks was to lay out 4.5 miles of road that followed the contours of the terrain and demonstrated the beauty of the site. This route became known as "the Tour" and was designed and used not only to display Green-Wood's charms but also to serve as an incentive for potential lot buyers. One unexpected side effect of the Tour was that Green-Wood quickly became a major recreational and tourist destination for New Yorkers, who had access to almost no public parkland at all.

Under Douglass's direction, Green-Wood was carefully

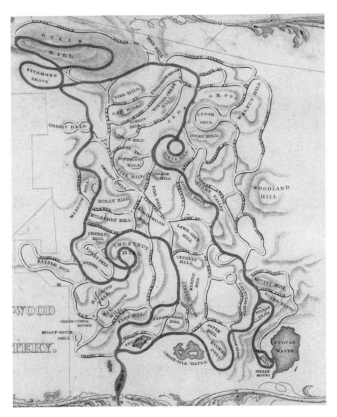

"The Tour." The original 1830s map and layout of Green-Wood Cemetery as envisioned by David Bates Douglass. His route conformed to the contours of the land to enhance the pastoral garden setting of the cemetery. The Tour enabled visitors to view the splendor of Green-Wood, visit interred family and friends, and perhaps select a site for themselves. Illustration from **Rural Cemeteries: Green-Wood, Illustrated**, by James Smillie.

and artistically designed to reveal every natural feature in its most advantageous light. Trees and shrubs were planted as screens and foils in the proper locations to provide just the right feeling and mood. Roads and paths followed land contours whenever possible and wound around lakes and ponds. Douglass even had songbirds imported from Europe to assist with the ambiance.

Although regarded as an aesthetic success, the early years were difficult for Green-Wood. New Yorkers and Brooklynites alike were unwilling to change from a local church graveyard burial to one that seemed both distant and insecure. Arrangements were quickly made to enclose the cemetery with a two-mile-long fence. The current fence, measuring some 21,120 feet in length, was erected beginning in 1860, at a cost of $40,000. As you enter Green-Wood, take note of this fence with its decorative cast iron finials that cap each post. Beginning in the year 2000, the cemetery began a fund-raising campaign to restore 280 missing finials. The reconstruction and replacement will cost almost $50,000—more than the cost of the entire original fence!

From the first interment on September 5, 1840, to December 1, 1842, only 162 burials took place. By 1843 the total had risen to only 352. But in 1844 a dramatic change occurred: 354 persons were buried in that year alone, and lot sales reached $20,000. This tremendous increase was caused by three factors: first, the growing acceptance of nondenominational burial, which made Green-Wood's nonaffiliation with any church acceptable; second, an easing of the financial effect of the depression of 1837, which gave people more disposable income; and third, the relocation of former senator, governor, and mayor DeWitt Clinton's casket from Albany to Green-Wood, which showed that the wealthy classes had accepted the place.

By 1855, just fifteen years after the first interment, 45,576 persons had been buried here and over one hundred thousand local people and tourists were visiting annually. Since that time the cemetery has expanded to 478 acres by purchasing neighboring land. There are an estimated six hundred thousand people buried here today.

GARDEN CEMETERIES

What is a garden cemetery? The garden cemetery emerged from the English landscape-garden movement of the early eighteenth century. Landscape gardeners altered and tamed the countryside to make it picturesque, literally to look like a picture.

Victorian garden cemeteries were strongly supported by ministers and religious liberals, who argued that they could be catalysts for civic virtue. They urged the young to visit and take away life lessons from the biographies of famous or accomplished people buried there. At the same time, visitors would come to understand the shortness and unpredictability of life. They were to return home with a new resolve to work hard and to do good. The cemetery was as much a civic space as a place for burial, and in some sense, when we visit a cemetery today, we are engaged in similar reflection on those whose lives we encounter.

Cemeteries in the Victorian age were also Romantic. They served as a place to mourn not just for a passed loved one but for a lost rural ideal. America in the mid-nineteenth century was a nation undergoing tremendous change. Many older Americans longed for the days of their youth, a time before mass immigration, modern political parties, tremendous urban centers, and technological advancements such as the railroad and telegraph. The garden cemetery allowed for the nostalgia of days gone by.

➤ We start our tour at the dramatic Gothic revival gates designed by architect Richard Upjohn. These gates were built between 1861 and 1863, by which time Green-Wood was an established success and its trustees wished for an imposing entrance.

Richard Upjohn (1802–1878) was one of America's most renowned nineteenth-century architects. Building primarily in the Greek revival and Gothic revival styles, he specialized in churches. His greatest surviving work in New York City is Trinity Church (1846) at the intersection of Broadway and Wall Street. (See chapter 1, our "Architecture of Capitalism" walk.) Upjohn later joined architect

Richard Morris Hunt in establishing the American Institute of Architects (AIA). Upjohn also helped found the Long Island Historical Society, now known as the Brooklyn Historical Society, located in Brooklyn Heights. (See our walk of Brooklyn Heights and the Brooklyn Bridge in chapter 5.)

Gothic revival architecture was one of the dominant styles of the Victorian era, an age of great romanticism. The period saw the construction of buildings that appealed to the imagination by stressing mystery, illusion, and nostalgia. Turning away from the rational and intellectual lines of Greek revival, this new movement replaced the old geometry and balance with texture, color, as well as a complex and lively asymmetry. The Gothic revival style reflects and celebrates the inherent irregularity of nature itself. This style was a perfect match for Green-Wood Cemetery and its vision of pastoral contemplation.

The entrance gates are a splendid example of Gothic Revival architecture. The center tower stands 106 feet tall and is flanked by two 90-foot peaks. While the towers are symmetrical, they are counterbalanced by the office wings, which are of differing shapes and sizes. The gates are made of red sandstone from Belleville, New Jersey, which is the same building material Upjohn used for Trinity Church. Take special note of the tremendous array of details and architectural elements throughout the gates. They contain, among other things, steep and colorful slate roofs, stone trefoils and quatrefoils, cast-iron bannerettes, a variety of columns, open gables, and detailed finials.

Embedded within the gates, above the entranceways, are four reliefs. Carved by John M. Moffitt in Nova Scotia yellow sandstone, they symbolize rebirth and resurrection. They are titled "Come Forth," "The Dead Shall Be Raised," "I Am the Resurrection and the Life," and "Weep Not." Higher up on the gates are smaller reliefs of Faith,

Hope, Memory, and Love. In 1966 the Green-Wood Cemetery main gates were designated a New York City landmark.

There are public restrooms within the gates, on your left, behind the office.

➤ Our tour continues by walking toward the left, uphill onto Battle Avenue. You will note that throughout the cemetery there are small, black iron street signs. These signs, along with our map and detailed route, will help you find your way in this most un-urban of settings. Our first stop is the David Stewart tomb, located on the corner of Battle and Arbor Avenues on your right.

This tomb brings together two of the greatest and best-known artists of the late nineteenth century. The tomb itself was designed by architect Stanford White, and the bronzes were created in 1883 by Augustus Saint-Gaudens. The tomb holds the remains of Pennsylvania coal and steel magnate David Stewart (1810–1891), the father of Isabella Stewart Gardiner (1840–1924), who was the doyenne of Boston's art scene and philanthropist extraordinaire.

The reliefs depict two robed angels. They were highly controversial at the time of their creation because most depictions of death were gloomy and filled with despair. Instead, Stanford White depicts the angels as musicians, perhaps heralding the ascension to heaven. White, having little patience for the criticism he was receiving, wrote to Saint-Gaudens that "some people are such God damned asses they always think of death as a gloomy performance instead of a resurrection."

A few feet farther along Battle Avenue and on the other side of the road, note the marble grave marker with the large cross and bronze emblem of the American Society for the Prevention of Cruelty to Animals (ASPCA). This is

Burying the victims from the December 5, 1876, Brooklyn Theater Fire. One this site, 103 bodies were interred in coffins donated by the City of Brooklyn. As shown, some two thousand mourners attended this winter ceremony. Illustration: **Harper's Weekly**, December 30, 1876, in John Grafton, **New York in the Nineteenth Century** (New York: Dover), 1977.

the grave of Louis Bonnard (1809–1871), a French émigré who developed and patented a number of profitable inventions in the cellar workshop of his Mulberry Street tenement. His inventions included a mechanical brick maker and a machine for molding cast iron. As he lay near death, Bonnard became convinced that he was to be resurrected as an animal and could be abused. He sent for Henry Bergh, founder of the ASPCA, and promised his fortune to the newly established organization. Bergh arrived to find his new benefactor living in abject poverty. Bonnard told Bergh that he was leaving his fortune to the ASPCA and asked the skeptical Bergh to open a trunk that was also in the room. When Bergh did so, he found it filled with money and jewels. Bonnard's family disputed the bequest, claiming the inventor was insane, but the courts upheld the donation and the ASPCA became one of the best-endowed charities in New York.

➤ Continue along Battle Avenue to the tall obelisk on the corner of Bayview and Battle Avenues.

This monument was erected by the City of Brooklyn to memorialize the 278 people who lost their lives during the Brooklyn Theater Fire on December 5, 1876; 103 of the victims are buried here.

Theater was a main source of entertainment for nineteenth-century America. One of the more prominent theaters, the Brooklyn, was located downtown, at the intersection of Johnson and Washington Streets. More than a thousand patrons had gathered on a Tuesday evening to watch the stage star Kate Claxton appear in the very popular *Two Orphans*.

As the play was ending, at approximately 11 P.M., someone told Claxton that a kerosene lamp had ignited a small fire amid the scenery backstage. As the actors were unsure what to do, Claxton supposedly whispered, "Go on, they will put it out, if we say anything there will be panic, go on." The fire could not be extinguished and it started to burn out of control. As the audience learned of the fire, Claxton tried to reassure the crowd, saying, "We are between you and the flames." Nonetheless, patrons fled in panic, clogging the few narrow exits. Within half an hour the roof of the building collapsed. In the end, 278 lives were lost.

Kate Claxton was found the next morning, dazed and burned, wandering in Manhattan near City Hall. She claimed she could not recall how she crossed the river—and this was years before the Brooklyn Bridge was completed. She was thereafter known as "Kate Claxton of the Big Brooklyn Fire."

The City of Brooklyn arranged for a mass grave in Green-Wood for the unidentified bodies and for those families who could not afford burial. Cemetery workers dug a seven-foot-deep crescent-shaped common grave, and 103 donated coffins were arranged with heads facing the center.

Two thousand mourners attended, accompanied by song, speeches, and flowers.

Kate Claxton continued acting until her retirement in 1904. She died twenty years later and is buried elsewhere in Green-Wood.

➤ **Across Battle Avenue from the Brooklyn Theater Fire monument stand a cluster of graves. These are of Henry Aaron Burr and his family.**

Henry Aaron Burr (1811–1884) was the great-nephew of the infamous vice president Aaron Burr and also a nephew of minister Jonathan Edwards. Henry Burr was famous in his own right an innovator in the hat industry. After working as the bookkeeper for milliner Elisha Bloomer, Burr decided in 1835 to open his own store across the street and became interested in perfecting a machine for forming hats. After numerous failures, he perfected his invention and received a patent. His machine dramatically reduced cost of hat making. By 1856, millions of his machines were in use worldwide. His invention was so successful that he was forced to sue for patent infringement fifty-six times, winning all but three cases. Burr was also a charter member of the Union Club and director of the Mechanics' National Bank, and he unsuccessfully ran for Congress as a Republican in 1862.

➤ **Continue uphill along Battle. A few feet beyond the Burr family, take a right onto Syringa Path. Walk up to the imposing statue of DeWitt Clinton. Along the way, note the Uhl-Ottendorfer family plot to your left.**

Anna and Jacob Uhl started the *Staats-Zeitung* (the City Paper) as a German weekly in New York in December 1834. It became a triweekly and then a daily in 1845. Jacob

Uhl died in 1851, and the paper was left under the direction of his wife, Anna, who in 1859 married Oswald Ottendorfer, a German immigrant who had been working at the paper for over a decade. The *Staats-Zeitung* became the preeminent German-language paper in New York, reaching a circulation of sixty-five thousand by 1880. Anna Ottendorfer, who remained active on the business side of the newspaper, died in 1885, but the paper continued as a daily until 1975. The Ottendorfers gave away much of their fortune to German American causes, including a free library whose building still stands on Second Avenue near Tenth Street in Manhattan.

The Uhl-Ottendorfers are one of many nineteenth-century newspaper publishing families to be buried in Green-Wood Cemetery. Also buried here are Henry Raymond of the *New York Times*, Horace Greeley of the *Tribune*, and J. Gordon Bennett of the *Herald*.

➤ **Continue along Syringa Path to the imposing statue of DeWitt Clinton. As you approach the statue, Clinton is standing with his back to you on a small grass island.**

DeWitt Clinton (1769–1828) was a remarkable man. The son of Revolutionary War general James Clinton, DeWitt chose a government career over a military one and secured a position as the personal secretary to his uncle Governor George Clinton around 1790. Within a decade DeWitt Clinton had become one of the most powerful politicians in New York State. After being appointed to the United States Senate in 1802, he returned home the next year to serve as mayor of New York. With the exception of two one-year terms, he was mayor from 1802 until 1815. During his terms he oversaw the creation of the New-York Historical Society and the Orphan Asylum, the improvement of sanitation, the adoption of the 1811 street-grid system, and the fortification of the harbor defenses in preparation for the feared British invasion during the War of 1812. Clinton ran for president in 1812, losing to James Madison by a slim margin. He also served as a three-term governor of New York State.

Clinton was also known as the "Father of the Erie Canal" because of his tireless support for this crucial infrastructure project, which assured New York's dominance of American commerce in the nineteenth century. He presided over the opening ceremonies of the canal in 1825.

The statue of Clinton was cast by Henry Kirke Brown from 1850 to 1853, and the base was designed by Richard Upjohn. It was sponsored by public subscription and displayed in Manhattan's City Hall Park prior to being placed here. Brown, by the way, also cast the George Washington–on–horseback sculpture at Union Square, where our Four Squares tour begins. (See chapter 4.) Note the two bronze reliefs on the base, which reflect the building of the Erie Canal.

➤ Sharing this small island of grass with DeWitt Clinton is Nathaniel Currier. His grave is a few feet to the south, among the trees.

Nathaniel Currier (1813–1888) was the senior partner of the lithography firm of Currier and Ives. During the second half of the nineteenth century, Currier and Ives produced thousands of images for mass consumption. Their work was excellent, but it was their unparalleled marketing skill that made Currier and Ives the most successful lithography firm in the nation. James Merritt Ives is buried elsewhere in Green-Wood.

➤ Opposite Clinton and facing his tomb, note the small, white marble statue of a young man.

This life-size statue of a young boy marks the grave of three-year-old Irwin Franklin, "Little Frankie." It was carved by the great American sculptor Daniel Chester French, who is best known for carving the statue of Lincoln seated at the Lincoln Memorial in Washington, D.C., and the statues in front of the U.S. Custom House in Lower Manhattan. Frankie, who died in 1880, was the son of Rear Admiral Aaron Ward (1851–1918). Father and son are buried adjacent to each other. Green-Wood Cemetery is filled with grave markers created by the master carvers of the nineteenth century. In between large commissioned works, this type of carving was quite often the "bread and butter" of their trade.

➤ **Leave this area by taking the Bay Side Path up to Highland Avenue. Turn left on Highland and continue along, past Green-Bank Path, to Fern Avenue and make a left. Fern Avenue ends at the base of Battle Hill. While walking along Fern Avenue, look downhill (to your left) at the tomb of John Anderson. His tomb in a classic Greek revival style, with four columns.**

John Anderson built his tomb himself in the early 1860s, twenty years before his death. It uses a Greek revival design that was popular in antebellum America. The style adheres to the Greek sense of order and proportion and is linked to what Americans believed were the enlightened and educated ideals of ancient Greek democracy. Greek revival was the design of choice for numerous academic and civic buildings. The style is represented in the tomb's fluted columns, Ionic capitals, pedimented gable, heavy cornices, unadorned friezes, and horizontal transoms. The four statuettes (two front and two back) are of the Four Evangelists, Matthew, Mark, Luke, and John, and were sculpted by

John Anderson's Greek revival mausoleum, with a wonderful view of New York Bay. The mausoleum was built in 1860, some twenty years prior to Anderson's death. Photo from **Green-Wood Illustrated**, 1891.

John Moffitt, who did the reliefs within the cemetery's entrance gates.

John Anderson (1812–1881) owned a tobacco shop on Broadway, across from City Hall Park. He specialized in "fine cut" tobacco that he packaged as Anderson's Solace Tobacco. In 1838 he hired an attractive young woman, Mary Cecilia Rogers, to draw young men to the shop. Mary Rogers and her mother had come to New York from New England after the depression of 1837, hoping to rebuild the family fortune in the growing city. While working for Anderson, Mary quickly picked up the nickname "the Beautiful Seegar Girl."

In July 1842, Mary disappeared. When she turned up three days later floating in the Hudson River, Anderson became the prime suspect. He was arrested, questioned, and immediately released, with details of his arrest and police statement hushed up by influential friends in the Democratic Party. Adding further mystery, although a number of men were questioned, Anderson's statement was the only one not released to the press.

Even though he was officially cleared, Anderson remained a suspect for many New Yorkers because the murder of Mary Rogers was one of the early crimes sensationalized by the press in the city. The *Herald, Sun*, and *Tribune* competed to create a "real-life mystery." Rumors that Rogers had died from a botched abortion led the state senate to pass a law criminalizing the practice, while law enforcement's inability to solve the crime led to the Police Reform Act of 1845. Rogers's story also became the basis for Edgar Allan Poe's *The Mystery of Marie Roget*. When Poe was hounded by the press to provide a solution to the continued mystery of the death of Mary Rogers, he responded that

> it will be seen that between the fate of the unhappy Mary Cecilia Rogers; so far as that fate is known, and the fate of one Marie Roget up to a certain epoch in her history, there has existed a parallel . . . but let it not for a moment be supposed that . . . it is my covert design to hint at an extension of the parallel, or even to suggest that the measures adopted in Paris for the discovery of the assassin . . . would produce any similar result.

After Mary Rogers's death, Anderson gave away much of his personal fortune. He supported Italian patriot Garibaldi; he gave $60,000 to the mayor of Jersey City to field troops for the Civil War; and he helped start a fund in Massachusetts to educate teachers in natural history.

The story continues even after Anderson's death, when his daughter contested his will, claiming he was insane. Anderson, she claimed, believed that Mary Rogers's ghost visited him regularly and that the ghost of Garibaldi inhabited his house. At the trial over his will, a witness in Anderson's favor testified that Anderson had indeed said his house was haunted—"by people who want money." Anderson's daughter lost her court battle.

➤ Continue along to the very end of Fern Avenue. On the right, about ten feet behind the Mulberry Avenue street sign, is the grave of Colonel Abraham Vosburgh. Note the symbolism on this column—the eagle holding a sword is a reference to Vosburgh's military service, and the broken column is indicative of a life cut short.

On April 22, 1861, Colonel Abraham Vosburgh (1825–1861) marched at the head of the Seventy-first New York State National Guard as it traveled to Washington, D.C., responding to President Lincoln's plea to defend the capital against Confederate attack. Without seeing any military action, Vosburgh died of consumption in Washington.

After President Lincoln laid a wreath on his body, the colonel was returned to Brooklyn for burial. The members of the Seventy-first Regiment erected this monument, which bears the inscription "Pro Patria" (For Country). It was originally surrounded by a cast-iron fence with posts shaped like bayoneted rifles and a gate decorated with a cast-iron Union cap, belt, and sword. The fence has since disappeared.

Vosburgh is far from the only officer buried in Green-Wood. From the Civil War alone there are nearly twenty generals from both sides, and there are thirteen Medal of Honor recipients as well.

➤ Turn around and continue walking around the Burnham family plot (keeping Burnham on your right) toward Battle Avenue.

The Burnham burial site is a classic late nineteenth-century family plot. It contains a central monument with an imposing statue, sculpted by John Moffitt, of a woman wearing a classical dress and holding a Bible. Engraved on the marble are the names and life spans of all buried here. Surrounding the plot is a stone wall. Many of these century-old plots originally had iron fences, but as they decayed, the fences were replaced by stone or concrete slabs.

Gordon W. Burnham (1803–1885) earned his millions as president of the Waterbury Clock, Waterbury Watch, and American Pin companies. He is buried here with his first two wives—Ann Griswold and Maria Louisa Brownell. Burnham died shortly before marrying a third time. He caught a chill while waiting in his unheated carriage for his fiancée Kate Sanborn's ferry, which was an hour late. The chill became pneumonia, and he died three days before his planned wedding. A staunch Democrat, Burnham had delayed his wedding until after the March 4 inauguration of Grover Cleveland so as not to be married under a Republican administration.

➤ Walk behind the Burnham plot and turn right onto Battle Avenue. Walk about one hundred feet farther along Battle Avenue for a short detour to the free-standing mausoleum of Marcus Daly. On arrival, be sure to note the magnificent stained-glass windows at the rear.

Born in Ireland, Marcus "Copper King" Daly (1841–1900) came to America at age fifteen with virtually no money or immediate prospects. In 1880, after years of struggling, he acquired enough money to buy a small mine near Butte, Montana. Although nominally a silver mine, in some places its veins held ore that was 55 percent copper. As luck would have it, Daly had hit the proverbial mother lode of copper at the same time that Thomas Edison was using copper to conduct electricity in his new lights. Soon, Daly's original Anaconda Mining Company was joined by a group of California financiers, and together they bought up many neighboring claims. At the peak of his influence, Daly's mines controlled nearly one-quarter of the world's mined copper. About twenty-five miles from Butte he built the city of Anaconda as a company town, diversified into coal mines and lumber, and became a millionaire several times over.

Daly was very active in Montana Democratic politics and was at constant war with his mining rival Andrew Clark. These formidable men fought with money and the press for control of the state. Clark's ambition was to become a U.S. senator; Daly's was simply to stop Clark. Clark spent $450,000 to keep the state capitol from being built in Daly's Anaconda. Clark won his battle and also, ultimately, the Senate seat—but not until 1901, after Daly's death.

➤ **Backtrack on Battle Avenue a few paces to the corner of Battle and Border Avenues. Climb up the steps marked "Battle Path" that lead to the Soldiers Monument, a monument to the New York Volunteers.**

Erected in 1869, the Green-Wood Cemetery's Soldiers' Monument honors the 148,000 New York men who fought "in aid of the war for the preservation of the Union and the Constitution." Two themes dominate—the sacrifice of the Republic's citizen-soldier and the union, stability, and prosperity with which the nation hoped to emerge from the Civil War. Built just four years after the end of the war, this monument is much more realistic in its vision of battle than the nostalgic memorials that were built in the 1880s and 1890s, when the blood and guts of the war had faded. The four life-size soldiers, supposedly cast from the bronze of captured Confederate cannons, represent the Union Army.

The soldiers originally held objects (an ax, rifle, rammer, and sword) that are now missing. In 1991, the casts of the four battle scenes depicted in relief on the sides of the central monument, which had been stolen, were refabricated and replaced.

➤ **Walk around the monument to the New York Volunteers and look for a low, white gravestone whose only inscription is "Grandmother." It is near granite cemetery marker 18495.**

This is the grave of Elizabeth Tilton (1834–1897). Elizabeth had been married to Theodore Tilton and was a schoolteacher for the Reverend Henry Ward Beecher of Plymouth Church in Brooklyn Heights. She and Beecher had an affair that was exposed by Victoria Woodhull. (See our Brooklyn Heights and Bridge tour in chapter 5 for the complete story). Theodore sued Beecher for "alienation of affection" and the story became national news.

Beecher was able to claim victory with a hung jury. But what happened to the Tilton family after the "trial of the century"? The family was torn apart. Theodore left the United States in 1883 and spent his life in Paris. Elizabeth was ostracized by everyone but her daughter and a few religious friends. She died alone and blind in 1897. Her marker simply reads "Grandmother" in an attempt to keep tourists from invading Elizabeth's final resting place. Beecher remained with his wife and is buried in a prominent tomb elsewhere in Green-Wood.

➤ **Continue along Battle Path to Minerva and the Altar to Liberty.**

Minerva and the Altar to Liberty was sculpted by F. Wellington Ruxell and unveiled in 1920. In Greek mythology,

An 1840s view of Green-Wood and New York Harbor from Battle Hill. Note the long line of carriages taking the Tour on a beautiful afternoon. This image is drawn from about where **Minerva** currently stands. Illustration from **Rural Cemeteries: Green-Wood, Illustrated,** by James Smillie, New York, 1847.

Minerva (also known as Pallas Athena), whose temple is the Parthenon, sprang fully formed from Zeus's head, clad in armor. She was the goddess of battle and protector of civilized life, as well as the inventor of the bridle and the person who first tamed horses for the use of humans. She was also the one who carried Zeus's thunderbolt for him. *Minerva* was unveiled on August 27, 1920, the 144th anniversary of the Battle of Long Island, which was fought on this spot in late August 1776.

This battle was the first for the Continental army after the Declaration of Independence some seven weeks prior. During the engagement, two thousand American troops under Brigadier General William Alexander, called Lord Stirling by his troops, battled Major General James Grant's British force that was three times larger. Much of the fighting occurred across the ridge where you are now standing—hence the name Battle Hill. It is said that atop this hill a group of American riflemen were surrounded, shot, and buried where they fell.

The Greek revival tomb directly behind *Minerva* is that of Charles M. Higgins (1854–1929). A Park Slope, Brooklyn, businessman, he was the inventor of India ink. It was Higgins's ambition to build a memorial to the first battle for American freedom. He led the movement to erect the statue of Minerva. As you look down the hill, note that this is the highest natural point in Brooklyn, 216 feet above sea level. If you stand directly in front of *Minerva*, you will also see that her left hand is raised in salute to the Statue of Liberty, standing due west in New York harbor.

As you are walking along Liberty Path, with the Higgins mausoleum to your left, note among the two evergreen shrubs to your right, the unassuming graves of Leonard Bernstein (1918–1990), his wife, and his sister. Born in Lawrence, Massachusetts, Bernstein was conductor of the New York City Symphony Orchestra from 1945 to 1948 and was with the New York Philharmonic from 1957 until being named conductor laureate in 1969. He was the first conductor successfully to use television as a tool for music education. Bernstein was also a prolific composer; his best-known piece is the 1957 musical *West Side Story*.

Bernstein's grave is usually piled with small stones. It is a Jewish tradition to leave a stone when visiting to honor the person who is buried, both to pay homage and to record your presence. Not only are stones all around us and easy to find, but they are related to the ground and last longer than flowers.

Continue along Liberty Path about thirty feet, and directly behind Higgins, hidden in a grove of trees, is the Edwin C. Litchfield plot. Litchfield (1815–1885) was a prominent Brooklyn lawyer and businessman. Along with his brother, Electus, he developed Brooklyn's street railways and the Gowanus Canal and acquired a significant tract of land from the Cortelyou estate, which the Litchfields developed into Park Slope. Litchfield also played a prominent role in the creation of Prospect Park. In 1892, after his death, the family estate—Grace Hill—was converted into the Parks Department building within the park. It has been renamed Litchfield Villa to honor its benefactor. The rumor is that his grave is turned away from Park Slope to protest the taking of his family home by the Parks Department.

➤ **Liberty Path comes to an end at Hemlock Avenue. Turn right on Hemlock and continue about one block to the intersection of Battle and Hemlock Avenues.**

On the far right corner stands the imposing Howe family grave site. It is overseen by the bust of the family patriarch, Elias Howe Jr.

Elias Howe Jr. (1819–1867) was born in Spencer, Massachusetts, to a large and impoverished family. Like many in the early nineteenth century, Howe went to work at an early age—six—and never received a formal education. He married at twenty-one and supported his family as a mechanic and part-time inventor. In 1846 he patented the first sewing machine. Although it was grossly inefficient and inconsistent, his machine sewed 250 stitches a minute, which was five times faster than could be sewn by a skilled hand. The introduction of Howe's sewing machine was met with great resistance from sewers and tailors who feared the loss of their jobs. Manufacturers were also reluctant to invest large sums of capital to mechanize when cheap human labor was in abundance.

Realizing that America was not ready for his machine, he sought a patent and then went to England to market his invention. Two years later he returned to America penniless. On his return, he discovered that his invention had been stolen. After five years of litigation he won his patent suit, gaining protection for the lockstitch that was formed by his eye-pointed needle and mechanical shuttle. Thereafter, Howe received a royalty on every sewing machine made in America. His annual income rose from $300 a year to $200,000 a year, or over $5 million today.

Directly behind Howe is buried the family dog, Fannie, who died in 1881. Carved on the marble marker is the following poem:

> Only a dog you say sir critic
> Only a dog, but as truth I prize
> The truest love I have won in living
> Lay in the deeps of her limpid eyes.
> Frosts of winter nor heat of summer
> Could make her fail if my footsteps led
> And the memory holds in its treasure casket
> The name of my darling who lieth dead.

➤ **Take a brief detour along Battle Avenue to the small Lake Path. On the near right corner is the tombstone of William Kingsley.**

William Kingsley (1833–1885), a Brooklyn contractor, was one of the earliest proponents of building a bridge between Brooklyn and Manhattan. In 1865, at age thirty-two, he employed engineer and fellow Brooklynite Colonel Julius Walker Adams to draw up a design, with cost estimates for materials and labor. Adams estimated that the Brooklyn Bridge could have been built for approximately $5 million. The Kingsley bridge was never built. In the end, the Roebling bridge cost $15 million.

Kingsley was active in Brooklyn politics and was a leader of the Democratic machine. His contracting company worked on several important public-works projects, including Prospect Park and the Hempstead Reservoir, but the Brooklyn Bridge project made him almost a million dollars alone, perhaps thanks to his association with Manhattan "Boss" William Marcy Tweed.

When the Tweed ring was broken in 1873, it became known that Kingsley, a major stockholder in the Brooklyn Bridge Company and general superintendent of the building project, was being paid 15 percent of the total construction expenses—over $170,000 per year. According to the Bridge Company's records, this payment was made at Tweed's suggestion. Following the removal of Tweed, Kingsley's annual salary was renegotiated to a flat $10,000 a year. Without the salary change, Kingsley would have garnered roughly $1.75 million by the time the bridge was finished in 1883.

Kingsley's grave marker was cut from a granite stone taken from the Brooklyn Bridge itself. The bridge trustees placed it here to commemorate his role in making the Great Bridge a reality.

➤ **Return to the grave of Elias Howe Jr. and Hemlock Avenue. Turn left onto Hemlock. Continue along for a while. Turn left onto Mulberry. Just after you pass the merge with Mulberry, keep an eye open for the grave of Andrew R. Culver on the right.**

The Culver grave's decorated marker is set a few yards back from the road. Done in white marble, it depicts the shattered trunk of a tree with the trappings of youth—a stack of books, a uniform and rifle, as well as a rope and ship's anchor. While we know little of his life, the grave reads that he died in 1871, at the age of seventeen years.

The marble grave marker is an excellent example of how tombstones describe a life. The dominant feature of the Culver grave is a strong tree trunk that has been shattered, a symbol of a young life abruptly and prematurely ended. The books and a globe are images of his life as a student. To the left is a Union Army uniform and rifle; perhaps young Andrew had ambitions of being a soldier.

TOMBSTONE SYMBOLISM

The grave markers in Green-Wood Cemetery contain many examples of funerary art. Many of the markers tell a graphic story about both the life and death of those interred. They illustrate Christian ideas of ascension to heaven, resurrection, and holy salvation. Here are a few symbols of which to make note:

"An intertwined alpha and omega—the first and last letters of the Greek alphabet. Taken from the book of Revelation (22:13), 'the first and the last, the beginning and the end.'

Fugit Hora—'the hours are fleeting' is a poetic translation; 'time flies' is another."

Animal symbols are quite common:

Unidentifiable birds—the soul in flight back to God

Dove—the Holy Ghost

Eagle—either a messenger from the heavens or military service

Butterfly—the Christian metamorphosis with resurrection

Lamb—purity, innocence, and meekness; the most common nineteenth-century symbol for children's graves.

Objects and shapes are also used as well. These can be carved in the stone or stand free as part of the grave marker. It is also common for a combination of symbols to be used.

Anchor—early Christian symbol of salvation and hope, also of death at sea

Broken column or tree trunk—a young life shortened by death

Orb—resurrection

Drapery over urn or column—sorrow or mourning

Angel—the messenger between God and man

➤ Walk along past Atlantic Avenue, where Mulberry will feed directly into Green-Bough. Continue downhill along

Green-Bough Avenue to the intersection with Fern Avenue. On the near right corner is the lavish white tomb of Charlotte Canda.

Charlotte Canda (1828–1845) was the daughter of Charles Canda, an officer in Napoleon's army who emigrated to America in the early nineteenth century and established a girls' finishing school in Manhattan. Charlotte was his only daughter. On a stormy and rainy night, February 3, 1845, a party was given to celebrate Charlotte's seventeenth birthday. As the party ended, Charlotte and her father escorted one of her friends home in the family carriage. At the friend's home on Waverly Place, Manhattan, not wanting a lady to walk alone after dark, Charles escorted the friend to the door. When he returned, the carriage was gone. The horse had bolted, crossed Broadway, and thrown Charlotte from the carriage, where she struck her head. Just as her father arrived at the scene, she died.

The Canda family were Catholic, and Charlotte was initially interred in the old St. Patrick's Cathedral cemetery on Mott Street in Manhattan.

This lavish monument was essentially designed by Charlotte herself. She had been drawing a memorial for her recently deceased aunt. Her father found the sketch, embellished it with roses, flowers, birds, and wreaths, many in the repetitive number of seventeen, Charlotte's age. The monument also stands seventeen feet high and seventeen feet deep. Similar to the Culver memorial, this monument incorporates many of Charlotte's favorite items, such as books, musical instruments, drawing implements, and her parrot. Charlotte appears in the gown she wore on the night of her death. A star above her symbolizes immortal life. Take note of the butterfly with wings extended, symbolizing her liberated spirit.

Charlotte Canda–"The French Lady." Canda died in a carriage accident at age seventeen. This lavish monument was adapted from a design by her own hand. This was one of the most popular visitation sites of the cemetery. Photo from **Green-Wood Illustrated**, 1891.

The Canda monument is estimated to have cost (in 1845) between $15,000 and $45,000—about $450,000 to $1.3 million today. In the 1850s, Charlotte's grave was the most popular one in the cemetery, attracting thousands yearly.

Charlotte was disinterred from St. Patrick's and buried here in 1848. Because the Candas were Catholics, the monument is on ground consecrated by the church. Although Green-Wood Cemetery is a nonsectarian site, each plot is individually owned and, as such, can be consecrated as holy ground. To the right of her grave, but just outside the consecrated ground, stands a monument with the coat of arms of Charles Albert Jarret de la Marie—a French nobleman who was Charlotte's fiancé. A year after her death, he committed suicide in the Canda residence. He could not be buried on consecrated ground but lies as close as the church would allow.

NINETEENTH-CENTURY CEMETERY TOURISM

Shortly after Green-Wood Cemetery opened, a local newspaper reported that visitors "began to be attracted from the city in considerable numbers daily." The press predicted that Green-Wood was destined to "become a popular and elegant place of resort, where some of the wild and lovely features of nature might be retained near the city."

At first people came by carriage, but by the 1860s, access was available by public horsecar from downtown Brooklyn or the Fulton ferries. At the same time, the cemetery began selling picture postcards and stereo cards for those who wanted souvenirs. In fact, the images in this chapter are from these picture postcards. In 1872, in **A Description of the New York Central Park**, art critic Clarence Cook remarked that rural cemeteries had become

> "famous over the whole country and thousands of people visited them annually. They were among the chief attractions of the cities to which they belonged. No stranger visited these cities for pleasure or observation who was not taken there, nor was it long before the smaller cities, and even towns and villages began to set aside land and to lay it out for the double purpose of burying ground and pleasure ground. . . . These cemeteries were all the rage. . . . The truth is, people were glad to get fresh air, and a sight of grass, and trees, and flowers, with now and then a pretty piece of sculpture . . . without considering too deeply whether it might not be better to have it all without the graves and the funeral processions."

These cemeteries were not just final resting places but America's first urban parks.

After the development of the public park and the dissemination of the pastoral landscape without graves, the recreational popularity of the "rural" cemetery began to wane in the last quarter of the nineteenth century. Frederick Law Olmsted, a critic of the idea of rural cemeteries becoming the "constant resort of mere pleasure seekers, travelers, promenaders and loungers" at first refused to design one—although he recanted later in life and designed Mountain View Cemetery in California.

Public parks were not the only reason for a decline in cemetery tourism. The immense number of casualties from the Civil War through World War I destroyed much of the sentimentalism and melancholy that had permeated the Victorian era. Equally important was the creation of museums to display art and sculpture, which made visiting cemeteries less desirable. Furthermore, cemeteries themselves began to forbid the common practice of picnicking and other activities that were associated more with leisure than with burial.

➤ Continue downhill along Green-Bough Avenue until it ends at Central Avenue. Directly in front of you are three small children's graves. The children are slightly behind and to the left of the Simonson family obelisk.

These are the graves of Little Georgie, Emily Louise, and Baby John. They are fine examples of Victorian children's markers. All of the children are depicted as though they are sleeping—the rest of the innocent. During the Victorian era, Americans began to move away from the Puritan ideas of original sin and instead began to see children as innocents, untouched by the evils and perils of the modernizing and rapidly changing nineteenth-century world.

Quite often, Victorian children's monuments contain

images of lambs, empty rocking chairs, or even toys. During this period, children who were wealthy enough were meant to enjoy life, as opposed to being considered miniature workers.

➤ **Cast your gaze over the children's graves and up the hill to the impressive mausoleum of Henry Evelyn Pierrepont.**

As noted at the beginning of this walk, Pierrepont (1808–1888) was the person primarily responsible for Green-Wood Cemetery. A city planner and businessman and the second son of Hezekiah B. Pierrepont, he worked to establish ferry connections across and up and down the East River, in addition to managing his family's properties. He is regarded as one of the first city planners in the United States and was active in planning the expansion of Brooklyn after its 1834 incorporation; one year later, Pierrepont was appointed chair of a commission to lay out the streets of the new city. He donated the original fence that surrounded the cemetery and, in 1842, purchased eight plots for himself and family. His monument, designed by Richard Upjohn, stands atop one of the few manmade hills in Green-Wood. When he died, Henry E. Pierrepont was the last survivor of the original trustees who created the cemetery.

Henry's father, Hezekiah (1768–1838), moved to Brooklyn in 1802 after building his fortune as a merchant adventurer. Upon arrival, he bought some sixty acres in Brooklyn Heights. He was the first important suburban real estate developer in America. As early as 1823 he was advertising and selling Brooklyn Heights lots to wealthy Manhattanites. In that year he advertised in the *Long Island Star*:

> Situated directly opposite the southwest part of the city [Manhattan], and being the nearest country retreat, and easiest of access

from the center of business that now remains unoccupied; the distance not exceeding on an average fifteen to twenty-five minutes walk, including the passage of the river; the ground elevated and perfectly healthy at all seasons; views of the water and landscape both extensive and beautiful; as a place of residence combining all the advantages of the country with the most of the conveniences of the city.

➤ **Walk toward your right, downhill on Central Avenue.**

Keep your eyes to the right and look for the smallish marble monument to the engineers from the monitor *Weehawken*. The marker has the masonic symbol and a carving of a steamship on it.

The monitor *Weehawken* followed in the pioneering footsteps of the famous armored warship *Monitor* that fought the *Merrimack* to a draw in 1862. The *Weehawken* helped blockade the Confederate port of Charleston beginning in January 1863, as part of a flotilla led by the *New Ironsides*. In April the ironclads attacked the harbor defenses. At least two thousand shots were fired by the Confederates at the ironclads. The *Keokuk* sank, and the *New Ironsides* actually sat for an hour directly on top of a torpedo containing a ton of powder, which the Confederates couldn't detonate due to a broken wire. The flotilla of monitors stayed around for months, sometimes shipping out for repairs. In October 1863, the *Weehawken* ran aground while attacking Fort Sumter. The *New Ironsides*, along with four other monitors, shelled the Confederate batteries, and the *New Ironsides* put itself between the *Weehawken* and the batteries to draw fire while Union tugs pulled out the *Weehawken*. Although the *Weehawken* was rescued, she sank two months later.

The gravestone reads:

> Sacred to the memory of the officers of the United States Navy who lost their lives by being drowned on the US Monitor Weehawken to which they were attached when she foundered off Charleston, SC, December 6, 1863.

> The remains were exhumed from the engine room of the wrecked Monitor where they nobly fell at their post of duty. 1863.

➤ **Continue downhill along Central Avenue for a longish walk. As you emerge from the lush tree cover, just where Vale Path meets Central Avenue, look up the steep hill toward your left. Try to discern a cluster of very simple black marble monuments. These unassuming markers are for the Tiffany family.**

The large central stone is the family patriarch Charles Lewis Tiffany (1812–1902). He is surrounded by his family, including his most famous son, Louis Comfort Tiffany (1848–1933). The internationally renowned jewelry and objet d'art company was founded by Charles Tiffany and his partner John B. Young in 1837. They sold primarily stationery and fancy goods from their shop at 237 Broadway. With the arrival of the third partner, Jabez Ellis, in 1841, the firm Tiffany, Young and Ellis began selling European jewelry and soon after started to manufacture gold and silver jewelry themselves. After thirteen years of partnership, Charles Tiffany bought out his associates and renamed the shop Tiffany and Company.

Charles's son, Louis, was destined to take over and run his father's business. Louis's talents, however, led him toward the artistic side of decorative arts. He studied painting in New York and Paris and traveled the world examining the patterns and designs of artisans' crafts. Louis's great talent appeared in his glass work, and during the 1870s he and his rival John LaFarge (also buried here in

Green-Wood Cemetery) revolutionized the stained-glass industry. In 1879, Tiffany opened his own company, Louis C. Tiffany and Associated Artists, and soon after was granted a patent for Favrile glass. His firm specialized in decorating the interiors of the mansions and private clubs of wealthy Manhattanites. In 1893 he built a factory for his firm, now renamed Tiffany Studios, in Corona, Queens. It was here that he and his staff would create thousands of windows, light fixtures, ceramics, and the many other items that are now found in museums and private collections throughout the world. Louis Comfort Tiffany also designed a number of stained-glass windows for vaults in Green-Wood Cemetery.

Louis was more interested in his art than in status. His grave simply states his name and his birth and death dates. Note, however, his two wives. Each calls herself "Wife of Louis Comfort Tiffany, N.A." This is a gesture to Tiffany's membership in the National Academy of Design. Also note how his second wife's grave marker stands a bit taller than his first wife's. Perhaps this is from the settling of the first grave. Perhaps not.

➤ **Continue downhill toward the Valley Water (the large lily pond with the fountain). When you reach the water, proceed toward your left along Valley Avenue. Take note of the very detailed blue-gray-colored August Jacklitsch monument. This monument is one of the few white bronze memorials in Green-Wood Cemetery.**

Only one company, the Monumental Bronze Company of Bridgeport, Connecticut, manufactured "white bronze" cemetery markers. They are cast in pure zinc and were made from the mid-1870s roughly to World War I. The grave markers were sold through a catalog or by a sales agent who had an office near the cemetery. The white bronze could be very similar to a carved marble or granite marker but allowed for greater detail than stone. For example, in the late 1890s it became very fashionable to plant the century plant (similar to a yucca) in American cemeteries. White bronze allowed families to recreate this plant on a tombstone—something that could not be carved in stone.

There was one major problem with white bronze monuments. They were mass-produced, with only the nameplates and inscriptions individualized. The tablets were then bolted onto the monuments. This made for easy removal by vandals, as well as a good place for bootleggers to hide liquor during Prohibition.

➤ **Continue along Valley Avenue to Hillside Path and the large monument to John Matthews.**

The monument for John "Soda Fountain King" Matthews (1808–1870) is one of our favorites. Crafted by Karl Muller in a combination of marble and terra-cotta in 1868, it was celebrated as the "Mortuary Monument of the Year." Matthews lies atop his tomb, staring up at various scenes from his life. The carvings are a combination of animals, plants, the Four Evangelists, and carvings of his own children's images. The four gargoyles on each corner serve as gutters, drawing rainwater off the roof and away from the tomb. The life-size statue seated above Matthews symbolizes grief and mourning. The center tower atop the roofline has been lost to decay and time. Be certain to walk around the Matthews tomb to see how the weather has aged the southern and western sides and left the rest virtually intact.

John Matthews pioneered a process of using marble chips mixed with sulphuric acid to create a carbonic acid gas. This gas, when combined with water, would carbonate

John "Soda Fountain King" Matthews's monument. Winner of the Mortuary Monument of the Year award, it was crafted by Karl Muller in 1868. Over time, the small limestone and marble tower has eroded and been removed. Photo from **Green-Wood Illustrated**, 1891.

the beverage. This beverage is essentially what is now known as seltzer water. By 1870, Matthews was supplying more than five hundred soda fountains with his beverage. His slogan was "Youth as it sips its first glass, experiences sensations which, like the first sensations of love, cannot be forgotten but are cherished to the last."

➤ Turn around and walk back toward the Valley Water. Take the small footpath, the Water Side Path, to your left. It will end at Lake Avenue. Proceed to your right along Lake Avenue to the intersection of Landscape Avenue. Turn left on Landscape. You are now directly behind the Chapel of Green-Wood Cemetery. Walk to your right, around to the front of the chapel.

Green-Wood did not have a chapel until the early twentieth century. When Green-Wood solicited bids, Carrere & Hastings submitted a plan for a chapel. When it was rejected, the architectural firm modified its plan, which became the main branch of the New York Public Library at Forty-second Street and Fifth Avenue. The firm of Warren & Wetmore, best known for designing Manhattan's Grand Central Terminal, completed in 1913, was chosen to build the chapel in 1912. It's a scaled-down version of Christopher Wren's Thomas Tower at Christ Church, Oxford. After many decades closed, the chapel reopened in April 2000. It is for individual contemplation but can be reserved for services. If there is no service being held at the time of your visit, please feel free to enter.

Alongside the chapel is the very large receiving tomb. Note the elaborate entrance, similar in style to the cemetery's entrance gate. Capable of holding fifteen hundred bodies, the tomb dates back to the original days of the cemetery. Before the advent of modern digging equipment, those who died in winter, when the ground was frozen, were held here until the spring thaw. The receiving tomb takes up the better part of the hill. Its vast size is evident from the series of black metal vents.

➤ Upon leaving the chapel, continue along Landscape Avenue toward the Twenty-fifth Street gates.

In summing up the beauty and serenity of Green-Wood Cemetery, perhaps the *New York Times* said it best in 1866: "It is the ambition of the New Yorker to live on Fifth Avenue, to take his airings in the [Central] Park, and to sleep with his fathers in Green-Wood." Returning to where we began, we can ponder what we learned about those who are buried here and perhaps understand the shortness and unpredictability of life. *Fugit hora.*

10 THE OTHER BOROUGHS

A Driving Tour

Note: This driving tour is designed for travelers in private vehicles (bicycles where allowed, motorcycles, or automobiles) and cannot be duplicated by bus and should not be attempted by bus. Many of the streets on this tour are residential, and it would be staggeringly inconsiderate to bring larger vehicles onto them. This tour abides by all traffic laws and regulations; please do the same. Furthermore, please respect all private-property rights for residences and institutions.

If you've been walking the other tours in our book, you are probably wondering what the many square miles not covered in them look like. You'll have to wait for a walking-tour guide to the rest of the city, but in the meantime, we offer our "The Other Boroughs: A Driving Tour."

It's certainly possible to drive this tour from start to finish in one day, but it will take you the good part of a day to do so, and that means starting early in the morning and not getting out to look around along the way. We assume that many folk will want to stop and walk around periodically. Keeping that in mind, it would probably take the heartiest and most patient traveler to drive the entire tour for the first time in one day. You're the best judge of how you like to do things. We've done the drive many times, but if you're doing it for the first time, you'll probably want to break it up into manageable chunks. For example, you can do any one borough individually or do two at a clip.

It is also important to remember that you'll be driving on all types of roads, from highways to tiny residential streets, and in all types of neighborhoods, from wealthy to poor. So be prepared for the phenomenal diversity of New York, bring everything you need for a long car trip, and get going.

STATEN ISLAND

Our "Other Boroughs Driving Tour" begins on the southernmost point of Manhattan—South Ferry. It is here you board the Staten Island Ferry for a refreshing twenty-five-minute, 6.2-mile journey to explore New York City beyond Manhattan. There is a $3 charge to take your vehicle onto the ferry. (It is free for pedestrians.) Car ferries run about every thirty minutes on weekdays and every hour on the half hour on weekends and holidays, but check the schedule because it is subject to change.

While crossing the harbor, you are allowed to leave your vehicle in the hold and step out onto the ferry's deck, which we recommend. You will pass a number of significant landmarks in the harbor. Immediately to your left will be Governors Island. This is the 176-acre former U.S. Army and then Coast Guard base that was closed in 1996. Almost half (eighty-five acres) of the island is a National Historic Landmark, and there are five individual land-marked structures as well. At this time the future of the island is unclear, but everything from casinos to universities has been proposed. The three-story fort protecting the is-

Staten Island Ferry, Lower Manhattan as seen in the mid-1990s. Ferries have run between Manhattan and Staten Island since the 1630s. The contemporary Staten Island Ferry has been operated by the City of New York since 1905. The ferries carry sixty-five thousand passengers a day and twenty million a year. The seven-ferry fleet makes the 6.2 mile crossing some thirty-four thousand times a year. Courtesy of NYC & Company–The Convention and Visitors Bureau.

land on this side is Castle Williams, built 1807–11. It is one of three forts on Governors Island.

> **Further into the harbor, to your right, are Ellis Island and the Statue of Liberty.**

Ellis Island first opened as New York's immigration reception center in 1892. The main building, which is now a museum, opened in 1900. Between first opening and 1924, some 16 million immigrants entered America through this building. One interesting note about the island itself: Ellis Island began as a 3.3-acre sandbar. To accommodate the buildings and increased demand for space, landfill was added to grow the island to its current 27.5 acres.

The Statue of Liberty, one of the best-known landmarks in the world, was a gift from France, dedicated on

October 28, 1886. Designed by sculptor Frédéric-Auguste Bartholdi, its copper "skin" is supported by a metal structure built by Gustave Eiffel. The stone base was designed by American architect Richard Morris Hunt.

Both Ellis Island and the Statue of Liberty can be reached by taking the Statue of Liberty Ferry (paid admission) from Battery Park, Manhattan.

Ferries between the harbor's islands began running as early as 1713, when sailing vessels were used to cross the harbor. The first steamer-ferry service between Staten Island and Manhattan was started by Daniel Tompkins when he launched the *Nautilus* in 1817. Regular ferry service has continued ever since. In 1905, municipal ferries began replacing the private companies.

STATEN ISLAND

➤ **Exit ferry terminal and drive straight one block to Richmond Terrace.**

We begin in one of the oldest and most historic parts of Staten Island. It was on the hills ahead of and above us that the British built a series of earthen redoubts to defend the island from invasion during the American Revolution. The area remained mostly rural until the 1830s, when Manhattanites began using it as a country retreat.

Today, St. George is the most populous part of Staten Island (seven thousand residents in 1990) and is the center of the borough's government.

➤ **Turn right on Richmond Terrace. As you turn, immediately to your left is Staten Island Borough Hall, at 2-10 Richmond Terrace.**

Built by architects Carrere & Hastings between 1904 and 1906, this is the main government building for the borough of Staten Island. It is designed to be immediately noticed by those arriving by ferry from Manhattan and stands as a symbol of Staten Island's equal membership in greater New York. This building is a New York City Landmark.

Directly adjacent to Borough Hall stands the Richmond County Courthouse, at 12–24 Richmond Terrace. The columned courthouse adjacent to Borough Hall was also built by Carrere & Hastings, but a decade later. These two buildings were meant to be part of a larger, but never built, civic center.

Carrere & Hastings was one of the city's more prominent early twentieth-century design firms. It built numerous structures throughout the city. But one must wonder if the fact that John Carrere was a Staten Island resident helped land this plum contract.

As you approach the intersection with Wall Street, look up the hill to your left and note the Staten Island Institute of Arts and Letters, just above the police station. The institute is a research center and museum dedicated to the heritage and history of Staten Island and its people.

It is impossible to discern the exact place where one neighborhood becomes another but you are now driving through the Village of New Brighton. When it was incorporated in 1866, it brought together a series of smaller areas known as Goosepatch, Vinegar Hill, and Tuxedo.

Take note of the street names. Many of them serve as reminders of the old Staten Island and have Dutch or early American names. Some prominent examples include Hamilton, Westervelt, and Van Tuyl.

➤ Just after the police station turn left on Hamilton Street. After two blocks, turn right on St. Marks Place.

It was here, along St. Marks Place, that a series of elegant hotels were built in the mid-nineteenth century. They offered a respite from the overcrowded city, with fresh sea air and a pastoral view across the Kill van Kull into rural New Jersey. That view has since been replaced by the shipyards and refineries of Bayonne just across the water.

➤ **As you travel along St. Marks Place, note Curtis High School to your left, at 105 Hamilton Avenue at St. Marks Place.**

Curtis High School sits on a diagonal on the corner of Hamilton Avenue and St. Marks Place. Built in 1904 in the collegiate Gothic style, it is the first public high school on Staten Island and the first municipal building built after the 1898 Consolidation of Greater New York. It's named for George William Curtis, a nineteenth-century writer and editor who had a country estate on the island. Curtis was an early advocate of women's suffrage and was a strong supporter of professional civil service as a cure for political corruption. Locally, he is known for sheltering Horace Greeley from pro-Confederate Staten Islanders during and before the Civil War. Curtis wrote for *Harper's* magazine and *The Nation*. He also published *Putnam's Monthly* with his friend and fellow Staten Islander Frederick Law Olmsted. Curtis High School is also a New York City landmark.

St. Marks Place runs through the heart of the St. George/New Brighton Historic District.

➤ **While driving along St. Marks Place, make note of Nos. 125, 119, and 103, three great examples of 1890s Queen Anne revival houses.**

Standing in the midst of the landmark district is St. Peter's Roman Catholic Church and Rectory, the oldest Catholic parish on the island. The neo-Romanesque church was built in 1900.

➢ **At the end of St. Marks Place, turn right on Westervelt Avenue.**

As you drive on Westervelt Avenue, note the lovely colonial revival home at No. 65.

➢ **At the end of Westervelt Avenue, turn left on Richmond Terrace and drive three blocks to Franklin.**

➢ **Turn left on Franklin and drive two blocks to Fillmore.**

➢ **Turn right on Fillmore, then turn right on Lafayette Street, to head back to Richmond Terrace.**

When you reach the intersection of Fillmore and Lafayette, note New Brighton Village Hall, at 66 Lafayette Street on the southwest corner of Fillmore Street. This boarded-up Second Empire–style brick building was New Brighton's former village hall. Built in 1871 by James Whitford, it has been vacant since 1968. Despite its dilapidated condition, it is a clear symbol of the wealth of this nineteenth-century village.

➢ **Turn left on Richmond Terrace.**

You are approaching the Tysen-Neville House—806 Richmond Terrace. Approximately two and a half blocks past Lafayette Street, look toward the left and take careful note of the small white building with the porch. Built around 1770 by sea captain John Neville, it is one of the few eighteenth-century buildings left on this part of Staten Island.

• • •

As you continue along Richmond Terrace, you will pass the iron fence and Greek revival buildings of Sailors Snug Harbor. Sailors Snug Harbor was created in 1801 with a bequest from shipping merchant Robert R. Randall as an institution for the care of "aged, decrepit, and worn-out sailors." Snug Harbor purchased this land in 1831 and built a campus of buildings for the care of retired seamen. By 1900 it housed over a thousand people. But as the number of American sailors diminished, so did the institution. In 1975 it relocated to North Carolina, and one year later the complex was turned into the Sailors Snug Harbor Cultural Center.

The most significant building is the 1831 Greek revival Administration Building. Easily seen from Richmond Terrace, with its Ionic portico, it is the oldest surviving work by architect Minard Lefever.

➤ **Turn left on Snug Harbor Road and make an immediate left into Sailors Snug Harbor.**

The Sailors Snug Harbor Cultural Center is a great place to drive and/or walk around. It houses a music hall, art galleries, classrooms, the Staten Island Children's Museum, and the newly created Chinese Scholars Garden.

➤ **Depart Snug Harbor the way you came and turn left on Snug Harbor Road.**

➤ **Turn left on Kissel Avenue.**

➤ **Turn right on Henderson Avenue (Kissel ends at Henderson). After approximately two blocks, turn left on Davis Avenue (second traffic light).**

➤ **Davis ends at Forest Avenue. Turn right on Forest Avenue.**

➤ After one block, turn left on Pelton Avenue.

➤ At the intersection with the fourth stop sign and the "dead-end" sign, turn right on Whitewood Avenue.

➤ Continue on Whitewood until it crosses Bement Avenue and becomes Tyler Avenue.

➤ Drive past the Julia Gardiner Tyler House—27 Tyler Street, on your right.

This wonderful house, with its columns and green trim, has been lovingly restored. Built about 1836 for Eliza Racey, this Greek revival manor became the home for Julia Gardiner Tyler, the widow of President John Tyler. It had been purchased for Julia by her parents in 1862.

➤ At the end of Tyler Avenue, turn left on Clove Road.

➤ Drive past the John King Vanderbilt House—1197 Clove Road.

Keep your eyes open to the left for this one. Built in 1836, this graffiti-covered wreck was once a fine example of Greek revival architecture. Its original owner was the cousin of "Commodore" Cornelius Vanderbilt (1794–1887), who was born on Staten Island. At an early age, Cornelius Vanderbilt began operating a ferry between here and Manhattan. From there he built a shipping empire, and he had become a millionaire by 1846. His statue stands in front of Manhattan's Grand Central Terminal, the Manhattan terminus for his New York Central Railroad.

➤ Turn right on Victory Boulevard (at the Getty gas station) for a fairly long drive, and then turn left on Manor Road (at fourth stoplight and Mobil gas station).

Victory Boulevard was created in 1817 as part of Staten Island resident and U.S. vice president Daniel Tompkins's Richmond Turnpike Company.

The intersection of Manor Road and Victory Boulevard is the heart of Castleton Corners, a small neighborhood that was colonial governor Thomas Dongan's land grant. Dongan was the first Catholic governor of the English colony, serving from 1682 to 1688. During his time as governor, he supported the "Charter of Liberties and Privileges," which proposed public elections, limited taxation, and Christian religious freedom.

➤ **After passing five traffic lights, at the flashing yellow light on Manor Road, take the right fork onto Brielle Avenue.**

➤ **Be careful, Brielle forks again. Take left fork to stay on Brielle.**

Drive past the New York City Farm Colony—Sea View Hospital and Home Historic District. Brielle Avenue runs straight through the center of the district. As you are driving, note the older run-down buildings on your right that are fenced off and partially obscured by trees. The Farm Colony was a fancy name for a poorhouse. Established in 1902, the able-bodied poor from throughout the city were sent here to work. The colony had a series of fields where the poor were taught to farm. In the late 1980s, there were some discussions about the city developing these buildings into viable housing, but nothing came of it.

As you come around the bend on Brielle Avenue, on the left you will see, surrounded by a chain-link fence, the Seaview Hospital. Founded in 1905, this was the largest tuberculosis hospital in the world. Most of the buildings are currently vacant, but it is still a functioning hospital, and the grounds are open to the public on a case-by-case basis.

➤ **Brielle Avenue ends at Rockland Avenue.**

➤ **Turn left on Rockland Avenue.**

➤ **Turn right at the first light onto Meisner Avenue.**

As you turn onto Meisner Avenue, you are entering the neighborhood known as Egbertville, a residential area named for the eighteenth-century farming landowners, the Egberts.

➤ **Drive past 190 Meisner Avenue.**

Watch on your left for this unique private residence, built around 1850. Note the small, all-glass monitor atop the roof. Such spaces were designed for watching the comings and goings of ships from the commanding heights over Lower New York Bay.

➤ **A few blocks after 190 Meisner, turn right on London Road. As it crosses Edinboro, go straight onto Rigby Street.**

➤ **Turn left onto Manor Court as Rigby dead-ends, after one short block.**

Drive past the William and Catherine Cass House at 48 Manor Court. This is New York City's only home designed by Frank Lloyd Wright, and a city landmark. Wright designed it in 1956 for the Madison, Wisconsin, builder Marshall Erdman. The prefabricated parts were shipped from Wisconsin and assembled here in 1958–59 by Wright's associate Morton Delson.

➤ You will have to turn around, as Manor Court is a dead-end street.

➤ Returning to Edinboro, turn right on Edinboro.

Drive past the landmarked Staten Island Lighthouse. The brick and limestone lighthouse was build in 1912 and houses a 350,000-candle-power light that guides ships into New York Bay. There is a better view of the lighthouse a bit further along in our tour, so don't despair about the partial view.

➤ Continue on Edinboro and make a right at the first stop sign onto Terrace Court.

➤ Terrace Court becomes Lighthouse Avenue.

As you curve around Terrace Court, look carefully left at the fantastic view of the Lower Harbor and the ocean from Lighthouse Hill, which will give you a sense of why Lighthouse Hill is considered one of the most exclusive neighborhoods on Staten Island.

Drive slowly along Lighthouse Avenue; otherwise you will miss the Jacques Marchais Museum of Tibetan Art at 338 Lighthouse. Look for a garage with green door, on your left. The museum is open to the public from November to April and houses the most extensive privately owned collection of Tibetan art outside Tibet.

As you begin to descend downhill, look up to the right at the lighthouse.

➤ At the end of Lighthouse Avenue, turn right on Richmond Road. Drive approximately two blocks and turn right on St. Patrick's Place.

As you drive a short distance on St. Patrick's Place, you'll see the namesake of the street, the landmarked Saint Patrick's Church, at No. 45. Built in the early 1860s, this is an excellent example of Romanesque revival design.

➤ **St. Patrick's Place ends at Clarke Avenue.**

➤ **The entrance to Historic Richmond Town is about one hundred yards to your right on Clarke Avenue.**

Located near the center of Staten Island, Historic Richmond Town is a great place to stop and walk around. This twenty-five-acre site contains twenty-seven historic buildings from throughout the island. The oldest extant schoolhouse in the nation is here, built in 1696. The "newest" of the structures dates from the mid-nineteenth century. Historic Richmond Town has a visitor center and offers guided tours and interpretive programming throughout the year.

➤ **After a visit to Historic Richmond Town, exit the parking lot and turn left on Clarke Avenue. At end of Clarke Avenue (approximately nine blocks), turn left on Amboy Road.**

➤ **Follow Amboy for four traffic lights to where it intersects with and becomes Richmond Road. Continue on Richmond to the Moravian Cemetery.**

About a block after you merge onto Richmond Road, keep a lookout for No. 2475. Located to your left and up on a hill, this 1850s Italianate villa is the former home of Gustave A. Mayer, the man who invented the Nabisco sugar wafer.

MORAVIAN CEMETERY

The entrance to the Moravian Cemetery is on Richmond Road, opposite Otis Avenue. This cemetery contains a "who's who" of Staten Island. Most of it is open to the public, and the older sections offer scenic views. Toward the back of the cemetery sit fourteen acres of the Vanderbilt family. The cemetery grounds were designed by Frederick Law Olmsted, and the large, seventy-two-crypt, Vanderbilt mausoleum, which holds the "commodore" and his family, by Richard Morris Hunt.

➤ Continue on Richmond Road, keeping the cemetery on your left, to the intersection of Richmond Road and Todt Hill Road. Turn left on Todt Hill Road (follow the cemetery fence up Todt Hill Road).

➤ After one block, turn right on Flagg Place.

The harbor view is to your right, while the splendid Flagg Estate is set off the road at No. 209. Now owned by the Scalabrini Fathers of St. Charles, this sweeping residence was the country home of Ernest Flagg, one of America's most prominent architects. Flagg also purchased a sizable tract of land on which he experimented with designing affordable middle-class housing. Called "The Cottages," these smaller stone and wood homes were part of his belief in home ownership for all people. The easiest cottage to view from Flagg Place is Wallcot, which stands at No. 285.

Note how we are climbing as we drive these roads. At 410 feet above sea level, Todt Hill is the highest point on the United States Atlantic Coast south of Maine. Todt Hill is one of the most affluent neighborhoods on Staten Island.

Historic Richmond Town. A one hundred-acre park, Historic Richmond Town represents three hundred years of Staten Island history. It contains twenty-seven historic buildings from throughout the island. Courtesy of NYC & Company–The Convention and Visitors Bureau.

➤ At the end of Flagg Place, turn left onto Richmond Road.

➤ Follow Richmond Road until it becomes Narrows Road.

➤ Continue on Narrows Road as it parallels the expressway.

➤ Be careful not to get onto Route 278, and do not follow signs for the Verrazano Narrows Bridge.

➤ As Richmond Road comes to an end, take the right fork onto Bay Street.

➤ Take a left on Lily Pond.

➤ Follow the signs for "Bay Street–Fort Wadsworth." After 1.8 miles, you will come to the entrance to Fort Wadsworth.

➤ **Go into Fort Wadsworth.**

There have been fortifications on this site since 1663, and it was one of the last British positions to surrender after the American Revolution. The present fort was built in 1847 and was dedicated to Brigadier General James Wadsworth in 1865, following his death at the Civil War's Battle of the Wilderness. Since the early 1990s this installation has been part of the Gateway National Recreation Area.

Within Fort Wadsworth, follow signs to the National Park Service Visitors Center and be certain to view the scenic overlook on Tompkins Road. The National Park Service has a short film on the history of New York's fortifications and offers daily guided tours of the site.

➤ **After viewing the fort, exit the grounds and continue straight on Bay Street, 0.5 miles to Hylan Boulevard.**

➤ **Turn right on Hylan Boulevard and follow it to the end.**

Drive to Alice Austen House, overlooking the Verrazano Narrows. Photographer Alice Austen's (1866–1952) work primarily focused on daily life in the late nineteenth century. This house, purchased in 1844 by her grandfather, was Austen's primary residence and is now a museum dedicated to her work.

➤ **Make a U-turn from the Austen House and drive Hylan Boulevard back to Bay Street.**

➤ **Turn right on Bay Street and drive four blocks to Chestnut Avenue.**

➤ **Turn left on Chestnut.**

➤ **Chestnut ends at Tompkins Avenue.**

➤ **Turn left on Tompkins Avenue.**

Directly in front of you, at the intersection of Tompkins and Chestnut, is the Garibaldi-Meucci Museum and historic home. Built around 1845, this was the home to Italian American inventor Antonio Meucci, who invented an early telephone. Guiseppe Garibaldi, the Italian liberator, lived here from 1851 to 1853 while in exile in America. The museum is maintained by the Sons of Italy and is open to the public.

➤ **Continue along Tompkins until you reach Hylan Boulevard.**

➤ **Turn right onto Hylan. Hylan Boulevard will cross over the expressway. Enter expressway (following signs for 278 East-Brooklyn).**

➤ **Cross Verrazano Narrows Bridge to Brooklyn.**

When the Verrazano Narrows Bridge was completed in 1964, as designed by Swiss engineer Othmar Ammann, it was the world's longest suspension bridge, measuring 4,260 feet between towers. It is not the longest anymore but is still beautiful. Many Italian Americans living in Bay Ridge near the Brooklyn approach to the bridge did not want their homes destroyed for its approaches, and naming it after Giovanni da Verrazano, who sailed into New York Harbor in 1524, certainly wasn't enough to alleviate their concerns. It took Robert Moses many years to beat back all the opposition to the bridge, but he eventually got his way, and eight thousand Brooklynites lost their homes and quite a number more moved across the bridge to Staten Island. The Staten Island side of the bridge is the starting point for the New York Marathon every November. Including the approaches, the bridge is 13,700 feet long; it is 228 feet above the water; each tower is 693 feet tall; and it costs $7 to go across—although the toll is collected only when traveling from Brooklyn to Staten Island, so you get a free ride.

BROOKLYN

Brooklyn is New York's most populous borough, but not its largest; that credit goes to Queens. Brooklyn was a separate city until it was united with New York City in 1898, but it still remains a place apart. The home of Coney Island, Bedford-Stuyvesant, Prospect Park, and Green-Wood Cemetery, the borough sits on the western end of Long Island and looks across the East River at Manhattan and across the Narrows at Staten Island. It shares a land border with Queens.

After driving around many of the open spaces in Staten Island, Brooklyn comes as a shock. It is a collection of neighborhoods mostly made up of modest-sized apartment buildings and attached rowhouses, although some spectacular free standing houses crop up. Brooklyn also has two beautiful parkways—roads lined with trees—designed by Frederick Law Olmsted and Calvert Vaux, who designed Central Park and Prospect Park.

Your drive through Brooklyn will take you along the waterfront, to old amusement parks, to one of the oldest cemeteries in the city, past what may be New York's most beautiful houses, and through neighborhoods of stunning ethnic variety.

➤ **Exit the Verrazano Narrows Bridge to the Belt Parkway East, which is also called the Shore Parkway on some maps. Signs will point toward JFK International Airport. As you exit the bridge, note Fort Hamilton, sister to Fort**

Wadsworth, on your left. The neighborhoods behind the fort are Bay Ridge and Dyker Heights.

➤ Drive 2.9 miles and exit the Belt Parkway at Cropsey Avenue (exit 6).

➤ At the end of the exit ramp, turn right onto Cropsey Avenue.

➤ Continue on Cropsey for a few blocks, staying in the middle lane and following the signs that say "Amusement Parks."

➤ As it crosses Neptune Avenue, Cropsey becomes West Seventeenth Street.

In front of you is the tall steel Parachute Tower built for the 1939 World's Fair and brought to Coney Island shortly afterward. Visitors used to be able to sit on a small seat and float by parachute and guide wire from the top to the ground.

➤ Seventeenth Street ends at Surf Avenue.

There is the new baseball field for the Brooklyn Cyclones, an AAA minor league team, at this intersection.

➤ Turn left on Surf Avenue and drive three blocks to Stillwell Avenue.

Nathan's has been serving hot dogs on the corner of Stillwell since 1916.

➤ Turn right on Stillwell, park, and get out for a look at the two-and-a-half-mile Coney Island boardwalk.

Coney Island is named for an Anglicized version of the Dutch word for rabbit; the animals were abundant here in the 1600s. It's been a vacation spot for New Yorkers from at least the mid-nineteenth century. Eventually, three of the most spectacular amusement parks in the nation were built here—Steeplechase Park, Luna Park, and Dreamland. They are all closed now. In their place stands Astroland, opened in 1954. Stop by for a ride or carny game.

If you go up on the boardwalk, you'll see a large pier to the right from which residents and visitors fish and go crabbing. From about where you're standing, the Polar Bear Club goes swimming every weekend during the winter. The New Year's Day swim brings out news cameras, tourists, and one-time swimmers from across the city.

➤ **Get back in your car and make a right on Surf Avenue.**

Note the flea markets in the stalls to your left. Most are run by recent Russian immigrants. At West Tenth Street, on your right, you'll pass the Cyclone, a landmark 1927 wooden roller-coaster on the site of the first roller-coaster in the world (which was built in 1884). Also on your right, at West Eighth Street, you'll pass the New York Aquarium, moved here from Battery Park in Manhattan by Parks Commissioner Robert Moses out of anger at those who stopped his project to build a bridge from Battery Park to Brooklyn.

➤ **Continue on Surf Avenue. As it begins to curve away from the water, pay attention and take the right fork that is marked with a very small sign for Brighton Beach Avenue. At the light at the elevated subway (the El), turn right onto Brighton Beach Avenue. Driving under the El is a unique experience that can be indulged in only a few cities, most notably New York and Chicago.**

Coney Island. The Mermaid Parade takes place every June in Coney Island. Each year it passes the original Nathan's hot-dog stand. Opened in 1916 by Nathan Handwerker, the Coney Island stand is a Brooklyn treasure. Courtesy of NYC & Company—The Convention and Visitors Bureau.

Brighton Beach is the best-known Russian neighborhood in the city, with about 150,000 Russians living here. The ethnicity of the neighborhood is apparent as you drive along under the El. Note stores and restaurants such as M & I International (249 Brighton Beach Avenue), Primorski (282 Brighton Beach Avenue), and Café Arbat (306 Brighton Beach Avenue). Brighton Beach developed along with Coney Island, helped by the presence of Brighton Beach Racetrack, which brought in visitors from 1879 to 1907.

➤ **Turn left on Coney Island Avenue as the El curves.**

At the corner is Mrs. Stahl's (1001 Coney Island Avenue), famous for its knishes. Note the bungalow communities to your right. The neighborhood was really a summer residence at first, but over the years the bungalows were converted to year-round homes. Further off to the right are the neighborhoods of Sheepshead Bay, from which you can leave on daily fishing trips, and Manhattan Beach, an expensive seaside community and home to Kingsborough Community College.

➤ Continue on Coney Island Avenue, crossing over the Brooklyn-Queens Expressway, and then take a left at the first light you come to, Avenue Z.

➤ Continue two lights to Ocean Parkway and turn right into the center of the road (not onto the service road).

➤ Drive to Avenue V and make a left.

➤ Avenue V turns into Gravesend Neck Road in a few blocks.

➤ Just after you pass under the El (F train) at McDonald Avenue, pull over.

The intersection of Gravesend Neck Road and McDonald Avenue was the town center of Gravesend, the only non-Dutch town of the original six settlements that made up Brooklyn in the seventeenth century. The original town stretched across much of the area you've just driven across and beyond. Gravesend was founded in 1643 by Lady Deborah Moody, an Anabaptist who fled religious intolerance in Massachusetts to New York. Here she became the first woman to vote at a town meeting. Depending on whom you ask, Gravesend comes either from the Dutch *grafes ande*, translated as both "end of the grove" and "count's beach," or from the British town of Gravesend.

The 1.6-acre Gravesend Cemetery (it stretches well back from the road) on your left has been here since the 1660s, though all the earlier gravestones are gone so Lady Moody's grave site is unknown. Next to it is the Van Sicklen Cemetery, named for a prominent neighborhood family.

Across from the cemetery is the Hicks-Platt House (27 Gravesend Neck Road), also called the Lady Moody House because a clever real estate developer in 1890 said she had lived here, although she never did. The original house was finished in 1645 but has been changed quite a bit. On the corner, just past the Hicks-Platt Houses, is P.S. 95. The first school building here went up in 1888, but this one dates from 1915.

➤ Turn left on Van Sicklen Street and drive one block.

➤ Turn left on Village Road South and drive another block.

➤ Turn left on McDonald Avenue and drive two blocks.

➤ Turn right on Avenue U, return to Ocean Parkway, and make a left.

➤ Note your mileage, because you'll be staying on Ocean Parkway for 3.2 miles.

Ocean Parkway, finished in 1876, before the automobile, stretches six miles from Coney Island to Prospect Park. Frederick Law Olmsted and Calvert Vaux, who designed Central Park in Manhattan and Prospect Park in Brooklyn, believed strongly in creating a series of scenic parkways throughout the city, and this is one of them. Ocean

Parkway originally had a central drive, greenery-filled malls (hence "parkway"), a bridle trail, and pedestrian walkways. The bridle trails are now service roads, but the beauty of the parkway remains.

As you drive along, note the large, elegant houses built earlier in the twentieth century, and those built later that attempt to blend in. Note how deep the lots are. After Gravesend, you will be driving through the neighborhoods of Midwood and then Kensington. Large Orthodox and Hasidic communities live along Ocean Parkway, which is lined with synagogues and religious schools. Note the Sephardic Community Center at the corner of Avenue S and Washington Cemetery at Avenue K.

➤ Drive Ocean Parkway for the 3.2 miles to Beverly Road (the first light after Avenue C) and turn right.

➤ Drive three blocks to Coney Island Avenue and turn left.

➤ Drive another three blocks to Albemarle and turn right.

➤ Continue between the small stone pillars with plaques that say "PPS" and mark the entrance to Prospect Park South.

This small historic district is home to large single-family houses that run a gamut of styles, from Tudor to Queen Anne to neo-Japanese, and sit incongruously hidden just off one of Brooklyn's busiest commercial streets. The neighborhood was created by developer Dean Alvord, who bought forty acres here in 1899. To create the neighborhood he wanted, Alvord required houses to be set back thirty-nine feet from the sidewalk, with eight feet left between street and sidewalk for greenery. Most of the houses were finished by 1905.

➤ **Drive slowly along Albemarle for five blocks, admiring the homes.**

Our favorites are the classical revival home, with a balcony behind a colonnade, at 1305 Albemarle; the Queen Anne at No. 1423; the Queen Anne/colonial revival hermaphrodite at No. 1440; and the large mansion at No. 1510, which originally had a conservatory and a stable.

➤ **Albemarle curves left, turning into Buckingham.**

➤ **Take the right fork as you drive up Buckingham.**

Some of the most beautiful homes along here include the porticoed one at 104 Buckingham, the shingle-style at No. 115, and the partially Japanese-style home at No. 131.

➤ **Leave the beauty of Prospect Park South when you intersect with the commercial strip at Church Avenue.**

➤ **Turn right on Church and drive two blocks.**

Note how incredibly busy this commercial strip is, only seconds from the Buckingham and Albemarle mansions.

➤ **Turn right on East Eighteenth Street.**

➤ **Drive two blocks to Albemarle.**

➤ **Turn left at Albemarle and drive four blocks.**

➤ **Turn left onto Flatbush Avenue.**

You are driving through Flatbush (from the Dutch *vlacke-bos*, "wooded plain"), although Flatbush is itself a collection of smaller neighborhoods, among them Ditmars Park and Prospect-Lefferts Gardens. Half a block down Snyder Street—the second street you pass on your right—at No. 35 is Flatbush Town Hall, built in 1875 before the town was incorporated into New York City. Unfortunately, you cannot see it clearly from Flatbush Avenue.

Drive another block and Erasmus Hall High School is on your right. Famous graduates include Barbra Streisand, Neil Diamond, Barry Manilow, and Bobby Fischer. If you look through the gate at the center of the block, the original, wooden 1786 Erasmus Hall is visible inside the quad. Erasmus was the first secondary school chartered by New York State, although it was set up by the Flatbush Reformed Dutch Church diagonally across the street from the high school. The present church building, finished in 1798, is the third one on this site. Also look at the parish house, set back from the street.

➤ **Continue on Flatbush Avenue through the shopping district until the avenue forks at Lincoln Street. Stay on Flatbush.**

➤ **Drive along, keeping Prospect Park to your left.**

Inside the park to your left, you will see the Lefferts Homestead, a copy of a Dutch home design, finished in 1783 and moved to its current spot in 1918. The present house was built by the Lefferts family with parts left from their earlier house, which was burned during the Revolutionary War.

PROSPECT PARK

The 526-acre Prospect Park was designed by Calvert Vaux and Frederick Law Olmsted in 1866–1873, as soon as they were finished with Central Park in Manhattan. Like Central Park, it encompasses different landscapes, including the Long Meadow, a long and hilly stretch of grass; a wooded ravine; a lake; several arches; and a number of buildings. Also like Central Park, the city first backed a mediocre design by Egbert Viele but abandoned it in favor of Vaux and Olmsted's. The park is as beautiful as Central Park, if not more so thanks to the very high hills that crop up in several places. Olmsted and Vaux had hoped that Prospect Park would be linked to Central Park by a series of parkways. Unfortunately, this never happened, but they did convince the city to build wide, tree-lined roads, such as Ocean Parkway and Eastern Parkway, leading to Prospect Park.

➤ Continue on Flatbush Avenue to Grand Army Plaza. (You'll see the giant arch at its center.) Turn right at the Brooklyn Public Library onto Eastern Parkway.

➤ Mark your mileage; your next turn is in 1.7 miles.

The entrance to the park, immediately to your left and facing the giant Soldiers' and Sailors' monument, was designed by Stanford White. It's a combination of columns, bronze urns, and two twelve-sided pavilions. In front of you, at Grand Army Plaza, is the Soldiers' and Sailors' Memorial Arch, which sits on a plaza designed by Olmsted and Vaux to mimic the Parisian plaza that holds the Arc de Triomphe.

To your right as you follow Eastern Parkway are the Brooklyn Public Library, the Brooklyn Botanic Garden, and the Brooklyn Museum. The library was founded in 1897, although it was not completed in this spot until 1941. The botanic garden opened in 1912. The museum, designed by Stanford White, was begun in 1897 and has an excellent Egyptian art collection. All three sites remind us that Brooklyn was, until 1898, a separate city and not part of New York City.

Continue on Eastern Parkway. To your left is the neighborhood of Bedford-Stuyvesant, and to your right is Crown Heights. Crown Heights is a neighborhood of West Indian immigrants, with a small population of Lubavitcher Hasidim. The neighborhood takes its name either from Crow Hill (a tall hill that had lots of crows on it) or because bigoted whites called the original African and African American settlers crows. Others say that "crows" were inmates at a nearby prison.

Continue four long blocks to Bedford Avenue. Look to your right down Bedford and you'll see a huge 1908 armory. A few blocks further you can make out a public housing project built on the site of Ebbets Field, home of the Brooklyn Dodgers.

Just before Nostrand Avenue, look to your right to see the Philadelphia Sabbath Cathedral (520 Eastern Parkway). At the corner of Kingston Avenue is 770 Eastern Parkway, synagogue for the Lubavitcher Hasidim and former home to Lubavitcher Rebbe Menachem Schneerson.

➤ **After driving the 1.7 miles, turn left on Buffalo (first street after Rochester Street).**

You're now in the center of Bedford-Stuyvesant, the largest black neighborhood in New York and former home to baseball great Jackie Robinson, boxer Floyd Paterson, and musician Eubie Blake.

➤ **Drive seven blocks and turn left when Buffalo Street ends at Bergen Street.**

On your left are the Weeksville Houses, which sit back from Bergen along what was Hunterfly Road. These four houses (now the Society for the Preservation of Weeksville and Bedford-Stuyvesant) are all that remain of the architecture of two mid-nineteenth century African American communities. Thirty years before the Civil War, William Thomas founded Carrville and James Weeks built a community that became Weeksville. Both Weeksville and Carrville had their own schools, churches, and an orphanage. The beautiful Eastern Parkway and streets built off it destroyed Carrville and Weeksville in the same way that the Cross Bronx Expressway destroyed Bronx communities in the twentieth century.

➤ Turn left on Berger and drive one block and turn right on Rochester Avenue.

➤ Continue five blocks to Atlantic Avenue and turn right.

As you drive along Atlantic Avenue, note that it is decidedly not a parkway like Ocean Parkway or Eastern Parkway.

➤ Continue along Atlantic up a ramp that goes over some railroad tracks. (Eastern Parkway intersects on the right.)

As you come off the ramp, look to your right at the abandoned but still interesting Twenty-sixth Ward Bank at the corner of Georgia Avenue.

➤ Get in the left lane and turn left at the second light after the ramp, which is called both Granville Payne Avenue and Pennsylvania Avenue.

➤ Drive two blocks and enter the Jackie Robinson Parkway (formerly the Interboro Parkway), which you will follow into the Borough of Queens.

➤ Take the Interboro (Jackie Robinson) Parkway to Van Wyck Expressway (exit 7)—4.9 miles

As you drive along the Interboro Parkway between Brooklyn and Queens, it appears that most of the route is lined by a giant cemetery. This observation would not be far from the truth; there are actually eighteen different cemeteries along the Interboro. From this angle, it is impossible to tell where one ends and the next begins. They hold a combined twenty thousand veterans of American wars and untold numbers of others.

The largest of the cemeteries is Cypress Hill. Buried here is Jackie Robinson, the first African American baseball player to break the color line in Major League Baseball on April 9, 1947, while playing for the Brooklyn Dodgers. Two years later he was named the Most Valuable Player in the National League. The Interboro was renamed for Jackie Robinson in the late 1990s.

Adjacent to Cypress Hills is Machpelah Cemetery. This is the resting place of the great magician Harry Houdini. In neighboring cemeteries are the graves of Yiddish writer Sholom Aleichem, actor Edward G. Robinson, gangster and World Series fixer Arnold Rothstein, and jurist Benjamin Cardozo.

➤ Take the Van Wyck to Northern Boulevard East (exit 13)— 3.3 miles

➤ As you exit the Van Wyck, be certain to take the left fork for Northern Boulevard East.

As you exit the Van Wyck, look toward your left for a nice view of the old World's Fair Grounds and Shea Stadium.

The Van Wyck Expressway is named for Mayor Robert Van Wyck, the first mayor of consolidated New York in 1898. His is an interesting name for a major roadway; Van Wyck is perhaps best known for being accused of accepting a $500,000 "gift" from a political supporter. Although he was cleared of wrongdoing by Governor Teddy Roosevelt in 1900, the gift became a reelection issue that cost Van Wyck his job.

QUEENS

We begin our Queens drive in one of the most historically significant neighborhoods in America (and we don't say this lightly). Flushing was established in 1645 under the auspices of Dutch governor William Kieft. The eighteen original freeholders were assured by Kieft of the right to religious freedom. With this promise, Flushing became one of the cornerstones of religious liberty in colonial America. Flushing also has a long history of ethnic diversity and tolerance. When it was first established, it was a predominantly English community within a Dutch colony. It was a haven for free blacks in the early nineteenth century and today may host more immigrants from different countries than any place in New York City.

➤ **Almost immediately as you drive off the elevated roadway along Northern Boulevard, you will pass (on your left) Chin Fook Funeral Home, on the corner of Prince Street.**

On this site stood the Prince House and Nursery, established in 1737 as the first tree nursery in America. The newly inaugurated president, George Washington, visited the nursery and the town of Flushing in 1789. Prince House was destroyed in the 1950s.

Up until the 1964 World's Fair, Flushing retained some of its small-town features, a moderate population density, limited high-rise buildings, and a limited commercial district. However, after the fair and the ensuing attention, as well as the great influx of Chinese and Korean immigrants in the early 1980s, Flushing became a true urban center.

As you pass the intersection of Main Street, note the small traffic island to your left. Officially known as Daniel Carter Beard Memorial Square, it is named for the Flushing native who was one of the founders of the Boy Scouts. The square also contains a number of other memorial markers. The flagpole commemorates the Spanish-American War. Until recently, an elm tree there recalled Washington's 1789 visit. Finally, a bit beyond the flagpole is the monument for those from Flushing who died to preserve the Union during the Civil War.

Behind the small park, also to your left, stands the old Flushing Town Hall, now the Flushing Council on Culture and the Arts. Built in 1862 in the early Romanesque style, this was the center of town "business" before the 1898 Consolidation of Greater New York It is interesting to note that Queens is the only borough that retains its pre-Consolidation town names. In fact, when writing letters to people in Queens, you write, for example, "Flushing, New York," not "Queens, New York."

➤ **Look to your right at the Friends Meeting House—South Side of Northern Boulevard, opposite Linden Place**

Built in 1694, this is the oldest house of worship in New York City. It stands in the traditional Quaker spirit of worship, without decoration or art, to allow undistracted worship. During the Revolutionary War it was converted into a prison and hospital by the British.

If you can find a place to park, you might want to step inside. The second story is supported by massive forty-foot hand-cut oak beams, and the original handmade ironwork is still in use. The Meeting House is on the National Register of Historic Places, and visitors are welcome.

The castlelike building adjacent to the Meeting House is the former National Guard Armory. Built in 1905, it is designed to appear imposing and defendable. It is now used by the police department's Queens North Task Force and is a temporary shelter for homeless women.

As you cross Union Street, look left across Northern Boulevard. You will see the collegiate Gothic Flushing High School, built in 1912–15 by C. B. J. Snyder. This building may look familiar; Snyder also built Curtis High School on Staten Island as well as Erasmus High School in Brooklyn. Flushing High School was chartered in 1875, making it the oldest free public high school in the city.

➤ **Turn right on Bowne Street.**

John Bowne House, at 37–01 Bowne Street (after first light on left), was built in the colonial saltbox style in 1661 by John Bowne, a native of England who migrated to Flushing by way of Boston, Massachusetts, in the 1650s. After converting to the Quaker faith, Bowne found Boston an intolerant place to worship and came here with a small group of his coreligionists in 1657. New Amsterdam Governor Peter Stuyvesant quickly disregarded his predecessor governor Kieft and declared the Dutch Reformed Church the only acceptable religious order. In response, thirty townspeople signed the "Flushing Remonstrance," a document protesting Stuyvesant's actions. It reads in part:

> You have been pleased to send up unto us a certain prohibition or command that we should not receive or entertain any of those people called Quakers. . . . We cannot condemn them in this case, neither can we stretch our hands against them, to punish, banish or persecute them. . . . [We] shall be glad to see anything of God in any of them, desiring to doe unto all men as wee desire all men should doe unto us, which is the law of both Church and State.

Styuvesant responded by sending troops to arrest and fine all those who signed the Remonstrance. The Quakers continued to gather in secret, and when John Bowne finished building his home in 1661, he invited the Quakers to meet in his kitchen. Governor Stuyvesant heard about these illegal meetings and, in 1662, arrested Bowne and sentenced him to prison and banishment. After seven months in jail, Bowne traveled to the Netherlands and argued before the Dutch West India Company for religious tolerance. They agreed with his principles, set him free, and rebuked Stuyvesant with a letter that strongly supported the principle of religious tolerance. On his return to Flushing, Bowne again invited the Quakers to meet at his home. They continued to do so until they built the Meeting House we saw on Northern Boulevard.

This community resistance to state authority over religious worship is regarded by many historians to be the foundation of the First Amendment to the Constitution of the United States—freedom of religion.

Nine generations of the Bowne family lived in this house, the last one moving out in 1945. At that time, the Bowne Historical Society assumed responsibility for the site. It is now called "A National Shrine to Religious Freedom" and is open to the public a few days a week.

➤ Turn right on Roosevelt Avenue. After three blocks turn left on Prince, then make a quick left on Fortieth Road. As

Fortieth Road ends after one short block, turn right on Main Street.

THE HEART OF ASIAN FLUSHING

As you turn onto Main Street, you enter the newest layer of this historically heterogeneous community. Main Street is the heart of Asian Flushing. This is a fantastic pan-Asian commercial district that reflects the diversity not only of the neighborhood but of Asian New York in general.

According to the census of 2000, nearly one in every ten New Yorkers described him- or herself as Asian. This number is a significant increase from one in fourteen just ten years earlier. Here in Queens, one in every six residents is Asian. Chinese remain the largest Asian group in New York, with Filipinos and Koreans as the next largest in population. Other Asians represented along Main Street include Taiwanese, Thais, Vietnamese, Cambodians, Laotians, Malaysians, and Indonesians.

If you can find a parking space, this is a great area to get out and walk around, exploring the shops and restaurants.

Coming up on your right, after you pass Sixty-third Avenue, is Mount Hebron Cemetery. On your left is the Queens College campus of the City University of New York system and CUNY Law School. The CUNY system was created in 1926 in an effort to create a municipal college system in New York City. Comprised of twenty schools and colleges, it is the largest urban education organization in the United States, with more than 180,000 students.

Continue along Main Street, crossing the Long Island Expressway (Route 495).

➤ **Turn right on Jewel Avenue (also known as Harry Van Arsdale, Jr., Road) through Flushing Meadows Park.**

Harry Van Arsdale Jr. (1905–1986) was a significant labor leader in New York City. In 1959 he was instrumental in the creation of the New York Central Labor Council of the AFL-CIO. At the peak of his power, his union had some nine hundred thousand members. He was also involved in the unionization of municipal employees, hospital workers, and taxi drivers.

As you drive this stretch of Jewel Avenue, note how this major thoroughfare is significantly different from Ocean Parkway or Eastern Parkway in Brooklyn. In Brooklyn, the nineteenth-century pre-automobile parkway combined utilitarian purpose with a strong sense of aesthetic sensibility. These roads, built primarily in the twentieth century and after the arrival of the car, were constructed with only utility in mind.

As you pass through Flushing Meadows–Corona Park you are, once again, given a great view of the old 1964 World's Fair Unisphere to the right.

➤ **Jewel Avenue becomes Sixty-ninth Road after the park.**

➤ **Turn left on 108th Street.**

➤ **As 108th Street crosses Queens Boulevard, it becomes Continental Avenue.**

➤ **Follow Continental under the Long Island Railroad (LIRR) tracks into Forest Hills Station Square.**

➤ **Turn left at Station Square onto Terrace Greenway North.**

➤ **Take the left fork around the small town park.**

As you pass under the train tracks, you enter Forest Hills Gardens. This 142-acre community was planned by Frederick Law Olmsted Jr. (son of the Olmsted of Central Park fame) in the style of an English Tudor village. Construction began around 1910, but with two world wars and the financial crash of 1929, the majority of the houses weren't built until the 1940s and 1950s. Olmsted, with his colleague Grosvenor Atterbury, designed the railroad station, the greens, and nearby houses. Forest Hills Gardens was originally envisioned by Margaret Olivia Slocum Sage, wife of financier/philanthropist Russell Sage and founder of the Russell Sage Foundation.

There is an interesting historical debate surrounding the apartment houses in this community. They were not part of the original plan but form a significant part of the housing stock. Of 1,600 housing units within the Gardens, 650 are in the eleven apartment buildings. One school argues that the apartment houses were built to block the noise of the railroad and the "outside" world. The other claims that Margaret Sage envisioned Forest Hills Gardens as a mixed-income community and not just estate homes for the wealthy.

As we slowly meander through the tree-lined streets, you can see how this is a picture-perfect model of an urban garden community. While there is significant variety among the houses, the overall style is uniform. The gently curved streets not only break with the monotony of the grid plan but also help prevent excessive speed.

➤ **After approximately six blocks and three stop signs, turn right on Rockrose Place.**

➤ **After two blocks, when Rockrose ends, turn right onto Terrace Greenway South.**

➤ As you return to the small town park, take the left fork. This will bring you back to Station Square and Continental Avenue.

➤ Crossing Continental Avenue, continue back the way you came on 108th Street.

➤ Drive on 108th Street into Corona (1.6 miles).

As you drive along 108th Street and pass under the Long Island Expressway, you enter the neighborhood of Corona. The original settlement of this area coincided with the arrival of the Long Island Railroad in 1847. The neighborhood was best known for its racetrack and the Tiffany glass factories in the late nineteenth century. A population explosion occurred after the 1917 development of mass transit. The neighborhood was largely Jewish and Italian up through the mid-1940s, when Puerto Ricans and, later, Dominicans began arriving.

The intersection of 108th Street and Corona Avenue is a perfect example of the ethnic diversity here today. If you park and walk around, you will see the long-term Italian shops and even a bocce ball court in the small park. Be certain to go to the Lemon Ice King of Corona, right on the corner of Fifty-second Avenue—the best ices in the city! At the same time, numerous shops represent the more contemporary immigrant communities—Colombian, Filipino, Ecuadorian, and Pakistani, just to name a few.

➤ Turn right on Fifty-second Avenue.

➤ Fifty-second Avenue ends at Flushing Meadows–Corona Park. Directly in front of you is the Terrace on Park restaurant.

Flushing Meadows-Corona Park, Queens. At 255 acres, Flushing Meadows-Corona Park is the second largest park in New York City. Temporary home to the United Nations from 1946 to 1950, the park also hosted two World's Fairs—1939 and 1964. The Unisphere was the centerpiece to the 1964 fair. Courtesy of NYC & Company-The Convention and Visitors Bureau.

➤ **Turn left on 111th Street.**

If you wish to visit the park, follow signs for the Hall of Science. Feel free to park your car here to walk around. (Note: This is also good place to park and walk back to 108th Street for an ice.)

Directly in front of you is Flushing Meadows–Corona Park. While automobiles are not allowed in the park, it's a good place to walk around. In this part of the park you can find the United States Tennis Association (USTA) National Tennis Center, the Queens Museum of Art, the 1964 World's Fair Unisphere, and the New York Hall of Science. At 1,255 acres, this is the second largest park in the city. To the north is Shea Stadium, built in 1964 and home to the New York Mets.

➤ Turn left on Forty-seventh Avenue and return to 108th Street.

➤ Turn right on 108th Street and continue to Thirty-seventh Avenue.

➤ Turn left on Thirty-seventh Avenue.

➤ After about thirty feet turn right onto a short, unmarked street. As this ends, turn right, and then, after one very short block, turn right onto 107th Street. (Driving this combination of residential streets can be a bit confusing. Watch carefully for 107th Street.)

Shortly after turning onto 107th Street, keep your eyes open for the modern red-brick house and garage on your left. This is the Louis Armstrong House, located at 34–56 107th Street. This National Historic Landmark was the home of jazz great Louis Armstrong for twenty-nine years, from 1942 until his death in 1971.

Born in the Storyville neighborhood of New Orleans, Armstrong was surrounded by the ragtime and blues music that would influence the rest of his life. His musical career got started in the marching band of the Colored Waifs Home, to which he had been sent in 1912. His professional career got a boost when jazz man King Oliver made Armstrong second cornetist in 1922. This brought Armstrong to Chicago. He came to New York as a trumpeter and joined Fats Waller and Edith Wilson's Broadway revue *Hot Chocolate* in 1929. Armstrong performed in numerous shows and films until his return to the stage in 1947. Some of his greatest hits include "Blueberry Hill" (1949), "Mack the Knife" (1955), and "Hello Dolly" (1962).

➤ Continue on 107th Street to Thirty-fourth Avenue.

> Turn left onto Thirty-fourth Avenue and into the Jackson Heights Historic District (which starts at Eighty-eighth Street and ends at Seventy-eighth Street and goes from Roosevelt Avenue to Thirty-fourth Avenue).

By now it should be apparent that Queens is physically and structurally different from the other boroughs. While Staten Island retains a colonial and early nineteenth-century feel, and while Brooklyn was developed in the latter half of the nineteenth century, Queens is decidedly of the twentieth century, with small towns like Flushing being established much earlier.

While driving along Thirty-fourth Avenue, you will enter the Jackson Heights Historic District when you cross Eighty-eighth Street. This area was farmland in the early twentieth century. Just prior to the Queensboro Bridge opening in 1909, this district had been ripe for speculative building. A group of investors called the Queensboro Realty Company bought up 350 acres and, over the next two decades, built this neighborhood.

What makes Jackson Heights such an innovation is the way in which the blocks were developed. Along the avenues, builders created five- and six-story cooperative apartment houses with large rear gardens. These gardens provided private outdoor space and generous light into the apartments. On the side streets they built smaller single-family attached houses. This combination of garden apartments and individual houses was revolutionary.

In the 1920s the Queensboro Realty Company tolerated the suburban practice of "red-lining," an exclusionary policy directed against unwanted buyers—here meaning Jews, Catholics, and African Americans—that prevented people from receiving mortgages and home loans. Today, Jackson Heights is a thriving ethnically diverse community. In the early 1990s it was home to the largest Argentinean community in New York City.

Be certain to drive slowly along Thirty-fourth Avenue. Take special note of the apartment houses between Eighty-first and Eightieth Streets, which are especially appealing.

➤ **Turn right onto Seventy-ninth Street and drive to the Grand Central Parkway (GCP).**

As you cross Twenty-fifth Avenue (just before GCP), note what appears to be a park on your right. This is actually the beginning of the La Guardia Airport approach. You might want to stop the car and watch jets come overhead. The airport strobe lights are lined up through the park.

➤ **Be careful crossing the parkway's service road.**

➤ **After crossing over the Grand Central Parkway, turn left onto Astoria Boulevard.**

➤ **From Astoria Boulevard, take the second left onto the Parkway—the sign will read "Triboro Bridge."**

The Triboro is actually three interconnected steel bridges that connect the Bronx, Manhattan, and Queens. Designers Othmar Ammann and Aymar Embury II, had the misfortune to begin construction on October 25, 1929, the same day the stock market collapsed. Work was then halted until 1933. The bridge finally opened in July 1936.

➤ **As you drive across the bridge, follow the signs toward the Bronx.**

Directly beneath you is what appears to be one large four-hundred-plus-acre island. It is actually two separate islands connected by landfill.

The first is Wards Island, named for its the post–American Revolution owners, Jasper and Bartholomew Ward. The city acquired the 255-acre island in the 1800s and used it for a potter's field, a hospital, and a mental institution called the City Asylum. Now called the Manhattan Psychiatric Center, the City Asylum is still based on the island. Wards Island is also the training ground for the New York City Fire Department. It's greatest claim to fame perhaps came in 1937, when one of the largest sewage treatment plants in the world was built here. (It's now closed.)

The second part is the 195-acre Randalls Island, named for the early nineteenth-century owner, Jonathan Randal (or perhaps Randell). The City of New York bought it in 1830 and has used it for numerous purposes. It has been a potter's field, an almshouse, and a reform school. It is now home to a twenty-five-thousand-seat sport arena and a golf driving range.

Paralleling the Triboro Bridge to the right is the New York Connecting Railroad Bridge, known to most New Yorkers as the Hell Gate Bridge. When this bridge was completed in 1917, it was the longest steel-arch bridge in the world. The bridge is two and a half miles in length and holds four sets of rail lines. The steel arch is a tremendous 1,017 feet. It was built for the Pennsylvania Railroad by Gustav Lindenthal (who also designed the Williamsburg and Queensboro Bridges) to provide direct train access between Manhattan, Queens, the Bronx, and points north.

THE BRONX

The Bronx is New York's northernmost borough and the only one wholly on the mainland of the United States. The borough is named for Jonas Bronck, an early settler. Parts of the western Bronx were annexed by New York in 1875, and the eastern parts joined the city at the 1898 Consolidation. The Bronx was the destination for millions of people moving out of Manhattan tenements in the nineteenth and twentieth centuries, who then moved on to the suburbs in the 1960s and 1970s. Over 20 percent of the Bronx is made up of parks, which may surprise other city residents who rarely visit. The borough is also home to large neighborhoods of very expensive private homes and some of the most grinding poverty in the city.

➤ From the Triboro Bridge, follow signs for 87 North (Major Deegan Expressway).

➤ The road forks after the toll; the Deegan is the left fork.

➤ After a quarter mile, take exit 2 (Willis Avenue).

➤ Exit onto East 135th Street in the South Bronx.

The designation "South Bronx" actually includes a collection of neighborhoods, including Mott Haven, Melrose, Morrisania, and others. Technically, you are in Mott Haven right now. In the nineteenth century, Jordan Mott built an ironworks here. His business was joined by piano factories and a collection of German, Irish, and Italian residents. Large industry was gone by the 1940s, and the neighborhood today largely is home to Puerto Ricans and African Americans, living in a collection of privately owned rowhouses, public housing, and apartment buildings.

➤ Continue along 135th Street to the second light, Alexander Avenue.

➤ Turn right on Alexander Avenue.

Yankee Stadium. One of the oldest and most famous ballparks in America, Yankee Stadium opened on April 18, 1923. Nicknamed "the House That Ruth Built," the stadium offers tours of the grounds that include the Yankees locker room and the monument park to past heroes, including Lou Gehrig, Babe Ruth, and Miller Huggins. Courtesy NYC & Company–The Convention and Visitors Bureau.

You're in a Bronx historic district and will pass a number of important buildings on Alexander Avenue. On your right, between 137th and 138th Streets, is St. Jerome's Roman Catholic Church (1898). At the corner of 138th Street, on your left, is the Fortieth Precinct (1924). Although you are in the South Bronx, this precinct is not "Fort Apache"— that was the Forty-first Precinct, to the northeast along Simpson Avenue, south of 167th Street.

Note the well-preserved rowhouses along Alexander between 139th and 141st Streets. The New York Public Library (1905) is on the left corner of 140th Street. On the right, at 141st Street, is the 1902 Tercera Iglesia Bautista (originally called the Alexander Avenue Baptist Church). Finally, on your left, note the large plaque for the East Side Settlement House between 141st and 142d Streets. As in Manhattan's Lower East Side, settlement houses offer services and classes for immigrants and others in the Bronx.

Before turning left on 142d Street, think about this: a few blocks to your right, along 142d, was the stone-carving studio of the Piccirilli brothers, who carved Daniel Chester French's design for the Abraham Lincoln statue that sits inside the Lincoln Memorial in Washington, D.C.

➤ **Turn left on 142d Street.**

➤ **Make your first right onto Third Avenue and drive four lights. Turn left on Courtland and drive a few blocks until you reach 149th Street. Turn left on 149th Street.**

The Hub, to your right, is one of the Bronx's main shopping areas. We've steered you just west of the Hub because the intersection of five streets that makes it hublike also makes for traffic jams. The Hub was the site of the first Alexander's Department Store and has housed theaters, burlesque houses, trolleys, and retail shops. It continues to be a shopping hub.

As you drive along East 149th Street, note the well-done ochre-colored brick Lincoln Hospital (1976), on your left at Morris Avenue, and the Eugenio Maria de Hostos Community College, called simply "Hostos" by New Yorkers and begun in 1968, at the corner of the Grand Concourse on your left.

➤ **Turn right on the Grand Concourse, which stretches four and a half miles from the South Bronx northward and is 180 feet wide at its broadest.**

The concourse was completed south to 161st Street between 1902 and 1909 and extended farther south in the 1930s. Especially in the 1920s and 1930s, the concourse became home to some of the Bronx's most elegant apartment buildings. Only the service roads were used for cars in the beginning, with the larger center stretch for horses and carriages. Now, of course, everything is a car lane.

Turn right onto the concourse from 149th Street at the plain 1937 Bronx General Post Office on your right, with excellent Ben Shahn murals in its lobby. Driving north on the concourse, at 153rd Street, on your right you pass an octagonal smokestack that was part of the Morgan Steam Laundry and then Cardinal Hayes High School (1941). Continue slowly. To your left is Franz Sigel Park, named for a German-born general who rallied many German Americans to the Union cause during the Civil War.

➤ **Turn left at 158th Street. The building on your right is the 1934 Bronx County Building.**

As soon as you make the turn, straight ahead you'll see Yankee Stadium, the "House That Ruth Built," rising up ahead. Jacob Ruppert, a brewer, had the stadium built for his team in 1923, and opening day was April 18. It was redone in 1976. Over the years, famous Yankees have included Babe Ruth, Lou Gehrig, Joe DiMaggio, Mickey Mantle, Roger Maris, and Reggie Jackson.

➤ **Continue three blocks right up to the stadium and turn right on River Avenue.**

This street is lined with sporting-goods stores. Most prominent are the series of baseball-related shops owned by "Stan." The stadium is open for tours year-round, daily at noon; go to the press entrance for admission.

➤ **Continue one block under the El (#4 train) and turn right on East 161st Street. Drive three blocks back to the Grand Concourse. Turn left onto the service road—not the main, center lanes—along the concourse.**

Now you'll begin to pass many of the famous buildings for which the concourse is known. Art Deco and Art Moderne buildings, often six stories, went up in the 1930s, and mixed in liberally are much taller and squatter 1920s apartment buildings.

Begin on your right, immediately across from the Bronx County Building, with the building known only as 888 Grand Concourse (1937)—not the best example of the decade but one to start with. On the north side of 161st Street is the former Concourse Plaza Hotel (900 Grand Concourse), which in its time was a Bronx social center, much as the St. George Hotel was in Brooklyn. Continuing north, you pass Joyce Kilmer Park at East 164th, on your left, named for the poet and author of "Trees." The park's Lorelie Fountain (1899) is dedicated to German poet Heinrich Heine.

The 1961 Bronx Museum of the Arts (1040 Grand Concourse) at 165th Street is built in the former Young Israel Synagogue, with a beautiful 1988 extension; note the red banner and low glass gazebo. The museum takes jurors on lunch break from nearby courthouses for free lunch and tours. On your left is the overgrown Andrew Freedman Home (1924), a former home for the aged. On your right is the Bronx County Housing Court.

Note the mural to the left of the lobby entrance of 1150 Grand Concourse. Across the concourse, to your left at 169th Street, is the former Temple Adath Israel (1927), now a Seventh-Day Adventist temple. Note the brilliant green glass brick around the lobby door of 1500 Grand Concourse (between 172d Street and Rockwood), built in 1935. The Bronx Lebanon Hospital Center at 173d Street (1942, expanded in 1991) is one of the borough's largest hospitals. The colossal-looking, though only thirteen-story, building on your left is the 1923 Lewis Morris Apartments (1749 Grand Concourse).

At the intersection of Grand Concourse, Eastburn, and 175th Street is the Pilgrim United Church of Christ, which looks much older than it is. The church was actually built in 1910, in a mix of Georgian and Turkish style.

Drive slowly, because at the intersection of East Tremont and Grand Concourse, on your right, is the 1914 Mount Hope Court Apartments (1882 Grand Concourse), also known as the Bronx Flatiron Building. Park safely on your right and look behind you: Mount Hope Court looks like Manhattan's Flatiron Building when you look back at it. The "point" of the iron is what you're seeing as you look south, back the way you came. Across the street, at 181st Street, is the wild-looking Art Moderne zigzag facade of 2121 Grand Concourse.

Slow down as you come to Burnside Street, for the Masonic Temple on your right.

➤ Here you want to exit from the service road to the central lanes of Grand Concourse. Get in your left lane and turn left at 181st Street.

➤ Drive to the top of the hill to University Avenue/Martin Luther King, Jr., Boulevard. Cross over University Avenue and continue on Hall of Fame Terrace. Note the new houses on your left. As the hill crests, slow down and turn left into Bronx Community College.

Bronx Community College (BCC) was begun in 1894 as the uptown campus of Greenwich Village's New York University (NYU). In 1973, NYU sold the grounds to the city, which turned the buildings into BCC.

Tell the guard at the gate that you want to have a look at the Hall of Fame Terrace, which is open to the public. The visitors' parking lot is to the immediate right after you go through the gate. Park there and walk through the iron gate at the north end of the parking lot and onto the terrace. The Hall of Fame (and much of the campus) was designed by McKim, Mead and White. It's a semicircular arcade with bronze busts of educators, lawyers, scientists, and others and gives visitors a great view westward. Although it isn't apparent from where you stand, the Hall of Fame was designed to hide the giant foundation walls of some of the buildings Stanford White designed for the campus.

➤ **Exit BCC and turn left on Hall of Fame Terrace, continuing the way you were going before turning in. Make your first right onto Sedgwick Avenue and follow it to the bottom of the hill.**

➤ **Turn right on Fordham Road and drive to the Grand Concourse. If you were to continue another mile, you would come to Fordham University, the Bronx Zoo, and the New York Botanical Garden. But turn left on the Grand Concourse again and continue north to Kingsbridge.**

On the corner is Poe Cottage, built in 1816. American author Edgar Allen Poe moved here in 1846, hoping the then-country air would cure his wife's tuberculosis. She died soon after they moved, but Poe stayed on until just before he died in 1849. He wrote "Ulalume" and "The Bells" here. The cottage was actually originally across the street but was moved to its current location in 1913.

➤ **Turn left on Kingsbridge Avenue.**

In three blocks, on your right, you will come to the giant, castlelike Kingsbridge Armory (1912), which some claim to be the largest in the world.

➤ **Four blocks further on, turn right on Sedgewick Avenue again.**

You are in Kingsbridge Heights, named for the first bridge to connect the Bronx and Manhattan. King's Bridge, built in 1693, took people over the Spuyten Duyvil Creek just to the west.

Continuing northward, Sedgewick runs along the west border of Jerome Park Reservoir. The reservoir, filled in 1905, is named for Leonard Jerome, Winston Churchill's grandfather, who had a racetrack also named after him nearby. Jerome sponsored the American Jockey Club in an attempt to raise the image of horse racing in the United States to something closer to the aristocratic status it held in England. Thankfully, the American democratic spirit allowed him to succeed only partially.

➤ **Sedgewick Avenue runs into Van Cortlandt Avenue West at a light. Make a 270-degree left turn onto Van Cortlandt Avenue West and drive a few blocks until you come to a light. Continue straight, and the road becomes Van Cortlandt Park South.**

➤ **Drive a few blocks and turn right on Review Place, which immediately curves into Broadway. In a few blocks you come to the last stop on the #1 train, Van Cortlandt Park. Make your first left turn after 242d Street (this is Manhattan College Parkway, but the sign is almost impossible to see; instead you will see a sign that says "Manhattan College.")**

➤ **Drive one hundred feet and turn right on Post Road, and go up the steep hill.**

➤ **At the top of the hill, turn left at West 246th Street.**

Follow West 246th as it curves through Fieldston, one of the most exclusive neighborhoods in the Bronx.

Fieldston is filled with 1920s English-style homes and houses two very expensive private schools: Fieldston, run by the Ethical Culture Society, and Horace Mann.

➤ Continue on 246th Street, admiring the houses, until you come to the Henry Hudson Parkway. Turn right on the service road that parallels the highway, but don't get on the highway itself. Drive to West 252d Street.

➤ Turn left here (see the sign for "Wave Hill"), cross over the highway, but once there, ignore the sign telling you to turn left for Wave Hill. Instead, continue straight on 252d Street.

You're now in Riverdale, perhaps even more exclusive than Fieldston because of its views of the Hudson River. Be careful on the roads here: they are narrow, winding, and potholed—intentionally, some would argue, to keep out visitors.

➤ Drive about five blocks until the road ends at Independence Avenue. Turn left and you will be following Wave Hill, on your right, a nonprofit, city-owned park.

Drive very slowly; the entrance is on your right. It costs $4 to get in except for Tuesday and Saturday morning before noon, when it's free, but it is well worth it. The grounds are beautiful, and it has an excellent herb garden and small greenhouse.

Wave Hill House, on the grounds, was a country home built in 1843 and over the years has been home to Teddy Roosevelt (summers of 1870 and 1871), Mark Twain

(1901–3), and Arturo Toscanini (1942–45). Bashford Dean, zoologist and curator of arms and armor for the Metropolitan Museum, lived in Glyndor House, another building on the grounds.

➤ Exit Wave Hill and turn right on Independence Avenue with Wave Hill on your right. Turn right on Ploughman's Road and drive one block to Palisade Avenue. Turn left on Palisade and drive along with mansions on your left and Riverdale Park and the Hudson River on your right. Continue until you turn left on West 232d St. Be careful—the sign is not apparent, and it will sneak up on you. Go to your first light and take the right at the sign for 9A/Henry Hudson Parkway West. Take the Henry Hudson back into Manhattan, crossing over the Harlem River and driving through Inwood Park. Continue south on the Henry Hudson Parkway to Midtown Manhattan.

SOURCES

Allen, Oliver E. *The Tiger: The Rise and Fall of Tammany Hall*. Reading, Mass.: Addison-Wesley, 1993.

Baker, Paul. *Stanny: The Gilded Life of Stanford White*. New York: Free Press, 1989.

Bender, Thomas. *New York Intellect: A History of Intellectual Life in New York City from 1750 to the Beginning of Our Own Time*. Baltimore: Johns Hopkins University Press, 1987.

Bernstein, Iver. *The New York City Draft Riots: Their Significance for American Society and Politics in the Age of the Civil War*. New York: Oxford University Press, 1990.

Bérubé, Allan. *Coming Out under Fire: The History of Gay Men and Women in World War II*. New York: Plume, 1990.

Binder, Frederick M., and David M. Reimers. *All the Nations under Heaven: An Ethnic and Racial History of New York City*. New York: Columbia University Press, 1995.

Blasius, Mark, and Shane Phelan, eds. *We Are Everywhere: A Historical Sourcebook of Gay and Lesbian Politics*. New York: Routledge, 1997.

Burrows, Edwin G., and Mike Wallace. *Gotham: A History of New York City to 1898*. New York: Oxford University Press, 1999.

Burton, Dennis. *Nature Walks of Central Park*. New York: Henry Holt and Company / A John Macrae Book, 1997.

Callender, James. *Yesterdays on Brooklyn Heights*. New York: Dorland Press, 1927.

Chauncey, George. *Gay New York: Gender, Urban Culture, and the Making of the Gay Male World, 1890–1940*. New York: Basic Books, 1994.

Cleaveland, N. *Green-Wood Illustrated*. New York: R. Martin Publishers, 1846.

Culbertson, Judi, and Tom Randall. *Permanent New Yorkers: A Biographical Guide to the Cemeteries of New York*. Chelsea, VT.: Chelsea Green Publishing Co., 1987.

Durso, Joseph. *Madison Square Garden: 100 Years of History*. New York: Simon and Schuster, 1979.

Edmiston, Susan, and Linda Cirino. *Literary New York: A History and Guide*. Boston: Houghton Mifflin, 1976.

Ewen, Elizabeth. *Immigrant Women in the Land of Dollars: Life and Culture on the Lower East Side, 1890–1925*. New York: Monthly Review Press, 1985.

Faderman, Lillian. *Odd Girls and Twilight Lovers: A History of Lesbian Life in Twentieth-Century America*. New York: Penguin Books, 1991.

———. *Surpassing the Love of Men: Romantic Friendship and Love between Women from the Renaissance to the Present*. New York: William Morrow, 1981.

Franklin, John Hope, and August Meier. *Black Leaders of the Twentieth Century*. Urbana and Chicago: University of Illinois Press, 1982.

Frick, John W. *New York's First Theatrical Center: The Rialto at Union Square*. Ann Arbor, Mich.: UMI Research Press, 1985.

Garrett, Charles. *The La Guardia Years: Machine and Reform Politics in New York City*. New Brunswick, N.J.: Rutgers University Press, 1961.

Geisst, Charles R. *Wall Street: A History*. New York: Oxford University Press, 1997.

Gilfoyle, Timothy J. *City of Eros: New York City, Prostitution, and the Commercialization of Sex, 1790–1920*. New York: W. W. Norton, 1992.

Graff, M. M. *Tree Trails in Central Park*. New York: Greensward Foundation, 1970.

Griffin, Farah Jasmine, ed. *Beloved Sisters and Loving Friends: Letters from Rebecca Primus of Royal Oak, Maryland, and Addie Brown of Hartford, Connecticut, 1854–1868*. New York: Alfred A. Knopf, 1999.

Halporn, Roberta. *New York Is a Rubber's Paradise: A Guide to New York City's Cemeteries in the Five Boroughs*. Brooklyn, N.Y.: Center for Thanatology Research, 1998.

Harlow, Alvin. *Old Bowery Days*. New York: D. Appleton & Co., 1931.

Headley, Joel Tyler. *The Great Riots of New York: 1712–1873*. 1873. Reprint, Indianapolis: Bobbs-Merrill, 1970.

Hodges, Graham. "Desirable Companions and Lovers: Irish and African Americans in the Sixth Ward, 1830–1870." In Ronald

Bayor and Timothy Meagher, eds., *The New York Irish*. Baltimore: Johns Hopkins University Press, 1996.

Hogan, Steve, and Lee Hudson. *Completely Queer: The Gay and Lesbian Encyclopedia*. New York: Henry Holt and Company, 1998.

Homberger, Eric. *The Historical Atlas of New York City*. New York: Henry Holt and Company, 1999.

Huggins, Nathan Irvin. *Harlem Renaissance*. New York: Oxford University Press, 1971.

Jackson, Kenneth T., ed. *The Encyclopedia of New York City*. New Haven: Yale University Press, 1995.

Kaiser, Charles. *The Gay Metropolis, 1940–1996*. New York: Houghton Mifflin, 1997.

Katz, Jonathan Ned. *Gay American History: Lesbians and Gay Men in the U.S.A*. Rev. ed. New York: Meridian, 1992.

Kinkead, Eugene. *Central Park: The Birth, Decline, and Renewal of a National Treasure*. W. W. Norton, 1990.

Klein, Carole. *Gramercy Park: An American Bloomsbury*. Boston: Houghton Mifflin, 1987.

Kwong, Peter. *The New Chinatown*. New York: Hill and Wang, 1987.

Lancaster, Clay. *Old Brooklyn Heights: New York's First Suburb*. 1961. Reprint, New York: Dover, 1979.

Latimer, Margaret, et al., eds. *Bridge to the Future: A Centennial Celebration of the Brooklyn Bridge*. Vol. 424 of *Annals of the New York Academy of Sciences* (1984).

Levinson, Leonard Louis. *Wall Street: A Pictorial History*. New York: Ziff-Davis, 1961.

Levy, Richard Michael. "The Brooklyn Bridge: An Engineering Masterpiece." *Foote Prints* 46:1 (1983). Foote Mineral Company.

Lewis, David Levering. *When Harlem Was in Vogue*. New York: Oxford University Press, 1981.

Lockwood, Charles. *Manhattan Moves Uptown: An Illustrated History*. Boston: Houghton Mifflin, 1976.

Maffi, Mario. *Gateway to the Promised Land: Ethnic Cultures in New York's Lower East Side*. New York: New York University Press, 1995.

McCullough, David. *The Great Bridge: The Epic Story of the Building of the Brooklyn Bridge*. New York: Simon & Schuster, 1972.

Meyer, Richard, ed. *Cemeteries and Gravemarkers: Voices of American Culture*. Logan: Utah State University Press, 1992.

Miller, Neil. *Out of the Past: Gay and Lesbian History from 1869 to the Present*. New York: Vintage Books, 1995.

Miller, Terry. *Greenwich Village and How It Got That Way*. New York: Crown Publishers, 1990.

Nadel, Stanley. *Little Germany: Ethnicity, Religion, and Class in New York City, 1845–80.* Urbana: University of Illinois Press, 1990.

Nestle, Joan. *A Restricted Country.* Ithaca: Firebrand Books, 1987.

Olmsted, Frederick, Jr., and Theodora Kimball, eds. *Forty Years of Landscape Architecture: Central Park.* 1928. Reprint, Cambridge, Mass.: MIT Press, 1973.

Osofsky, Gilbert. *Harlem: The Making of a Ghetto.* 2d ed. New York: Harper & Row, 1971.

Reed, Henry Hope, Robert M. McGee, and Esther Mipaas. *Bridges of Central Park.* New York: Greensward Foundation, 1990.

Richman, Jeffrey. *Brooklyn's Green-Wood Cemetery: New York's Buried Treasure.* Brooklyn, N.Y.: Green-Wood Cemetery, 1998.

Riis, Jacob. *How the Other Half Lives.* New York: Charles Scribner, 1890 and 1901.

Riordan, William. *Plunkitt of Tammany Hall.* New York: E. P. Dutton, 1963. [Originally published in 1905 as *Very Plain Talks on Very Practical Subjects.*]

Rischin, Moses. *The Promised City: New York's Jews, 1870–1914.* Cambridge, Mass.: Harvard University Press, 1962.

Rosenzweig, Roy, and Elizabeth Blackmar. *The Park and the People: A History of Central Park.* Ithaca: Cornell University Press, 1992; paperback, New York: Henry Holt and Co., 1994.

Sante, Luc. *Low Life: Lures and Snares of Old New York.* New York: FSG, 1991.

Scherzer, Kenneth A. *The Unbounded Community: Neighborhood Life and Social Structure in New York City, 1830–1875.* Durham: Duke University Press, 1992.

Schoener, Allon, ed. *Harlem on My Mind.* 1968. Reprint, New York: New Press, 1995.

Sexton, Andrea Wyatt, and Alice Leccese Powers. *The Brooklyn Reader: Thirty Writers Celebrate America's Favorite Borough.* New York: Crown, 1994.

Shapiro, Mary. *A Picture History of the Brooklyn Bridge.* New York: Dover, 1983.

Tchen, John Kuo Wei. *New York before Chinatown: Orientalism and the Shaping of American Culture, 1776–1882.* Baltimore: Johns Hopkins University Press, 1999.

Thompson, Daniel. *Ruggles of New York: A Life of Samuel B. Ruggles.* New York: Columbia University Press, 1946.

Trachtenberg, Alan. *The Brooklyn Bridge: Fact and Symbol.* Chicago: University of Chicago Press, 1965.

Walker, Altina. *Reverend Beecher and Mrs. Tilton: Sex and Class in Victorian America.* Amherst: University of Massachusetts Press, 1982.

Walsh, George. *Gentleman Jimmy Walker: Mayor in the Jazz Age.* New York: Praeger, 1974.

Weisser, Michael. *A Brotherhood of Memory: Jewish Landsmanshaftn in the New World.* New York: Basic Books, 1985.

Wiegold, Marilyn. *Silent Builder: Emily Warren Roebling and the Brooklyn Bridge.* Port Washington, NY: National University Publications/Associated Faculty Press, 1984.

Willensky, Elliot, and Norval White. *AIA Guide to New York City.* New York: Harcourt Brace Jovanovich, 1988.

Zink, Clifford, and Dorothy White Hartman. *Spanning the Industrial Age: The John A. Roebling's Sons Company of Trenton, New Jersey, 1848–1974.* Trenton: Roebling Community Development Corp., 1992.

ABOUT THE CONTRIBUTORS

SETH KAMIL holds advanced degrees in American history from Columbia University. He is founder and president of Big Onion Walking Tours and Big Onion Historical Consulting. Kamil's dissertation is titled "The Management of Misery: Homelessness in New York City, 1857–1940." He is author of "Tripping Down Memory Lane: Walking Tours on the Jewish Lower East Side." an essay in *Remembering the Lower East Side* (Indiana University Press, 2000), and a contributor to the *Encyclopedia of New York City*.

ERIC WAKIN is a Ph.D. candidate in U.S. history at Columbia University and has received M.A.s in Asian studies and political science from the University of Michigan, Ann Arbor. He is currently an e-business advisor at Ernst & Young. Eric is a native of New York who was born in Manhattan and raised in Queens. He is the author of *Anthropology Goes to War: Professional Ethics and Counterinsurgency in Thailand* (University of Wisconsin/Center for Southeast Asian Studies, 1992); *Asian Independence Leaders* (Facts on File, 1997); and coauthor of two travel guides for Lonely Planet. He has been a Big Onion guide since 1995.

LEONARD BENARDO has advanced degrees in political science from Columbia University and a degree in history from the University of Michigan. He is presently Regional Director for Russia, Ukraine, the Baltics, Poland and Hungary at the Open Society Institute in New York. Leonard is a life long devotee of New York City—its people, history and architecture. His love for the city knows no bounds. Leonard has been a tour guide with Big Onion since 1997.

ELIZA STARR BYARD is a Ph.D. candidate in United States history and Whiting Fellow in the Humanities at Columbia University. Her dissertation is titled "Inverts, Perverts, and National Peril: Federal Responses to Homosexuality, 1890–1955." Eliza has worked on numerous projects for public television, including coproducing *Out of the Past*, a look at lesbian and gay history in the United States that won the Audience Award for Best Documentary at the 1998 Sundance Film Festival. She received her B.A. from Yale in 1990 and holds an M.A. and an M.Phil. in United States history from Columbia University. Eliza has been a Big Onion guide since 1996.

MARK ELLIOTT is a Ph.D. Candidate in history at New York University; he received an M.A. in history from the University of California at Riverside in 1993. His scholarly interests include American political, legal, and intellectual history and center on issues of race and democratic ideals in American history. Elliott's dissertation is on the career of Albion W. Tourgee. Mark has been a Big Onion guide since 1997.

CINDY R. LOBEL is a doctoral student in American history at the Graduate Center of the City University of New York. She is currently working on her dissertation, which looks at New Yorkers' eating and dining habits in the first half of the nineteenth century. She holds a B.A. in history from Tufts University. Cindy has been a Big Onion guide since 1998.

INDEX